ADOPTION &
PRENATAL ALCOHOL
AND DRUG EXPOSURE

Edited by
Richard P. Barth,
Madelyn Freundlich,
and David Brodzinsky

Child Welfare League of America • The Evan B. Donaldson Adoption Institute
Washington, DC

The Child Welfare League of America (CWLA), the nation's oldest and largest membership-based child welfare organization, is committed to engaging all Americans in promoting the well-being of children and protecting every child from harm.

CHILD WELFARE LEAGUE OF AMERICA, INC.
440 First Street, NW, Third Floor, Washington, DC 20001-2085
E-mail: books@cwla.org

CURRENT PRINTING (last digit)
10 9 8 7 6 5 4 3 2 1

Cover design by Luke Johnson and Tung Mullen
Text design by Peggy Porter Tierney

Printed in the United States of America
ISBN # 0–87868-720-3

Library of Congress Cataloging-in-Publication Data
Adoption and prenatal alcohol and drug exposure : research, policy and practice/ edited by Richard P. Barth, Madelyn Freundlich & David M. Brodzinsky
    p. cm.
    Includes bibliographical references.
    ISBN 0-87868-720-3 (alk. paper)
    1. Special needs adoption--United States--Congresses. 2. Children of prenatal substance abuse--United States--Congresses. 3. Children of prenatal alcohol abuse--United States--Congresses. I. Barth, Richard P., 1952- II. Freundlich, Madelyn. III. Brodzinsky, David. IV. Child Welfare League of America.

HV875-55 .A3635 2000
362.73'4'0973--dc21
                                                                99-045583

Contents

Contents

Figures

Preface

Prenatal alcohol and drug exposure has had and continues to have a significant impact on children and families, as well as on health, public health, and child welfare systems. Within the child welfare system in the United States, parental alcohol and drug abuse generally and prenatal substance exposure in particular have had a substantial effect on the numbers of children reported for abuse and neglect, the number of children entering foster care, and the length of time that children remain in foster care while efforts are made to either reunify them with their parents or find other alternatives that will provide them with safe and permanent families. In contrast to earlier perceptions—that these children would not be "adoptable"—child welfare professionals have begun to consider adoption as the permanency plan for children who cannot or will not be reunited with their birth parents.

At the same time, prenatal substance abuse is affecting children outside the child welfare system—both children whose birth parents make the decision to place their children for adoption through private agencies or intermediaries in this country and children in countries outside the United States served through international adoption. As a consequence, the issues that adoption professionals face in planning for substance-exposed children in foster care likewise confront professionals working in the private adoption sector.

With the growing recognition of the impact of prenatal substance exposure on children who are being or could potentially be served through adoption, questions have arisen for both professionals and prospective adoptive parents. What is the impact of prenatal substance exposure on children's immediate health and well-being? What are the long-term implications for children's health and development when there is a history of prenatal exposure to alcohol or drugs? What role does a positive postnatal environment play in remediating the effects of prenatal substance exposure? How can prospective adoptive parents best be counseled regarding the effects of prenatal substance exposure so that they can make an informed decision about adopting a child with such a history? What ongoing services and supports are needed for adoptive families and their substance-exposed children to maximize positive outcomes? What policies need to be in place to support adoption planning and services for children who are prenatally exposed to alcohol or drugs?

In October 1997, with the support of The Robert Wood Johnson Foundation, The Evan B. Donaldson Adoption Institute convened a conference, Adoption and Prenatal Alcohol and Drug Exposure: The Research, Policy and Practice Challenges, in order to bring together leading experts to address these questions and begin charting a course for the further development of practice and policy that support substance-exposed children and their adoptive families. The conference, featuring presentations by researchers, practitioners, and policymakers with expertise in prenatal alcohol and drug exposure and adoption, drew a multidisciplinary group of professionals from child welfare, health care, mental health, and the law, who both learned from and contributed to the knowledge base in this critical area of adoption practice and policy.

This edited volume, also supported by The Robert Wood Johnson Foundation, is a collection of contributions from a number of experts who presented at the October 1997 conference. It is organized in three major sections: research on the effects of prenatal alcohol and drug exposure and its implications for adoption; programmatic approaches and practice considerations related to serving substance-exposed children and their adoptive families; and policy issues that bear on adoption planning and services for this vulnerable group of children.

Following an introductory chapter that briefly outlines selected research regarding the short and long term outcomes for children who are prenatally exposed to alcohol or drugs and the implications of this research for adoption practice and policy, critical research in four areas is presented. Dr. Richard Barth and Dr. Devon Brooks report on their findings on the outcomes of adopted children who are drug exposed, as compared to outcomes for children who are not drug exposed, eight years after adoption. Dr. Remi Cadoret and Dr. Kristin Riggins-Caspers present their findings from their research on psychopathological outcomes among adult adoptees with histories of fetal alcohol exposure. This section concludes with the chapter by Dr. Heather Carmichael Olson, Dr. Barbara Morse and Victoria McKinney which comprehensively reviews the research on alcohol related disorders, including both Fetal Alcohol Syndrome and the broader range of effects from prenatal alcohol exposure, and describes the impact of these conditions on children and their adoptive families.

The second section focuses on practice and program issues. The opening chapter in this section by Susan Edelstein, Dr. Jill Waterman, Dorli Burge, Carolyn McCarty, and Joseph Prusak describes a comprehensive program model that prepares prospective parents to adopt drug-exposed children and provides services to children and families post-placement and post-finalization. In the next chapter, Dr. Jane Ellen Aronson, a pediatrician with expertise in international adoption medicine, describes the impact of fetal alcohol exposure on children adopted from abroad, particularly from Russia, and the unique diagnostic and treatment issues presented in international adoption. In the third chapter in this section, Dr. Mary Dozier and Kathleen Albus focus on attachment issues for young children who are adopted, including children with histories of prenatal substance exposure, and they describe an intervention to enhance caregiver-child relationships.

The section on policy issues related to prenatal alcohol and drug exposure features two chapters. The first, by Dr. Stephen Kandall, describes from a historical perspective societal attitudes toward maternal substance abuse, particularly during pregnancy, and the effects of those attitudes on public policy in the areas of alcohol and drug treatment for women, child protective service interventions, and planning for children who are removed from their parents' custody because of substance abuse. In their chapter, Judith Larsen and Harvey Schweitzer, lawyers with substantial child welfare and adoption experience, identify key legal issues that impact adoption planning and services for substance exposed children, particularly in light of recent changes in federal law. The volume concludes with a chapter that synthesizes the contributions from research, practice, and policy to an understanding of the issues involved in the adoption of children affected by prenatal alcohol and drug exposure and outlines directions for future research, practice and policy development.

This volume would not have been possible without the significant contributions of The Robert Wood Johnson Foundation which provided financial support for its development; Leigh Nowicki whose editorial expertise and assistance were invaluable; and Lisa M. Grant, who provided essential administrative support. It is the hope of the Evan B. Donaldson Adoption Institute that this publication will serve as a key resource for practitioners, policymakers, researchers, and others with an interest in and commitment to adoption for substance-exposed children who cannot or will not be raised by their birth families.

Madelyn Freundlich
Executive Director
The Evan B. Donaldson Adoption Institute

1

The Impact of Prenatal Substance Exposure: Research Findings and Their Implications for Adoption

Madelyn Freundlich[1]

No aspect of the dramatic growth in alcohol and drug abuse over the last two decades has received greater attention than drug use by pregnant and parenting women. With the advent of "crack" cocaine in the mid-to-late 1980s—an inexpensive, easy-to-use, and readily available drug—maternal substance abuse grew significantly [Schaffer 1994]. Within a few years of the introduction of "crack," some 739,000 pregnant women were using drugs each year [Gomby & Shiono 1991], and it was estimated that 11% of all newborns were affected to some degree by prenatal substance exposure [Chasnoff 1989; Vega 1993]. The impact of prenatal exposure to drugs and, to a lesser degree, alcohol has become an issue of critical public health and child welfare concern. Increases in admissions to Neonatal Intensive Care Units because of prenatal cocaine exposure and higher incidences of serious medical problems among substance-exposed neonates have generated serious health care concerns [Schaffer 1994]. Significant increases in child abuse and neglect reports and growth in the population of young children entering foster care because of prenatal substance exposure have generated serious child welfare concerns [Child Welfare League of America 1992]. At the same time, mental health and education professionals have become increasingly concerned about the implications of prenatal substance exposure for children and their families. As attention has focused on prenatal drug and alcohol exposure, professionals from a range of disciplines have sought guidance in the research to understand the impact of prenatal substance exposure on children and their prospects for the future.

This chapter, designed to briefly set the research context for the subsequent chapters in this volume, provides a selective review of the research findings on the effects of prenatal alcohol and drug exposure over the past twenty years. It highlights the important trends in the research, describing studies on the short-term effects of prenatal substance exposure and, in somewhat greater detail, the research on the longer-term development effects. It outlines the limitations on the existing research and the gaps in the current research-based knowledge. The chapter concludes with a consideration of the general implications of this research for adoption policy and practice.

Research on the Effects of Prenatal Alcohol and Drug Exposure

Research on the effects of prenatal alcohol and drug exposure has occurred in two distinct phases. The first phase of research began in the 1970s and continued through the early 1990s. Findings during this phase were by and large pessimistic, with an emphasis on early neurological damage among children prenatally exposed to drugs or alcohol and predictions that these children would be unable to function normally intellectually or socially. Beginning around 1993, the tone of the research shifted, as longer-term studies showed dramatic variation in the outcomes for children prenatally exposed to substances. It became clear that there were many cases in which children, despite histories of prenatal substance exposure, demonstrated normal long-term development. As the research has continued, studies have expanded beyond a consideration of the outcomes that may be associated with prenatal drug and alcohol exposure, to a focus on the relationship between prenatal and postnatal environmental factors and longer-term outcomes for children.

The Early Research

Early research on prenatal substance exposure, beginning in the 1970s as treatment programs for drug-addicted women became available, focused primarily on the in utero and perinatal effects of alcohol and heroin. In 1973, the term "Fetal Alcohol Syndrome" (FAS) was coined. Research associated FAS with distorted facial features and neurological damage as a consequence of the entry of alcohol into the fetal brain. The biological damage associated with FAS was determined to be severe, permanent, and irreversible, and individuals affected by FAS were found to be mentally retarded and likely to engage in socially unacceptable or illegal behavior. Researchers also determined that many individuals exposed prenatally to alcohol did not have full-blown FAS. They found that as a result of prenatal alcohol exposure, many children manifested either the neurological damage or the physical effects that typify FAS, but not both. These conditions were labeled Fetal Alcohol Effects (FAE) [Streissguth et al. 1988].

Unlike the research focused on the effects of prenatal alcohol exposure, the studies of prenatal exposure to heroin conducted in the 1970s did not find distinct physical and developmental deficiencies that amounted to a lifelong syndrome. The research, however, did identify immediate neonatal central nervous system dysfunction, termed Neonatal Withdrawal Syndrome (NWS) or Neonatal Abstinence Syndrome (NAS), as a consequence of prenatal heroin exposure. The research suggested that NWS involved gastrointestinal, respiratory, and reflex difficulties in the days to weeks immediately following birth, during which the heroin—to which the exposed fetus developed a tolerance—left the neonate's system [Zuckerman 1993; Coles & Platzman 1993].

Follow-up studies, in the early 1980s, expanded the range of drugs under scrutiny. Whereas earlier research focused on the effects of central nervous system depressants such as heroin and other opiates, studies during the 1980s began to consider the effects of prenatal exposure to stimulants such as hallucinogens, cigarettes, and marijuana. Research on the effects of stimulants on fetal and infant development during this period, however, was more limited than the ongoing research on the effects of prenatal alcohol and heroin exposure. The reasons for the limited work on the effects of tobacco and marijuana are not entirely clear, but may relate to the lack of funding for such research and the inability to identify significant effects or syndromes associated with these drugs [Koren et al. 1989].

In the early 1990s, research began to focus on the effects of prenatal exposure to crack and cocaine. Findings were, by and large, pessimistic. Much of the published research suggested that children prenatally exposed to cocaine would sustain long-term physical damage requiring significant and expensive medical attention. Very preliminary published research and media accounts during this period further indicated that children prenatally exposed to drugs would lack the ability to bond, academically achieve, socially adapt, or develop basic living skills [cf. Barth 1993].

The Current Research

More recent studies on prenatal drug and alcohol exposure, published after 1993, offer findings that differ significantly from the earlier research. The more recent studies, as opposed to the uniformly negative findings and predictions from the earlier research, suggest a broad range of outcomes, including the absence of significant problems. The fact that more optimistic findings have emerged from this research can be attributed to several factors. First, more recent studies utilize samples statistically significant in size that contrast with the small populations studied in earlier research. The subjects of earlier research were drawn from high-risk pools of infants referred for evaluation due to the serious nature of their problems, and consequently, these studies appear to have been biased toward poor outcomes [Aylward 1992]. It has been pointed out that these early studies of severely affected infants, ironically, may have understated the scope of the problem because they did not take into account the less extreme effects of prenatal substance exposure which affect larger numbers of children [Kleinsfeld 1993].

Second, current research has benefited from the ability to follow subjects over time and observe the longer-term consequences of prenatal substance exposure. Infants who were originally identified with FAS in the 1970s, for example, are now in their twenties, and longitudinal studies of these individuals reveal that the effects of prenatal alcohol exposure differ greatly among individuals. Recent research indicates that although damage sustained as a result of prenatal alcohol exposure is always permanent and often severe, persons prenatally exposed to alcohol may be able to achieve some level of academic and social success by using adaptive skills [Kleinsfeld 1993].

Finally, current research has expanded its area of study, considering factors in addition to prenatal drug and alcohol exposure that may impact outcomes for substance exposed children. Researchers particularly have focused on the interactions of children with their social environment and have found that postnatal environmental factors have an effect on long-term developmental outcomes that are as, if not more, important than prenatal exposure to drugs or alcohol [Ornoy et al. 1996; Lutiger et al. 1991]. Studies suggest that unstable postnatal environments are associated with poorer outcomes for children who are prenatally substance exposed [Streissguth et al. 1988], while children with similar prenatal histories who are reared by nurturing and responsive caregivers are more likely to achieve developmental norms and interact appropriately in social situations [Kronstat 1991; Zuckerman 1993].

Current Research: The Short-Rerm Effects of Prenatal Exposure.

Research describing the effects of prenatal exposure to drugs and alcohol on newborns is the most clear because there are few confounding factors that make interpretation difficult, and there is close proximity between exposure and the opportunity to observe effects [Coles & Platzman 1993]. These studies have contributed to an understanding of how fetal development may be affected by maternal drug and alcohol use, although the exact mechanisms remain unclear. It is known that alcohol is a teratogen, an agent that may affect fetal growth and development and cause defects in the structure or function of the central nervous system [Streissguth et al. 1996]. Individuals diagnosed with Fetal Alcohol Syndrome, for example, show clear deficits in judgement, social behavior, cognition, and attention and memory [Streissguth et al. 1991; Coles 1994]. Toxic effects on the developing fetus also have been observed in connection with prenatal substance exposure. The most common effects of prenatal drug and alcohol abuse, low birthweight, and small head circumference, are associated with toxicity resulting from the constriction of the pregnant woman's blood vessels due to substance abuse and the reduction in the amount of oxygen and nutrients available to the fetus [Volpe 1992]. The quality of prenatal care and sociological factors also may affect fetal development. If a mother fails to seek appropriate and timely prenatal care, the opportunities to identify and prevent health problems before birth may be significantly limited and fetal development may suffer [Levy & Koren 1990; Randal 1991]. Sociological factors such as poverty, which is also likely to be accompanied by poor nutrition, may likewise affect fetal development [Coles & Platzman 1993].

A summary of the potential short-term effects of prenatal exposure to a range of drugs, adapted from Brady and associates [1994], is provided in Table 1. As the table indicates, there are more generalized findings associated with prenatal exposure to certain drugs, and there are effects that have been suggested by only a limited number of studies. Research on certain drugs is so limited by sample size, lack of controls, and other factors, that any findings are inconclusive. The effects of prenatal alcohol exposure in two categories— Fetal Alcohol Syndrome (FAS) and Alcohol Related Birth Defects [ARBD] or Fetal Alcohol Effects (FAE)—are best understood.

Although the increased risks associated with prenatal exposure to certain drugs have been generally identified, birth outcomes associated with prenatal substance exposure vary significantly from one child to another, ranging from, at one extreme, the nonviability of the fetus to, at the other, the birth of a healthy, well-functioning infant. Research suggests that outcomes are associated with differences in the type of substance the mother uses during pregnancy; the stage of fetal development at the time of exposure; the duration of prenatal exposure to drugs or alcohol; other biologic maternal factors; and unexplained fetal predispositions [Kronstat 1991]. Studies have found that approximately 60% of newborns who have been prenatally exposed to drugs or alcohol exhibit problems related to substance exposure, with the most common physical effect being small head size and the most common behavioral effect being over-sensitivity to stimuli [Chasnoff 1989; Schaffer 1994]. Stimuli-sensitive infants often respond with self-protective behavior; they either become agitated and difficult to calm, as evidenced by jitters, tremors, or high-pitched cries, or they shut out the stimulation and fall into deep sleep [Chasnoff et al. 1992]. Research suggests that these self-protective behaviors may have important implications for later development, as difficulties in achieving calm and regulating arousal affect an infant's ability to orient to stimuli and may be a precursor to later intellectual and social growth [Chasnoff 1986; Mayes 1992]. These problems may impede the ability of the infant to absorb new information through interaction with people and objects in the environment and, as a result, affect future development [Chasnoff 1986].

The research makes clear, however, that it is not possible to predict long-term developmental or behavioral problems on the basis of acute symptomatic responses to prenatal substance exposure. Infants vary in their degree of sensitivity to stimulation as a result of a range of factors. Infants with no history of prenatal substance exposure may be highly sensitive to stimulation. There is also variation among infants affected by prenatal substance exposure. Sensitivity to stimulation may be a sustained state, or it may be a temporary symptom of drug withdrawal as the infant establishes the ability to achieve calm as drugs exit her system [Coles & Platzman 1993]. Finally, the nature and quality of caregiving may affect an infant's ability to regulate arousal and may play a significant role in abating or exacerbating the infant's acute symptomatic responses. A caregiver, for example, may intrude on an overstimulated infant and cause even a child who was not prenatally exposed to drugs or alcohol to exhibit distracted, impulsive, and restless behavior. By contrast, a caregiver who appropriately reduces stimuli for an overexcited infant and stimulates an under-aroused infant may assist the child in learning to concentrate and respond to others appropriately [Zuckerman 1993].

Current research: The long-term effects.

Researchers have found that by the end of the first year, most infants who manifest physical and behavioral indicators of prenatal sub-stance exposure achieve height and weight within normal param-

Table 1-1. Short-Term Effects of Prenatal Exposure to Alcohol and Drugs (Adapted from Brady et al. 1994)

Drug Type	Potential Effects of Prenatal Exposure	
	Generalized Findings from the Research	Other Effects Found in Some Studies
Cocaine	• Preterm delivery • Smaller-than-normal head size; low birthweight • Low scores on the APGAR (which assesses the condition of newborns) • Disorganized behavioral states in the prenatal and neonatal periods, which may indicate central nervous system damage	• Increased risk of motor dysfunction • Withdrawal symptoms • Longer-term language development and attention problems
Opiates	• Preterm delivery • Smaller-than-normal head size; low birthweight • Neonatal abstinence syndrome: neurological effects (hypertonia, tremors, sleep disturbance, seizures), autonomic nervous system dysfunctions, gastrointestinal abnormalities and respiratory problems	• Increased risk of SIDS • Longer-term effects related to below average weight/height, adjustment problems and psycholinguistic problems
Amphetamines and Methamphetamine	• Research inconclusive; some findings of aggression and problems relating to peers may be result of postnatal environment	• Research inconclusive; some findings of aggression and problems relating to peers may be result of postnatal environment

PCP
- Research very limited (very small samples, lack of controls); studies suggest a number of possible consequences such as preterm delivery, neonatal withdrawal, poor consolability and neurobehavioral symptoms such as irritability and tremors
- Research very limited (very small samples, lack of controls); studies suggest a number of possible consequences such as preterm delivery, neonatal withdrawal, poor consolability and neurobehavioral symptoms such as irritability and tremors
- Problems in verbal and memory domains

Marijuana
- Low birth weight

Alcohol: FAS
- Shortened gestational period
- Complications in delivery
- Neonatal neurobiological abnormalities
- Increased risk of spontaneous abortion and stillbirth

Alcohol: Alcohol Related Birth Defects [ARDB] or Fetal Alcohol Effects [FAE]
- Shorter gestational periods
- Reduced birth size and weight
- Postnatal growth retardation
- Central nervous system involvement (acute sensitivity to sound, irritability, attention problems)
- Facial abnormalities
- Cognitive impairment (use and understanding of language; ability to process information)
- Physical abnormalities which may affect linguistic development; impaired vision, hearing, and articulation
- Shorter gestational periods
- Reduced birth size and weight
- Neurobehavioral deficits in attention and memory
- Poor integration and quality of responses
- Distractibility and poor organization

eters and overcome behavioral effects such as agitation or sleepiness [Schuler et al. 1995]. Child development studies likewise have found that the majority of toddlers and preschoolers with histories of prenatal substance exposure test within normal ranges on developmental tests used to evaluate cognitive and motor development [Coles & Platzman 1993; Nulman et al. 1994; Lester 1998]. Many researchers have concluded on the basis of these findings that the effects of prenatal drug exposure taper off over time for most children as they make use of their natural adaptive biological abilities [Richardson et al. 1996].

Other researchers, however, question whether tests that indicate normal cognitive and motor development for preschool age children have predictive reliability in relation to long-term intelligence, social interactions, and overall potential for achievement, including scholastic and job performance [Schaffer 1994]. They highlight situations in which older children prenatally exposed to drugs or alcohol have significant problems related to attention deficits, hyperactivity, and impulsive or aggressive behavior [Schaffer 1994]. Some researchers hypothesize that prenatal substance exposure may affect aspects of behavioral development, even if it does not impair cognitive development. Nulman and associates [1994], for example, found that young children with histories of drug and alcohol exposure had average scores on tests of mental abilities and complex reasoning, but did not perform as well on tests of motor skills and language. The impact of prenatal substance exposure on longer-term cognitive development, however, remains uncertain. Skills related to intelligence are not fully developed in early childhood, and, as a consequence, research findings that toddlers and preschoolers score within normal ranges on cognitive functioning do not rule out the possibility that children may develop problems when they reach intellectual maturity and are required to perform in challenging academic settings [Nulman et al. 1994].

Both statistical and case study methods of research on the long-term effects of prenatal drug and alcohol exposure suggest a high level of variability in children's developmental outcomes. Child development, like fetal and infant development, appears associated with type, quantity, and timing of drug consumption and other factors related to maternal health and functioning during pregnancy [Schaffer 1994]. Dissimilarity in children's postnatal environments further adds to the variability of outcomes for children prenatally exposed to drugs and alcohol. Poor developmental outcomes are associated with postnatal risk factors that include poverty, unstable home conditions, violence in the home environment, and inadequate interaction with adult caregivers [Schaffer 1994]. These factors are also associated with child abuse and neglect and foster care entry, which carry with them additional risks to children's health and development [Schaffer 1994].

Positive long-term developmental outcomes are associated with a nurturing environment that begins in early childhood [Zuckerman 1993]. Flexible yet consistent environments have been found to promote the development of children prenatally exposed to drugs or alcohol who exhibit symptomatic behavior [Kleinfeld 1993]. Although nurturing and stable home environments cannot reverse low IQ scores or neurological damage [Aronson et al. 1985], research suggests that positive postnatal environments can maximize children's ability to perform scholastically, socially, and personally [Nulman et al. 1994; Zuckerman 1993].

Research on postnatal environment factors has identified aspects of a nurturing environment that appear to promote the development of substance-exposed children. Attachment is likely to be fostered when a single caregiver is consistently available to the child and offers the child nurturing and support. Similarly, children appear more willing to explore and learn from their environments when they interact with a single, nurturing, dependable caregiver. Studies also show that caregivers can promote children's biologic maturation. Specifically, research has found that children's development is promoted when caregivers adjust the environment to enhance children's responsiveness, consistently provide affection to children who have difficulties achieving calm, orient children who are consistently under-aroused toward sight and sound, and respond appropriately to the child's sleepy and alert states. Inconsistent and punitive responses by caregivers, on the other hand, are associated with poorer developmental outcomes, even for healthy children without histories of prenatal substance exposure [Zuckerman 1993].

Limitations on the Research

In spite of the important information that research has provided on the short- and long-term effects of prenatal alcohol or drug exposure, issues relating to collection and evaluation of data place limitations on the research knowledge base. The limitations relate to three factors. First, information obtained on drug and alcohol use during pregnancy may be of limited scope and accuracy. Data on prenatal substance use is not uniformly collected from pregnant women, and toxicology testing is not done on all newborns. Research, as a result, largely has relied on self-reporting of drug or alcohol use during pregnancy [Zuckerman 1991; Kronstat 1991], limiting participation in studies to women who choose to take part in research. The accuracy and completeness of information that is obtained on prenatal drug and alcohol use also may be limited, particularly information related to the nature of substances used during pregnancy and the timing and frequency of use [Zuckerman 1991]. Women may not accurately recall these aspects of substance use or may be reluctant to report the full extent of these behaviors.

Second, research primarily has studied prenatal substance exposure within certain socioeconomic and racial groups. Studies have concentrated to a far greater extent on the developmental effects of cocaine, the drug of choice for lower income groups and African Americans, than on marijuana, the drug of choice for higher income groups and Caucasians [Chasnoff et al. 1980]. Research also has tended to focus on the effects of prenatal substance exposure on newborns delivered in publicly-funded hospitals, which generally serve lower income communities and communities of color [Coles 1992], and on children in the child protective service system to which African American and poor women are far more likely than Caucasian and nonpoor women to be reported [Chasnoff et al. 1980]. The primary focus of the research on poor minority women significantly restricts the ability to generalize the findings, leaving open many questions regarding outcomes for the prenatally substance-exposed children of women who are in the middle- to upper-income bracket or who are Caucasian.

Third, research is limited because it cannot isolate the impact of prenatal alcohol and drug exposure from other factors bearing on developmental outcomes. Research suggests that a significant percentage of pregnant women who abuse substances engage in drug, alcohol and tobacco use, making it impossible to isolate the effects of any one substance [Zuckerman 1991]. The impact of prenatal exposure to drugs and alcohol is further affected by maternal factors such as nutritional status; use, timing, and quality of prenatal health care; and maternal medical problems such as liver damage related to alcohol abuse [Zuckerman 1991; Frank et al. 1996]. Finally, research cannot fully take into account the biological vulnerability of the fetus and the extent to which fetal factors interact with prenatal substance exposure and maternal factors [Zuckerman 1991].

Research and Adoption of Children Prenatally Exposed to Drugs and Alcohol

Over the past decade, prenatal drug and alcohol abuse has significantly effected child welfare agencies across the United States. Substance abuse by parents has precipitated substantial increases in reports of child abuse and neglect, a dramatic rise in the number of children entering foster care, and a heightened demand for adoption planning and services, particularly for infants and young children.

Studies have documented the connection between parental drug and alcohol involvement and child abuse and neglect. One study found that drug and alcohol dependence is a problem for at least half of the families known to the public child welfare system [Dore et al. 1995]. In a recent survey of the 50 states, 80% of the states identified parental substance abuse as one of the two most prevalent problems in families reported for child maltreatment [National Committee to Prevent Child Abuse 1996]. Studies also suggest that a significant number of children affected by prenatal drugs or alcohol exposure are reported as neglected or abused. Estimates are that from

48% to 80% of the 3 million infants prenatally exposed to drugs and alcohol each year need child welfare services before their first birthday [Gomby & Shiono 1991; Curtis & McCullough 1993; Child Welfare League of America 1996].

As the number of reports of abuse and neglect for children affected by prenatal drug or alcohol exposure has grown, the number of these children entering foster care likewise has risen. The Child Welfare League of America [1998] found that parental substance abuse was one of the key factors contributing to the dramatic growth in out-of-home care placements between 1986 and 1995. Similarly, a study by the Urban Institute found that more than half of the placements in foster care are attributable, at least in part, to parental substance abuse [Newmark 1995]. Drug use by pregnant and parenting women has been a significant aspect of parental substance abuse and the need for foster care services. Data from New York, Illinois, and Michigan—states with significant foster care populations—indicate that the number of infant admissions to foster care more than doubled between 1984 and 1989 because of maternal drug use [Wulczyn & Goerge 1991]. Parental drug involvement also has been associated with prolonged stays in foster care. Barth and Needell [1995] found that drug-exposed infants remain in foster care far longer than children who are not drug-exposed.

Child welfare systems have encountered significant challenges in permanency planning for children affected by prenatal alcohol and drug exposure. As it has become apparent that reunification of children with substance-involved parents may not be an appropriate or timely alternative in many cases, adoption has come to be considered a viable alternative for substance-exposed children. As they have weighed adoption as a permanency option for these children, practitioners and prospective adoptive parents have turned to the research on health and developmental outcomes in an attempt to gain a better understanding of the short- and long-term effects of substance exposure.

Findings from the early research suggesting that children affected by prenatal substance exposure were irreparably damaged caused practitioners and potential adoptive parents throughout the late 1980s and early 1990s to question the wisdom of adoption [Barth 1993; McCullough 1991]. Media accounts heightened concerns about adoption as an option for substance-exposed children. Newspaper and magazine articles highlighted the disastrous outcomes believed to be uniformly associated with prenatal substance exposure [Lyons & Rittner 1998] and recounted stories in which adoptive parents returned young children to child welfare agencies or abused infants in their care because of their demanding and inconsolable behavior [Blakeslee 1990; McFadden 1990].

Adoption began to be viewed more favorably with the publication of research beginning in the mid-1990s indicating that nurturing caregivers could promote relatively positive health and developmental outcomes for children prenatally exposed to drugs or alcohol. Studies finding relatively normal intellectual, psychological, and social development among many children prenatally exposed to drugs or alcohol suggested that these children could form close attachments and become part of an adoptive family. Studies reporting successful results from intervention programs designed to address the developmental effects of prenatal substance exposure also supported more optimistic views of adoption as a service for substance-exposed children. Researchers reported that even in cases of FAS, improved intellectual functioning and social interaction could be achieved with special education services and programs offering adaptive social skill strategies [Streissguth et al. 1988]. As journalists noted these studies and began to report more positive outcomes for substance exposed children [Rainey 1998; Wren 1998], public perceptions of these children and their long-term prospects began to shift. These research and media developments set the stage for a consideration of adoption as a viable alternative for substance-exposed children.

Most recently, research has begun to compare outcomes for adopted children affected by prenatal substance exposure to outcomes for children with different prenatal histories and postnatal environments. The limited body of research in this area suggests positive outcomes associated with adoption. Ornoy and associates [1996] compared outcomes for adopted children affected by prenatal heroin exposure to outcomes for heroin-exposed children reared by birth parents and for nonexposed children reared in neglectful and abusive environments. They found that heroin-exposed adopted children achieved higher scores on tests of mental and motor development than the other two groups of children. The research of Barth and Brooks, as they report in this volume, compares outcomes for adopted children who are drug-exposed and adopted children who are not drug exposed. Finding that the two groups of children are more similar than different on key developmental outcomes eight years postadoption, Barth and Brooks highlight the benefits of postnatal environmental factors associated with adoption.

A number of issues remain to be studied as child welfare professionals continue to assess the viability of adoption as a permanency planning alternative for substance-exposed children and provide adoption planning and services for children and their adoptive families. Tools are needed to assess more fully the status of substance-exposed children, particularly in relation to their future developmental needs. Further research is needed that compares long-term developmental outcomes of children prenatally exposed to drugs or alcohol and reared by their birth families and by adoptive families. Research also is needed on the experiences of families who adopt substance-exposed children. Research that tracks families' experiences as children move through all developmental phases could provide child welfare professionals with a fuller understanding of the education, preparation, and support needs of adoptive families and how their needs can best be met.

Conclusion

Research on the effects of prenatal drug and alcohol exposure conducted over the past twenty years provides a significant knowledge base on which adoption practice and policy may build. Research provides an understanding of the short-term effects of prenatal substance exposure and guidance on the range of potential long-term developmental outcomes associated with prenatal and postnatal factors. Although there is still much that remains to be understood, this research can assist adoption professionals in strengthening their own practice in the recruitment, preparation, and support of adoptive parents; educating prospective adoptive parents about the health and developmental outcomes associated with prenatal substance exposure; assisting prospective adoptive parents in making fully informed decisions regarding the adoption of a substance exposed child; and supporting adoptive families when children present developmental or behavioral problems related to prenatal alcohol or drug exposure. It likewise has value for mental health professionals who prepare and counsel adoptive families and education professionals who develop and provide preschool and school-based programs for substance-exposed children and their families.

Notes

1. The author gratefully acknowledges the research assistance of Aline Kahn.

References

Aronson, M. (1995). Children of alcoholic mothers. *Acta Raediatrica Scandinavica, 74*, 27–35.

Aylward, G. (1992). The relationship between environmental risk and developmental outcome. *Developmental and Behavioral Pediatrics, 13*(3), 222–229.

Barth, R. (1993). Revisiting the Issues: Adoption of drug exposed children. *The Future of Children, 3*(1), 167–175.

Barth, R. & Needell, B. (1995). Outcomes for drug-exposed children four years post-adoption. *Children and Youth Services Review, 18*(1 /2), 37–56.

Blakeslee, S. (1990, May 19). Parents fear for future infants born on drugs. *New York Times*, pp. A1, A8–A9.

Brady, J., Posner, M., Lang, C., and Rosati, M. (1994). *Risk and reality: The implications of prenatal exposure to alcohol and other drugs.* Rockville, MD: U.S. Department of Health and Human Services.

Chasnoff, I. J. (1989). Drug use in women: Establishing a standard of care. *Annals of the New York Academy of Science, 562*, 208–210.

Chasnoff, I. J., Burns, K. A., Burns, W. J., & Schnoll, S. H. (1986). Prenatal drug exposure: Effects on neonatal and infant growth. *Neurobehavior, Toxicology, and Teratology, 8,* 357–362.

Chasnoff, I. J., Griffith, D. R., Freier, C., & Murray, J. (1992). Cocaine/poly-drug use in pregnancy. *Pediatrics, 89,* 284–289.

Chasnoff, I. J., Landress, H., & Barrett, M. (1980). The prevalence of illicit drug or alcohol use during pregnancy and discrepancies in mandatory reporting. *New England Journal of Medicine, 322,* 1202–1206.

Child Welfare League of America (1992). *Children at the front: A different view of the war on alcohol and drugs.* Washington, DC: CWLA Press.

Child Welfare League of America (1996). *Alcohol and other drugs: A study of state child welfare agencies' policy and programmatic response.* Washington, DC: Child Welfare League of America.

Child Welfare League of America (1998). *Child Welfare Stat Book.* Washington DC: CWLA Press.

Coles, C. (1992). How the environment affects research on prenatal drug exposure: The laboratory and the community. In *Measurement Issues in Epidemiological, Prevention, and Treatment Research on the Effects of Prenatal Drug Exposure on Women and Children* (NIDA Research Monograph 117) (pp. 272–292). Rockville, MD: National Institute on Drug Abuse.

Coles, C. (1994). Critical periods for prenatal alcohol exposure: Evidence from animal and human studies. *Alcohol Health and Research World, 18*(1), 309–315.

Coles, C. & Platzman, K. (1993). Behavioral development in children prenatally exposed to drugs and alcohol. *The International Journal of the Addictions, 28,* 1393–1433.

Curtis, P. & McCullogh, C. (1993). The impact of alcohol and other drugs on the child welfare system. *Child Welfare, 72,* 533–542.

Delaney-Black, V., Covington, C., Templin, T., Ager, J., Martier P., & Sokol, R. (1998). Prenatal cocaine exposure and child behavior. *Pediatrics, 102,* 945–950.

Dore, M., Doris, J., & Wright, P. (1995). Identifying substance abuse in maltreating families: A child welfare challenge. *Child Abuse and Neglect, 19,* 531–543.

Frank, D. A., Bresnahan, K., & Zuckerman, B. S. (1996). Maternal cocaine use: Impact on child health and development. *Pediatrics, 26*(2), 49–76.

Gomby D. & Shiono, P. (1991). Estimating the number of substance exposed infants. *The Future of Children, 1*(1), 17–25.

Kleinfeld, J. (1993). Introduction. In Kleinfeld, J. & Wescott, S. (Eds.) *Fantastic Antone Succeeds: Experiences in Educating Children with Fetal Alcohol Syndrome* (pp. 1–20). Fairbanks, AK: University of Alaska Press.

Koren, G., Shear, H., Graham, K., & Einarson, T. (1989). Bias against the null hypothesis: The reproductive hazard of cocaine. *Lancet, 2,* 1440–1442.

Kronstat, D. (1991). Complex developmental issues of prenatal drug exposure. *The Future of Children, 1*(1), 26–35.

Lester, B. M., LaGrasse, L. L., & Seifer, R. (1998). Cocaine exposure and children: The meaning of subtle effects. *Science, 282,* 633–634.

Levy, M. & Koren, G. (1990). Obstetric and neonatal effects of drugs of abuse: Emergency aspects of drug abuse. *Emergency Medical Clinicians of North America, 8*(3), 633–352.

Lutiger, B., Graham, K., Einarson, T. R., & Koren, G. (1991). Relationship between gestational cocaine use and pregnancy outcome: A meta-analysis. *Teratology, 44,* 405–414.

Lyons, P. & Rittner, B. (1998). The construction of the crack babies phenomenon. *American Journal of Orthopsychiatry, 68*(2), 313–320.

Mayes, L. C. (1992). Prenatal cocaine exposure and young children's development. *The Annals of the American Academy of Pediatrics, 521,* 11–27.

McCullough, C. (1991). The child welfare response. *The Future of Children, 1*(1), 61–71.

McFadden, R. (1990, June 19). Tragic ending to the adoption of a crack baby. *New York Times,* p. B1.

National Committee to Prevent Child Abuse. (1996). *Current trends in child abuse reporting and fatalities: NCPCA's 1995 annual fifty state survey.* Washington, DC: Author.

Newmark, L. (1995). *Parental drug testing in child abuse and neglect cases: Major findings.* Washington DC: The Urban Institute.

Nulman, I., Rovet, J., Altman, D., Bradly, C., Einarson, T., & Koren, G. (1994). Neurodevelopment of adopted children exposed in-utero to cocaine. *Canadian Medical Association Journal, 151,* 1591-1597.

Ornoy, A., Michailevskaya V., & Lukashov, I. (1996). The developmental outcome of children born to heroin dependent mothers raised at home. *Child Abuse and Neglect, 20,* 381–396.

Rainey, J. (1998, September 15). "Crack babies" show fewer problems than predicted, experts say. *Los Angeles Times,* pp. A1, A23.

Randall, T. (1991). Intensive prenatal care may deliver healthy babies to pregnant drug abusers. *Journal of the American Medical Association, 265*(21), 19–20.

Richardson, G., Conroy, M., & Day, N. (1996). Prenatal cocaine exposure on the development of school age children. *Neurotoxicology and Teratology, 19,* 627–634.

Schaffer, J. (1994). *When love is not enough: The foster children of crack-cocaine.* New York: Resources for Children with Special Needs, Inc.

Schuler, M., Black, M., & Starr, R. (1995). Determinants of mother infant interaction: Effects of prenatal drug exposure, social support, and infant temperature. *Journal of Clinical Child Psychology, 24,* 397–405.

Streissguth, A. P., Aase, J. M., Clarren, S. K., LaDue, R. A., Randels, S. P., & Smith, D. F. (1991). Fetal Alcohol Syndrome in adolescents and adults. *Journal of the American Medical Association, 265*(15), 1961–1967.

Streissguth, A. P., Barr, H. M., Hogan, J., & Bookstein, F. L. (1996). *Understanding the occurrence of secondary disabilities in clients with Fetal Alcohol Syndrome and Fetal Alcohol Effects.* Seattle: University of Washington Publication Services.

Streissguth, A. P., La Due, R., & Randels, S. (1988). *A manual on adolescents and adults with fetal alcohol syndrome with special reference to American Indians.* Seattle, WA: U.S. Department of Health and Human Services.

Vega, W., Kolody, B., Hwang, J., & Noble, A. (1993). Prevalence and magnitude of perinatal substance exposure in California. *New England Journal of Medicine, 329,* 850–854.

Volpe, J. (1992). Effect of cocaine use on the fetus. *New England Journal of Medicine, 327*(6), 399–407.

Wren, C. (1998, September 22). For crack babies, a future less bleak: The drug's effects are real, experts say, but can be reversed. *New York Times,* p. D4.

Wulezyn, E. & Goerge R. (1991). Foster care in New York and Illinois: The challenge of rapid change. *Social Service Review, 69,* 278–294.

Zuckerman, B. (1991). Drug exposed infants: Understanding the medical risk. *The Future of Children*, *1*(1), 26–35.

Zuckerman, B. (1993). Developmental considerations for drug- and AIDS-affected infants. In R. P. Barth, J. Pietrzak, & M. Ramler (Eds.), *Families living with drugs and HIV: Interventions and treatment strategies* (pp. 37–58). London: The Guilford Press.

2

Outcomes for Drug-Exposed Children Eight Years Postadoption

Richard P. Barth & Devon Brooks

The success of new, national public child welfare policies depends upon the willingness of the American public to adopt children in foster care. President Clinton's Adoption 2002 aims to double the number of children adopted or placed in other permanent arrangements between 1998 and 2002. The Adoption and Safe Families Act [1997] requires that reasonable efforts be made to ensure that children who cannot be reunified with their parents are placed for adoption—in their own states or across state lines. To promote adoption for these children, a variety of strategies is being implemented, including shorter time frames for decision making regarding permanency plans for children, and the placement of children in homes where there is a high likelihood of adoption even while attempts at reunification with the birth family continue. However, these strategies will not succeed in achieving their objectives unless families are willing to adopt children in foster care who were born drug-exposed.

Although there are no definitive data on the proportion of children available for adoption who have experienced prenatal drug exposure, there is some indication that this group is sizable. The U.S. General Accounting Office [1998] estimates that in the states of California and Illinois, between 65% and 75% of the children who have been in foster care for at least 17 months have substance-involved parents. Although there was no effort to assess the proportion of children born prenatally exposed to drugs, the report found that more than 80% of the mothers of these children abused substances for at least five years [U.S. General Accounting Office 1998].

In recent years, with the sharp influx of drug-exposed newborns and their siblings, children have entered foster care at increasingly younger ages. More than 25% of all children placed in foster care are now under one year of age at the time they enter care [Wulczyn et al. 1997]. Parental drug use during pregnancy has become a powerful predictor of subsequent child abuse reports and foster care entry [Albert & Barth, 1996; Wulczyn 1994], and infants are more likely to enter foster care than children of any other age group [Berrick et al. 1997; Wulczyn et al. 1997].

Today, infants most often are placed in foster care because of parental substance abuse. Approximately one in three infants in care will ultimately be adopted [Berrick et al. 1997], and given indicators related to maternal substance abuse, it is likely that a sizable proportion of these children will have histories of prenatal substance exposure. Barth and Needell [1996] found in their study, for example, that 31% of parents adopting through public agencies indicated with substantial certainty that their adopted children were drug-exposed, while another 48% were unable to rule out this possibility.

The willingness of potential adoptive parents to accept drug-exposed children is related to their willingness to accept the long-term risks of assuming full responsibility for a child via adoption. The acceptance of these risks is partially a result of beliefs about probable outcomes for drug-exposed children who are adopted. Initial media and scientific reports on the long-term future of drug-exposed children and the short-term difficulty of caring for them [e.g., Blakeslee 1990; Howard 1990] were so pessimistic that they often discouraged prospective adoptive parents from considering these children. They also dissuaded social workers and judges from giving serious consideration to moving these children from temporary foster care placements into permanent adoptive families. Little research-based information has been provided since then to correct early impressions regarding outcomes for drug-exposed children who are adopted.

Potential adoptive parents may have other reasons for concern. Recent attention to the importance of prenatal, infant, and genetic factors places adoption of children in foster care under a harsh light.

Perry and colleagues [1995] have concluded that abused children may experience lasting changes in the structure of their brains and diminished capacity for thought and action as a result of the trauma of abuse. In the context of the effects of prenatal substance exposure on children, however, these findings may suggest differential outcomes for drug-exposed children depending on their preplacement histories. Children who are adopted by families with whom they are placed directly from the hospital may avoid some trauma; children who first are discharged to drug-affected families, however, may experience a double dose of cognitive insult.

Although adoptive parents generally expect to have a major and positive impact on their children, they may be concerned that parental devotion will not be enough to help adopted children overcome early adversity. Concerns may arise as a result of theories such as that put forward by Judith Harris [1998], a parent of both an adopted and a biological child, who has gained much attention for her argument that genetic and peer influences, rather than parental influences, dominate the determination of child outcomes. Cadoret and colleagues [this volume] also indicate reasons for concern about prenatal alcohol exposure and its impact on long-term life outcomes.

Beyond implications for the child welfare system and foster care in particular, research on adoption of drug-exposed children has implications for a more general understanding of adoption and child development. Because adoption permanently changes a child's living environment and relationships, it is the most comprehensive intervention available for children. Studies of the adoption of socially disadvantaged children show strikingly positive changes in the developmental and cognitive performance of those children [Dumaret 1985; Hodges & Tizard 1989a; Rutter et al. 1981; Scarr & Weinberg 1976]. At the same time, other recent adoption literature emphasizes the limits of the benefits of family formation by adoption and preserves the possibility that adopted children do not fare as well as other children [e.g., Sharma et al. 1998]. How well each of these opposed expectations best predicts the cognitive, social, and behavioral outcomes for drug-exposed children who are adopted is unclear.

Previous Research on Outcomes for Drug-Exposed Children

Research that attempts to clarify the impact of prenatal drug exposure on the cognitive functioning of children is limited and imperfect. Griffith, Azuma and Chasnoff [1994] conducted a three-year study of behavioral and cognitive outcomes for ninety-three children exposed prenatally to cocaine and other drugs and for twenty-four polydrug/noncocaine-exposed children. Among these 117 children, 34% lived with birth mothers who continued to use drugs and the remaining children lived with birth mothers who ceased to use drugs within one year after birth (26%) or with kin or foster parents (40%). These drug-exposed children were compared to 25 non-exposed children living with their birth mothers. All mothers in the study were enrolled in prenatal care and received subsequent pediatric and developmental follow-up. The impact of drug-exposure on children's outcomes was very modest. Prenatal cocaine exposure accounted for a small proportion (9%) of the variance in verbal reasoning, marijuana accounted for 13% of the variance in abstract/visual reasoning, and the combination of cocaine, marijuana, and alcohol accounted for 5% of the variance in abstract visual reasoning. Children in the polydrug and cocaine drug-exposure groups were rated as more destructive and externalizing than the control group of children. No comparisons were made, however, between children in each group who were living in drug-free environments. As a consequence, the relative impact of prenatal drug exposure and postnatal exposure to a drug-affected parent and environment is unclear.

A second, important cohort study is described in several papers by Nulman and Koren and their colleagues. Their prospective study is of 30 mothers who admitted to social cocaine use and their children, matched with 30 drug-free control subjects and their children [Nulman et al. 1994]. The matching did not result in equivalence between the two groups on paternal education or socioeconomic status, maternal smoking, or alcohol use. The researchers found no differences between the two groups of children on physical or cognitive development at 1.6 years of age. Koren and colleagues [1998], who followed this same sample of children through the age of six years, concluded that there were mild to moderate direct neurotoxic effects of cocaine on IQ and language, but they did not control for maternal characteristics that could determine both IQ and language independently of drug-use. The researchers further concluded that adoption reduced the impact of parental drug exposure and resulted in mild to moderate effects as compared to those measured in children exposed in utero to cocaine and reared by their birth mothers.

Richardson and colleagues [1996] studied the offspring of 28 mothers who reported light to moderate cocaine use during pregnancy. They found no significant effects of prenatal cocaine exposure on the growth, intellectual ability, academic achievement, or teacher-rated classroom behavior of the children through six years of age. The cocaine-exposed children, however, were found to have less ability to sustain attention on computerized tasks.

In a meta-analysis of five studies that met methodological criteria, Lester and colleagues [1998] determined that there were modest but important relationships between prenatal substance exposure and the outcomes of interest. The effects on IQ represented a decrease of 3.26 points (and an effect size of .33). According to the authors' calculations, this decrease in IQ points nearly doubled the number of children who would have tested above the cut-off IQ score for special education services, but who, as a result of prenatal substance exposure, now qualified for special education services. The effect sizes for expressive and receptive language were nearly twice as large (.60 and .71, respectively), indicating that substance-exposed children were about two-thirds of a standard deviation below the comparison groups of non-drug affected children. The authors computed the odds that exposed children would have language problems at the clinical level at about four times the odds for comparison children. The authors concluded that the effects of prenatal substance exposure are subtle but important, and that prevention and intervention services are critical to ensuring that greater long-term public health and social service costs are not generated.

Additional concern about the outcomes associated with adoption arises from questions about children's ability to attach to their adoptive families. The common lore of social work practice is that attachment is critically important and a major point of vulnerability for adopted children and parents [Johnson & Fein 1991]. Some evidence on adoption of children from residential care (children not identified as drug-exposed) indicates that "children who in their first years of life are deprived of close and lasting attachments to adults can make such attachments later" [Hodges & Tizard 1989b, 96]. The development of such attachments is not inevitable, however, varying according to parent traits and, especially, the level of disturbance demonstrated by children before they leave institutional care. In their study of special needs adoptions, Groze and Rosenthal [1993, 10] found modest associations between predictors of attachment (such as age at time of placement, length of time in prior placements, and history prior to adoptive placement) and attachment, noting that "many children develop close attachments even with problematic preplacement histories." The proportion of drug-exposed children in their sample, however, is likely to have been small, and the ability to generalize the findings to these children is in doubt. Dozier [this volume] also raises questions about the risk of insecure attachments among adopted children.

While acknowledging the limits of available research, Gittler and McPherson [1990] indicate that toddlers prenatally exposed to drugs are less securely attached to caregivers. From their clinical perspective, Moore and Camarda [1993] in their article, "Drug-Exposed Children, Fresh Reasons for Concern" write, "drug-exposed infants tend to be seriously limited in their ability to form an adequate relationship with their primary caregiver. It is the quality of this first relationship which is most decisive in laying the foundation for the child's future development" [1993, 11]. The research and clinical literature highlight the need for professionals and potential adoptive parents to understand the dual impact of adoption and drug exposure on attachment.

Method

The present study was conducted to address some of the limitations described in the studies referred to above and to provide more information on the long-term outcomes of drug-exposed and adopted children.

Sample and Procedure

Between June 1988 and July 1989, social workers asked approximately 2,589 adoptive parents about their interest in taking part in the California Long-Range Adoption Study (CLAS). Of the 2,238 parents who expressed an interest in participating in CLAS, 2,058 parents were mailed questionnaires and were asked to provide information about the children they had recently adopted. Due to incomplete address information, the remaining 180 parents could not be contacted and therefore were excluded from the study. Sixty-nine percent (n = 1,296) of the parents who received questionnaires (n = 1878) provided information about their 1,396 adopted children.

The second wave of the study was conducted in 1993, four years after the placements of the adopted subjects. Using mailed questionnaires, 80% (n = 1,119) of the children studied in the first wave of CLAS were followed up in Wave II. Due to missing or discrepant data, however, only 1,008 cases (72% of the original sample) could be matched between Waves I and II.

In 1997—approximately eight years after the placements—the second follow-up commenced. Participants were asked to complete mailed questionnaires about their adopted children. Attempts also were made to contact adoptive parents who, despite expressing initial interest in participating in the study, did not participate in either of the first two waves of CLAS. In total, 1,455 questionnaires were mailed to parents for whom current addresses were available. Completed questionnaires were returned for 888 children (61% of the mailing). Of these, questionnaires were completed in all three waves of CLAS for 679 children (representing 49% of the original child sample). Of the 1,008 children studied four years postadoption, 642 (64%) were studied again at eight years postadoption. Children whose parents did not participate in all three waves, children from Wave III who could not be matched to the Wave I/II data set, and children who were adopted internationally were excluded from the present analysis. The analysis also excluded children reported in any wave as having Fetal Alcohol Syndrome (FAS), Down's Syndrome, and/or HIV. Finally, children whom we could not classify as drug-exposed or non-drug-exposed, due to either missing or discrepant data (see below), were excluded. Our final sample of 233 children consists of 112 (48%) non-drug-exposed and 121 (52%) drug-exposed subjects.

Questionnaire

A mailed questionnaire asked adoptive parents about various aspects of adoption, the characteristics of their family, and the characteristics of and outcomes for their adopted children. Among the child outcomes assessed were education, general adjustment and behavior, and physical health. The questionnaire also contained items related to the respondents' sense of closeness with their adopted child, as well as items related to their satisfaction with both the adoption experience and the adopted child. Many items in the Wave III questionnaire were also included in the questionnaires from previous waves, providing a unique opportunity to assess changes in the respondents' attitudes about and perceptions of adoption and children's development and well-being over time.

Classification of Subjects

In Wave I, participants were asked three questions regarding knowledge of their adopted child's exposure to drugs prenatally. We initially classified children as drug-exposed if the answers to all three questions indicated prenatal drug exposure and as not drug-exposed if 'no' was indicated on all three indicators. Children whose parents reported at least one but less than three indicators of drug exposure or whose parents indicated "still unknown" were classified as unknown.

At four years, responses to the three indicator questions resulted in a change of 17 children from the classification of drug-exposed (7% of the two-year postadoption sample with this classification) to unknown, and 106 children from the classification of not drug-exposed (35% of the two-year sample with this classification) to unknown. To examine the possibility that the change in responses at four years from non-drug-exposed to drug-exposed was the result of children's problems that may have convinced the parent that the child was prenatally exposed to drugs, the behavior of the 106 children who were reclassified was compared to that of the 201 who remained classified as not exposed to drugs. At the four-year point, no differences existed between the two groups [Barth & Needell 1996].

We included additional items concerning prenatal drug exposure in the questionnaires for Waves II and III. Discrepancies between Wave II responses and Wave III responses resulted in a change in the classification of 18 children previously classified as either drug-exposed or non-drug-exposed to unknown. These cases involved children previously classified as drug-exposed and then identified as not drug-exposed in Wave III and children previously classified as non-drug-exposed and then identified as drug-exposed in Wave III. We did not repeat an analysis comparing reclassified children to children who were not reclassified at eight years because the number of reclassifications of children was quite low.

At four years, respondents who indicated that their children were prenatally exposed to drugs were asked about all types of drugs to which their children were exposed and the approximate level of exposure. Respondents indicated that 62% of their drug-exposed children were prenatally exposed to crack cocaine, 63% to other forms of cocaine, 59% to heroin, 75% to marijuana, and 30% to PCP. Nearly 85% were also exposed to alcohol and 90% to tobacco. Although known to have untoward effects, prenatal exposure to alcohol and tobacco smoking were not treated as drug exposure for the purposes of this study. To better understand the reliability of information on the nature and level of prenatal exposure, respondents were asked to identify the source of their knowledge about drug exposure. They indicated that they knew about the prenatal drug exposure primarily on the basis of information from their social worker (54%), the birth mother directly (35%), or from the birth records (11%).

Data Analysis

Both bivariate and multivariate analyses were used to compare groups. Associations between categorical variables were tested using the Pearson chi-square test, and differences in means were tested by independent sample and paired t-tests. We developed maximum likelihood logistic regression models to predict the outcome variable of interest. Models were constructed using variables that were significant in the bivariate analysis or considered theoretically relevant. When conducting logistic regression analysis, we compared levels of a variable to the effect of that variable on the odds of the event occurring. A frontward stepwise approach with a selection criterion of .01 was used to build the models.

Results

Attrition

In order to determine whether the Wave III sample was different in any significant way from the samples from Waves I and II, we conducted a logistic regression analysis. The analysis, which is summarized in Table 1, suggests that selection bias in Wave III due to attrition is minimal. Of the child characteristic variables and the child functioning variables from Wave II that we tested as predictive of participation in Wave III, only one variable was significant. Specifically, having indicated in Wave II that the adoption was open at the time of placement increased the likelihood of nonparticipation in Wave III by 1.2 times (p < .05). Children's drug exposure status was not significant, nor was their ethnicity, kinship status, adoption type, or gender. Though it was included in the final model in order to increase the parsimony of the model, children's functioning at Wave II also was not significant. With regard to the "child functioning" variable, the logistic regression analysis suggests that children with poorer functioning in Wave II were no more or less likely to be omitted in Wave III than children with better functioning.

Family and Child Characteristics

As can be seen in Tables 2 and 3, the background characteristics of the families and children we studied differed significantly by group, depending on the drug exposure status of the child. For instance, drug-exposed children were more likely than non-drug-exposed children to be adopted by parents having attained lower levels of

Table 2-1. Attrition Analysis[1]: Effect of Child Characteristics and Functioning in Wave II on Participation in Wave III (N = 719)

	B	SE	df	Sign.	Effect on Odds[2]
Variables remaining in the final model[3]					
Open adoption (yes) *	-.2181	.0874	1	.0126	.8041[4]
Functions wells (BPI scale)					
(yes)(n.w)	.1507	.0935	1	.1069	1.1627

·2Log likelihood	879.17
Goodness of fit significance	.47
% Correctly predicted by model	69.26

[1]*The original sample for the attrition analysis consisted of Wave I and Wave II matched cases (N = 1,008) studied at four years post adoption. Additional cases were excluded due to missing data, yielding a final sample of 719 cases.*

[2]*Values greater than 1 indicate an increase in the odds of participating in Wave III.*

[3]*Variables excluded from the full model: drug exposure status, child's ethnicity, kinship status, type of adoption, and child's gender.*

[4]*Indicates that having an open adoption increases the odds of non-participation in Wave III by 1.24 times.*

formal education as reported in Wave III. More precisely, drug-exposed children were less likely than their non-drug-exposed counterparts to have been adopted by parents who either graduated from a four-year college or completed a graduate or professional program ($p < .05$). The difference in parents' formal educational attainment is reflected in the mean income from employment and investment for families. Parents of drug-exposed children reported making over 30% less than the parents of non-drug-exposed children ($62,232 vs. $89,878).

Compared with children from the non-drug-exposed group, children from the drug-exposed group were placed for adoption at a slightly older age and were more often adopted through a public agency. Roughly one-half of the drug-exposed children we studied

Table 2-2. Family Characteristics

Family Characteristic	Base	Non Drug-Exposed (%)	Drug-Exposed (%)
Respondent	231		
Mother		83.8	84.2
Father		16.2	15.8
Kinship (yes)	232	7.1	10.8
Respondent's current marital status	233		
Single		3.6	4.1
Married or living with partner		90.2	91.7
Other (separated, divorced, widowed)		6.3	4.1
Respondent's ethnicity	224		
White or Caucasian		86.1	85.3
Hispanic or Latin		7.8	9.1
Black or African American		2.8	2.6
Other		4.6	1.7
Ethnicity of spouse or partner	212		
White or Caucasian		88.2	86.4
Hispanic or Latin		7.8	9.1
Black or African American		2.0	4.5
Other		2.0	0.0
Mean age of respondent (years)	232	45.8	45.0
Mean age of spouse or partner (years)	218	48.4	47.0
*Respondent's highest level of education**	233		
High school		14.3	24.0
Vocational school or Junior college		13.4	22.3
Four-year college		30.4	25.6
Graduate or professional school		42.0	28.1
*Education of spouse or partner***	218		
High school graduate		9.6	24.6
Some college or completed vocational school		25.0	29.8
College graduate		28.8	20.2
Completed graduate or professional school		36.5	25.4
*Mean family income from employment and investments (dollars)***	196	89,878	62,232
Family structure	233		
Single adopted child		1.8	0.0
Only other adopted children		67.9	57.9
Only other birth children		8.0	16.2
Other adopted and birth children		22.3	28.9

*$p < .05$; **$p < .01$; $p < .001$

Table 2-3. Child Characteristics

Child Characteristic	Base	Non Drug-Exposed (%)	Drug-Exposed (%)
Gender (female)	233	50.0	46.3
Mean age (years)	233	10.6	10.6
Age when placed with family*	231		
Less than 1 year		64.0	52.5
1–2 years		12.6	26.7
3+ years		23.4	20.8
Mean age when adoption was finalized (years)	229		
Ethnicity			
White or Caucasian		65.2	54.2
Hispanic or Latino		17.0	27.5
Black or African American		7.1	10.8
Other		10.7	7.5
Inracial adoption (yes)	230	86.4	80.8
Type of adoption	231		
Public		42.7	69.4
Private		18.2	12.4
Independent		39.1	18.2
Open adoption (yes)	225	60.2	52.1
Respondent was a foster parent to child (yes)**	213	31.7	53.6
Placed in foster care with other families (yes)***	220	39.0	70.4
Respondent received AAP[1] for child in 1995 (yes)	91	75.9	69.4
Mean monthly AAP received in 1995 (dollars)	65	523.59	363.93
Respondent is currently receiving AAP (yes)	91	79.3	69.4

[1]Adoption Assistance Program subsidy or other monthly payment from the state.

* $p < .05$; ** $p < .01$; *** $p < .001$

were placed as infants (less than one year old), while nearly two-thirds of the non-drug-exposed children were placed as infants (p < .05). Though not significant, a comparison between the two groups of children by adoption type (public agency, private agency, independently) revealed that approximately 70% of drug-exposed children were adopted through public agencies. Non-drug-exposed children, on the other hand, were about as likely to have been adopted independently as they were to have been adopted through a public agency. Consistent with our findings on adoption type, drug-exposed children (54%) were more likely than non-drug-exposed children (32%) to have been placed in foster care with the adopting parent (p < .01) and also with other foster families (70% vs. 39% respectively; p < .001). When asked if their child's adoption was open or closed at the time of placement, 52% of parents of drug-exposed and 60% of parents of non-drug-exposed children said that the adoption was open at the time of placement.

Child's Preadoptive History

Respondents were asked whether their child had a history of any of the following conditions prior to being placed with them for adoption: physical abuse, sexual abuse, neglect, and multiple placements prior to adoption. As can be seen in Table 4, parents of drug-exposed children were more likely than parents of non-drug-exposed children to report that their children had histories of neglect (p < .01 in 1993; p < .05 in 1997) and/or multiple placements (p < .05 in 1993). Among drug-exposed children, roughly 40% had histories of neglect and/or multiple placements, whereas only about 25% of non-drug-exposed children were reported in 1993 and/or 1997 as having been neglected and placed in multiple homes before being adopted. Children were similar in terms of histories of physical and sexual abuse.

When parents were asked in 1997 to indicate if their children had any developmental disabilities, those who had adopted drug-exposed children were more likely than those who had adopted non-drug-exposed children to report that their children had physical/mental disabilities (21% vs. 9%, p < .05), developmental disabilities (26% vs. 11%, p < .01), and learning disabilities (41% vs. 22%, p <

Table 2-4. Child's Preadoptive History as Reported at Four and Eight Years

	1993		1997	
	Non Drug- Exposed $(n = 112)$	_Drug- Exposed_ $(n = 112)$	_Non Drug- Exposed_ $(n = 112)$	_Drug- Exposed_ $(n = 112)$
Child Preadoptive History	%	%	%	%
History of physical abuse prior to adoption				
No	76.6	75.0	75.0	71.8
Yes	9.9	15.2	12.5	13.6
Unknown	13.5	9.8	12.5	14.5
History of sexual abuse prior to adoption				
No	76.6	80.5	74.8	79.8
Yes	10.8	6.2	12.6	5.5
Unknown	12.6	13.3	12.6	14.7
History of neglect prior to adoption††*				
No	71.2	58.4	68.6	50.0
Yes	21.6	38.9	25.7	42.0
Unknown	7.2	2.7	5.7	8.0
History of multiple homes†				
No	74.8	63.2	69.5	57.7
Yes	21.6	36.0	26.7	39.6
Unknown	3.6	.9	3.8	2.7

* $p < .05$; ** $p < .01$; *** $p < .001$ (1993)

† $p < .05$; †† p , $.01$; ††† $p < .001$ (1997)

.01). Parents of drug-exposed children also were much more likely than parents of non-drug-exposed children to report in 1993 that their child had emotional/behavioral problems (30% vs. 15%; p < .05). Despite their drug exposure status and reported histories of neglect, however, 98% of children in the drug-exposed group were described as having "good" or "excellent" physical health. This finding is comparable to the percentage of parents of non-drug-exposed children reporting that their children were in good to excellent health (97%). Children's development at four and eight years is reported in Table 5.

Children's Educational Outcomes

Table 6a illustrates that in many regards, the drug-exposed children in our study were no different than non-drug-exposed children, yet they seemed to have deeper involvement with special education services. At eight years postadoption, the majority of children from each group—roughly 75%—were in elementary school and described by their parents as doing well in school (or making A's or B's). Less than 6% of parents reported that their children disliked school. Parents of drug-exposed children were no more likely than parents of non-drug-exposed children to report that their child had repeated a grade in school (13% vs. 6% respectively; n.s.), while parents of non-drug-exposed children were more likely to report that their child had been suspended and/or expelled from school (n.s.). In response to questions about the types of special education classes in which their children were enrolled, we found that although drug-exposed children were nearly twice as likely to be enrolled in classes for the learning disabled (57% vs. 30%, $p < .01$), they were no more likely than their non-drug-exposed counterparts to be enrolled in most other special education classes.

Children's Adjustment and Behavioral Outcomes

As to their adjustment at eight years (Table 6b), children appear more similar than different. For example, while the presence of Attention Deficit Hyperactivity Disorder (ADHD) was fairly high overall (as assessed by the IOWA Conner's Scale for ADHD), there were no significant differences between the groups. Except for children nine and younger, non-drug-exposed children were either about as likely or more likely than drug-exposed children to have been classified as having ADHD. According to scores on the Behavioral Problem Index (BPI) (Tables 7a through 7d), drug-exposed children were only slightly more likely than non-drug-exposed children to score in the 75th percentile on the hyperactivity subscale in Wave III (35% vs. 27%) (see Table 7c). Again, though, according to BPI scores, there were no significant differences between groups

Table 2-5. Child's Development as Reported at Four and Eight Years

	1993		1997	
	Non Drug- Exposed (n = 112)	Drug- Exposed (n = 112)	Non Drug- Exposed (n = 112)	Drug- Exposed (n = 112)
Child Development	%	%	%	%
Physical/mental disability*				
No	87.4	83.0	90.5	78.6
Yes	10.8	13.4	8.6	20.5
Unknown	1.8	3.6	1.0	.9
Developmental disability†**				
No	86.4	72.6	88.6	70.9
Yes	10.9	22.1	10.5	26.4
Unknown	2.7	5.3	1.0	2.7
Learning disability††**				
No	80.9	62.3	74.8	54.4
Yes	10.9	23.7	22.3	41.2
Unknown	8.2	14.0	2.9	4.4
Emotional/behavioral problems†				
No	81.1	63.2	73.3	58.6
Yes	15.3	29.8	24.8	36.9
Unknown	3.6	7.0	1.9	4.5
Physical health				
Poor to fair	0.0	.8	3.7	1.7
Good to very good	35.7	39.7	29.4	29.4
Excellent	64.3	59.5	67.0	68.9
Has required care for a disability or severe illness (yes)			19.3	23.5

* $p < .05$; ** $p < .01$; *** $p < .001$ (1993)

† $p < .05$; †† $p , .01$; ††† $p < .001$ (1997)

in the prevalence of ADHD. In fact, there was an overall decrease in the percentage of children scoring in the 75th percentile on the BPI, suggesting that at eight years postadoption there were fewer behavioral problems exhibited by children from either group.

The ADHD behaviors manifested by children in both groups appear to have had an impact on their adjustment in multiple

Table 2-6a. Child's Educational Outcomes at Eight Years

Educational Outcomes	Base	Non Drug-Exposed (%)	Drug-Exposed (%)
Current grade level	227		
K-6		70.6	78.8
7-12		23.9	19.5
Other		5.5	1.7
Average grades in school	222		
"A" average or Excellent		22.9	30.1
"B" average or Good		50.5	40.7
"C" average or O.K.		20.2	25.7
"D" or "F" average or needs improvement		6.4	3.5
How child feels about school	227		
Dislikes		4.6	5.9
Enjoys/dislikes about the same		26.6	26.6
Enjoys		68.8	67.8
Has repeated a grade (yes)	228	6.4	13.4
Has been suspended (yes)	232	10.8	9.1
Has been expelled (yes)	233	6.3	3.3
Has been enrolled in classes for the learning disabled (yes)**	96	30.2	56.6
Has been enrolled in classes for speech or language difficulties (yes)	96	30.2	45.3
Has been enrolled in classes for the emotionally or behaviorally disturbed (yes)	96	7.0	5.7
Has been enrolled in classes for the gifted and talented (yes)	96	27.9	13.2

*$p < .05$, ** $p < .01$, *** $p < .001$

domains (Table 6b). For instance, 52% of the parents of drug-exposed children and 43% of the parents of non-drug-exposed children said that ADHD behaviors had interfered with their children's performance at school. Regarding the impairment on children's peer relationships, 40% of the drug-exposed group and 39% of the non-drug-exposed group reported that ADHD had an impact in this area.

Drug-exposed children were more likely (though not significantly so) to have taken medications for ADHD behaviors. Thirty

Table 2-6b. Child's Adjustment at Eight Years

Adjustment and Behavioral Outcomes	Base	Non Drug-Exposed (%)	Drug-Exposed (%)
Adjustment compared to other children the same age	228		
Poor to fair		11.0	6.7
Good to very good		46.8	44.5
Excellent		42.2	48.7
Adjustment compared to other children in the family	183		
Poor to fair		12.4	8.5
Good to very good		48.3	52.1
Excellent		39.3	39.4
ADHD classification (yes) (9 years and younger) Subscale 1 (Inattention/Overactivity) (score Æ 11)	105	9.8	18.2
Subscale 2 (Aggression/Defiance) (score Æ 9)	107	7.9	9.1
ADHD classification (yes) (10 years and older) Subscale 1 (Inattention/Overactivity) (score Æ 9)	117	42.9	37.3
Subscale 2 (Aggression/Defiance) (score Æ 6)	116	45.2	43.2
ADHD behaviors have interfered with school performance (yes)	224	42.5	51.7
ADHD behaviors have interfered with child's relationships with other children (yes)	224	38.9	37.9
Child has ever taken medications for ADHD behaviors (yes)	227	21.3	30.3
Child is currently taking medications for ADHD behaviors (yes)	60	79.2	86.1
Child has had trouble with the police (yes)	232	7.2	3.3
Child has had drug or alcohol problems (yes)	226	2.8	.9
Child has seen a counselor for emotional or behavioral problems (yes)	230	38.7	40.3
Child's overall mental health	231		
Poor to fair		9.9	7.5
Good to very good		44.1	55.8
Excellent		45.9	36.7
How difficult child has been to raise	230		
Not difficult at all		40.9	43.3
A little difficult		31.8	37.5
Quite difficult to extremely difficult		27.3	19.2

* $p < .05$, ** $p < .01$, *** $p < .001$

Table 2-7a. Mean BPI Scores at Four and Eight Years: Non Drug-Exposed

BPI Scale	1993	1997	Paired Difference	95% CI
BPI Summary	11.85 (SD=6.39)	11.20 (SD=7.85)	.65 (SD=6.72)	(-.69; 1.99)
Anxious Depressed**	1.79 (SD=1.33)	2.29 (SD=1.81)	-.50 (SD=1.68)	(-.83; -.18)
Headstrong	2.92 (SD=1.57)	2.81 (SD=1.78)	.10 (SD=1.57)	(.20; .41)
Hyperactivity	1.95 (SD=1.46)	2.17 (SD=1.76)	-.21 (SD=1.58)	(-.51; .09)
Immature-Dependent***	1.88 (SD=1.36)	1.21 (SD=1.29)	.67 (SD=1.47)	(.39; .95)
Peer conflict	.92 (SD=.99)	.78 (SD=1.00)	.14 (SD=1.14)	(-.08; .35)
Antisocial	2.23 (SD=1.64)	2.00 (SD=2.01)	.23 (SD=1.63)	(-.08; .54)

*$p < .05$; ** $p < .01$; *** $p < .001$

percent of parents of drug-exposed children reported that their children had taken medications in the past, compared with 21% of respondents of non-drug-exposed children. Among parents reporting that their child had ever taken medications for ADHD behaviors, 85% of those from the drug-exposed group, compared with 79% of their counterparts, reported that their children were still taking medications at the time of the study.

Despite drug-exposure status, most parents reported that their children were not difficult to raise. About 20% of drug-exposed children were reported as being "quite difficult" or "extremely difficult" to raise, which is slightly less than the percentage of non-drug-exposed children reported in these categories.

As Table 8a shows, regardless of drug exposure status, children appear in general to be functioning adequately. Sixty-four percent of

Table 2-7b. Mean BPI Scores at Four and Eight Years: Drug-Exposed

BPI Scale	1993	1997	Paired Difference	95% CI
BPI Summary	12.1 (SD=6.83)	11.4 (SD=7.77)	.72 (SD=5.67)	(-.33; 1.77)
Anxious Depressed**	1.66 (SD=1.37)	2.1 (SD=1.71)	-.44 (SD=1.51)	(-.72; -.17)
Headstrong	2.86 (SD=1.60)	2.73 (SD=1.65)	.14 (SD=1.46)	(-.13; .40)
Hyperactivity	2.42 (SD=1.58)	2.51 (SD=1.70)	.09 (SD=1.50)	(-.37; .18)
Immature-Dependent***	1.93 (SD=1.28)	1.29 (SD=1.25)	.64 (SD=1.34)	(.40; .89)
Peer conflict	.77 (SD=1.01)	.79 (SD=.99)	-.02 (SD=.95)	(-.19; .16)
Antisocial	2.35 (SD=1.94)	1.97 (SD=2.00)	.38 (SD=1.64)	(.08; .68)

$* p < .05; ** p < .01; *** p < .001$

drug-exposed children and 73% of non-drug-exposed children were classified as functioning "well with few problems" (as indicated by their scores on the "Functioning Scale"). Of the child and family characteristic variables that were tested for their impact on children's functioning at eight years postadoption (as indicated by scores on the "Functioning Scale"), only two variables were found to be significant: (1) the child's age at placement and (2) the respondent's level of educational attainment by Wave III. The respondent's education and the child's age at placement were both significant alone and together in predicting children's functioning. Drug exposure status was not found to affect the likelihood that a child would function either poorly or well (Table 8b).

We completed additional analysis because we noted that although more educated parents may do better with drug-exposed

Table 2-7c. Percentage of Adoptions Scoring in the 75th Percentile on the BPI at Four and Eight Years

| | 1993 | | 1997 | |
	Non Drug-Exposed (n = 112)	Drug-Exposed (n = 112)	Non Drug-Exposed (n = 112)	Drug-Exposed (n = 112)
BPI Scale	%	%	%	%
BPI Summary	3.6	.8	23.4	17.4
Anxious-Depressed	50.0	46.2	46.3	38.3
Headstrong	41.1	39.5	45.3	36.7
Hyperactivity†	38.7	52.9	26.9	35.3
Immature-Dependent	34.3	35.3	36.4	36.1
Peer conflict	55.9	43.7	26.6	27.7
Antisocial	37.3	42.9	36.7	36.1

* p < .05; ** p < .01; *** p < .001 (1993)

† p < .05; †† p , .01; ††† p < .001 (1997)

children [see Brooks and Barth 1998, which draws on a different sample], they have been found to be at higher risk with regard to adoption outcomes in general [Barth & Berry 1988; Boyne 1983]. Employing the whole matched Wave I, II, III data set, we found that age of placement was not related to children's functioning when the respondent's level of educational attainment was high school or less. The outcomes for children of different ages were significantly different, however, when the respondent's level of education was vocational program/junior college or 4-year college/graduate school. Age at placement was more important when adopting parents had attained higher levels of education.

Family Relations, Closeness, and Satisfaction

In almost every instance, drug-exposed children and their parents were similar to non-drug-exposed children and their parents in terms of family relations (Table 9), closeness (Table 10), and satisfaction with adoption (Table 11). Worth noting is that parents of children

Table 2-7d. Change in Behavior Between 1993 and 1997

BPI Scales	Base	Non Drug-Exposed (%)	Drug-Exposed (%)
Anxious-Depressed	225		
% Where behavior worsened		26.2	25.4
% Where behavior stayed the same		32.7	33.1
% Where behavior improved		41.1	41.5
Headstrong	224		
% Where behavior worsened		35.8	39.0
% Where behavior stayed the same		28.3	28.8
% Where behavior improved		35.8	32.2
Hyperactivity	225		
% Where behavior worsened		28.7	29.9
% Where behavior stayed the same		38.0	35.0
% Where behavior improved		33.3	35.0
Immature-Dependent	224		
% Where behavior worsened		48.6	50.4
% Where behavior stayed the same		33.6	35.0
% Where behavior improved		17.8	14.5
Peer conflict	226		
% Where behavior worsened		31.2	23.1
% Where behavior stayed the same		43.1	58.1
% Where behavior improved		25.7	18.8
Antisocial	225		
% Where behavior worsened		39.8	39.3
% Where behavior stayed the same		31.5	34.2
% Where behavior improved		28.7	26.5

*$p < .05$, ** $p < .01$, *** $p < .001$

from both groups were more likely in 1997 than in 1993 to indicate a substantial degree of dissatisfaction about adoption. In Wave II, 86% of parents of drug-exposed children and 87% of parents of non-drug-exposed children reported being very satisfied with the adoption. Yet, four years later, only about 65% of parents from either group reported being very satisfied. Between four and eight years, parents' satisfaction with adoption decreased, with about 30% of all parents being less satisfied with their adoptions in 1997 than they

Table 2-8a. Overall Functioning at Eight Years

BPI Scales	Base	Non Drug-Exposed (%)	Drug-Exposed (%)
Overall functioning (n.s.)	199		
Functions well or with few problems[1]		72.8	63.6
Functions poorly[2]		27.2	36.4

[1]Scoring below the 75th percentile.

[2]Scoring at or above the 75th percentile.

were in 1993. Though there exists a marked decrease in satisfaction with the adoption at eight years postadoption, more than 90% of all respondents reported that if they had it to do over, they would adopt this child again.

Uncertainty about drug exposure status was not a key determinant of overall satisfaction with the adoptive placement and does not distinguish dissatisfaction and satisfaction. Certainty about drug exposure status, however, is significant when discriminating between being satisfied and very satisfied with adoption. This finding is consistent with much other adoption literature indicating that when families know the challenges they may face, they are much more satisfied, even if those challenges are greater [Barth & Berry 1988].

Discussion

This study is the only substantial investigation of the outcomes for drug-exposed children after adoption. According to their adoptive parents, children who are prenatally exposed to drugs appear to function very much like other adopted children on educational attainment and emotional or behavioral adjustment. These findings offer considerable support for the argument that drug-exposed children are, for the most part, not significantly different from other adopted children. Still, the slightly elevated rates of parental reports of learning problems and placement into learning disabilities programs leave the picture somewhat cloudy.

The findings of high levels of satisfaction among adoptive parents are consistent with the two- and four-year findings from the

Table 2-8b. Effect of Child and Family Characteristics on Functioning Poorly (or Well) at Eight Years (N=180)[1]

-2 Log Likelihood	199.67
Goodness of Fit	34
Significance	72.22
% Correctly Predicted By Model	

Variables remaining in the final model[2]	B	SE	df	Sign.	Effect on Odds
Age when placed with family				.0012	
Less than one year	-.7200	.2363	1	.0023	.4868[3]
1–2 years	-.1919	.2835	1	.4985	.8254
3+ years	.9118	.2884	1	.0016	2.4889
Respondent's education				.0162	
High school	-.3604	.3323	1	.2782	.6974
Vocational school or Junior college	1.0204	.3234	1	.0016	2.7743
College graduate	-.2294	.2909	1	.4304	-.7950
Graduate/ professional school	-.4307	.2844	1	.1300	.6501

1. Cases in which respondents indicated that they were "uncertain" about their child's history prior to adoption (e.g., multiple homes, sexual abuse, physical abuse, neglect) were excluded from this analysis.

2. Variables excluded from the full model: drug exposure status, adoption type, child's gender, kinship status, child's ethnicity, open/closed adoption, history of maltreatment, and history or multiple homes.

3. Indicates that being placed as an infant increases the odds of functioning well by 2.05 times.

earlier study of this sample [Barth, 1991; Barth & Needell, 1996] as well as other studies of special needs adoption [Barth & Berry 1988; Nelson 1984; Rosenthal & Groze 1992]. The high levels of closeness between parents and their children, drug-exposed and non-drug-exposed alike, are also consistent with extant research [Rosenthal & Groze, 1992].

Table 2-9. Family Relations Eight Years

Family Relations	Base	Non Drug- Exposed %	Drug- Exposed %
How often child experiences difficulty getting along with others	184		
Never to hardly ever		27.8	41.5
Sometimes		54.4	40.4
Often to all the time		17.8	18.1
How the presence of other children has affected the respondent's experienc or raising child	185		
It hasn't really affected the experience		39.6	48.9
Made it much more to a little more difficult		19.8	19.1
Made it a little to much easier		40.7	31.9
How often birth children tease the child because he/she is adopted	88		
Never to hardly ever		91.9	94.1
Sometimes		8.7	5.9
Often to all the time		0.0	0.0

* p < .05; ** p < .01; *** p < .001

The absence of studies of the adoption of drug-exposed children requires comparison to other studies of children who experienced some improvement in environment in their early years. The closest of these studies is that of Griffith, Azuma, and Chasnoff [1994, p. 26], which reported on the positive outcomes for children who had not experienced multiple placements and children who were not living with drug-affected mothers; the study also confirmed that children were much more likely to display problems if they were being raised in a home where drugs continued to be used. In findings which echo our results, they concluded that "the majority of the children exposed prenatally to drugs scored within the average ranges for intellectual abilities and displayed no significant behavioral problems" [1994, p. 26].

Table 2-10. Closeness at Four and Eight Years

Closeness	1993 Non Drug-Exposed (n = 112)	1993 Drug-Exposed (n = 112)	1997 Non Drug-Exposed (n = 112)	1997 Drug-Exposed (n = 112)
	%	%	%	%
How often child is affectionate or tender with the respondent				
Very often to sometimes	92.9	95.9	91.0	95.0
Not very often	5.4	3.3	8.1	4.2
Almost never or never	1.8	.8	.9	.8
How satisfied respondent is with how affectionate or tender child is				
Very to somewhat satisfied	92.0	95.9	93.7	95.8
Not very satisfied	5.4	4.1	3.3	3.3
Very dissatisfied	2.7	0.0	.8	.8
How much child seems to appreciate how much respondent does for her/him				
Very to somewhat appreciative	92.8	92.5	87.3	90.8
Not very appreciative	5.4	6.7	10.9	5.8
Not at all appreciative	1.8	.8	1.8	3.3
Satisfaction with appreciativeness of child				
Very to somewhat satisfied	91.0	91.6	89.1	90.8
Not very satisfied	7.2	7.6	9.1	7.5
Very dissatisfied	1.8	.8	1.8	1.7
How close respondent feels toward child†				
Very to somewhat close	96.4	100.0	97.3	97.5
Not very close	3.6	0.0	2.7	1.7
Not at all close	0.0	0.0	0.0	.8
Mean Closeness Scale score[1]	18.1	18.4	17.8	18.1
Respondent's current attachment with child				
Somewhat to very warm and close			92.8	95.0
Neither distant nor warm and close			5.4	4.2
Very to somewhat distant			1.8	.8

[1]Higher Scores on the Closeness Scale indicate greater closeness and satisfaction with the relationship between the child and respondent.

* $p < .05$; ** $p < .01$; *** $p < .001$ (1993)

† $p < .05$; †† $p , .01$; ††† $p < .001$ (1997)

Table 2-11. Satisfaction at Four and Eight Years

| | 1993 | | 1997 | |
	Non Drug-Exposed (n = 112)	Drug-Exposed (n = 112)	Non Drug-Exposed (n = 112)	Drug-Exposed (n = 112)
Satisfaction	%	%	%	%
How satisfied respondent is *with adoption*				
Very to somewhat dissatisfied	3.6	.8	23.4	17.4
Satisfied	9.0	13.4	10.8	17.4
Very satisfied	87.4	85.7	65.8	65.3
Change between 1993 and 1997 in how *satisfied respondent is with adoption*				
Satisfaction stayed the same or increased			71.8	71.4
Satisfaction decreased			28.2	28.6
How child seems to feel about adoption				
Feels negative to mostly negative	1.4	0.0	11.1	3.5
Feels neutral about it	23.0	17.2	15.7	13.0
Feels positive to mostly positive	75.7	82.8	73.1	83.5
The effect of adoption on the respondent's *marriage or long-term relationship*				
Strengthened relationship	61.5	49.1	57.3	61.9
Has had no effect	35.6	44.6	32.0	34.5
Weakened the relationship	2.9	6.3	10.7	3.5
If they had it to do over again, would *thee respondent adopt the child*				
Definitely/most likely would	98.2	97.4	90.1	93.3
Do not know	0.0	0.0	2.7	0.0
Definitely/most likely would not	1.8	2.6	7.2	6.7

* $p < .05$; ** $p < .01$; *** $p < .001$ (1993)

† $p < .05$; †† p , .01; ††† $p < .001$ (1997)

Our study is, in great part, consistent with the meta-analysis by Lester and associates [1998] and the earlier research review of the outcomes for drug-exposed children by epidemiologists, Robins and Mills [1993]. Noting that studies lack precise estimates of the drugs involved in the prenatal exposure and the length or timing of exposure, Robins and Mills [1993, p. 29] observed that, "overall, the impression from the literature is that drug exposure does cause serious problems and even disastrous ends to pregnancy in a small minority of cases. The other impression from the literature is that, in the great majority of drug-exposed pregnancies, whatever effects noted on growth and behavior are transitory and are no longer apparent after a few months. Unfortunately, defects in these studies leave open the possibility that they may be exaggerating the more serious outcomes or underestimating the long-term effects of exposure to drugs in utero."

Our study findings are vulnerable to the dual concerns of weak measures of exposure in utero as a result of dependence on adoptive parent reports, and the possible presence of many cases of undetected drug exposure in control groups, which might mitigate real differences. The sole reliance on parental self-report makes interpretation of the developmental findings difficult.

The study is not, however, vulnerable to common problems arising in prior research: difficulties in assessing functioning for very young children (our sample is the oldest yet); the fact that adverse rearing environments may override the evidence for in utero effects (adoption equalizes environments somewhat); and the fact that children with the gravest effects are lost to follow-up (we had no evidence of this). Further, these findings are not as vulnerable as the findings from other studies regarding "the fact that the follow-up interval is too short to display the more subtle effects that will become obvious after more complex intellectual tasks are posed by school and work" [Robins & Mills 1993, p. 28]. Although an even longer follow-up would be helpful, the average age of the drug-exposed children in our sample exceeds 10 years.

Given that an element of adoption may involve the desire to have a normal family life, it is almost inevitable to ask whether adopted children will have outcomes similar to birth children and, in the context of prenatal substance exposure, whether adopted children who are drug-exposed will have similar outcomes as adopted children who are not drug-exposed. Because this study lacks a comparison group of children raised by their birth parents, arriving at the answers to these questions requires tapping into the broader literature on both prenatal drug exposure and adoption. Nulman and associates [1992] made a direct comparison of a small sample of children raised by their birth parents and drug-exposed children who were adopted and, while finding no differences in intelligence, did find early language delays among cocaine-exposed children. The authors, however, failed to consider that the birth parents may have contributed genetic material that was not as likely to result in expressive language or intelligence, and they attributed the differences solely to toxic neurological effects. Issues related to genetic considerations have been raised in other studies, including Graham and colleagues [1992], who compared children who were born exposed to cocaine and those who were not exposed and found that parents of children exposed to cocaine had significantly lower educational attainment.

Sharma, McGue and Benson [1998] and Brooks and Barth [1999] have shown that adopted adolescents and young adults perform less successfully in school than their nonadopted siblings, suggesting that there may be factors in addition to or in lieu of drug exposure that contribute to academic difficulties for adopted children. This finding may not be reassuring to parents considering adoption of drug-exposed children. It may contribute, however, to a coherent picture of the outcomes of adoption of drug-exposed children, as it suggests that some difficulties in learning and behavior for drug-exposed adopted children may originate in genetic or prenatal environments and may be vulnerable to postnatal experiences. It should be noted that learning and behavioral difficulties for substance-exposed children may not be significantly greater than the difficulties experienced by other adopted children. The learning and behavioral problems of drug-exposed adopted children, in fact, may be significantly less than for drug-exposed children raised by their birth parents, and who experience substance impaired parenting [Chasnoff 1997; Howard et al. 1995].

The present research is the only sizable study that compares adopted children who have and have not been prenatally exposed to drugs, demonstrating what other studies can only surmise. This study makes clear that adopted drug-exposed children have modestly more difficulties than non-drug-exposed adopted children, and that adopting parents of drug-exposed children appear to have an adequate understanding of these differences and appropriate expectations for their children. As a consequence, they report levels of satisfaction with adoption and commitment to their children that are every bit as high as parents who adopted non-drug-exposed children.

From a public policy perspective, our findings are certainly good news. Information about the general well-being of drug-exposed children who have been adopted can combat continuing concern about the likelihood of successful adoption outcomes for these children. Although there are many reasons that very young children in non-kinship foster care remain in care for extensive periods of time, it is clear that a history of prenatal drug exposure and evidence of drug exposure at birth offers no empirical justification for extended waits in foster care. Our study, comparing adopted children who are and are not identified as drug-exposed, finds the two groups of children to be remarkably similar to one another. Evidence that adoptive parents are highly satisfied with their adoptions—whether or not children are prenatally drug-exposed—should be helpful to adoption agencies in their discussions with potential adoptive parents. Our findings suggest that certainty about drug-exposure is not likely to be a key determinant of the parent's satisfaction with the child and adoption experience.

The finding that adopting parents of drug-exposed children had attained lower levels of formal education and had lower incomes is consistent with the finding that these children were more likely to be adopted by their original foster parents rather than by persons who later seek to adopt them. Findings do not support the prediction that drug-exposed children will have lower educational achievement because of typically lower educational achievement on the part of birth parents and adoptive parents.

The finding that the outcomes for the sample of adopted children are sensitive to the age at which they are placed is predictable and important. Since there is much evidence that adoption as an infant eases adjustment to adoption, the fact that more drug-exposed children were placed for adoption as infants suggests a protective factor. Children born prenatally exposed to drugs may be more likely to be adopted at an earlier point in time than other children, which may help to compensate for the other risks that they face. Other findings—such as those of Goerge and Harden [1993] that many drug-exposed infants are discharged to the home initially and then enter foster care, and of Barth [1997] that toddlers have a much lower likelihood of adoption than do infants—suggest that drug-exposed children who are not adopted as infants may be less likely to ever be adopted.

Finally, we take note of the declining parental satisfaction for all adoptive families and expect that this pattern has much to do with the general stresses of children asserting their independence as they enter adolescence. Because there are no significant differences between the drug-exposed and non-drug-exposed groups, there is little reason to believe that this pattern is attributable to children's prenatal backgrounds. Without a sample of families who did not adopt, it is even difficult to make the case that these families are having more problems than is typical. It may only be possible to conclude that parenting is harder when children are between the ages of 10 and 18, and that the proportion of adoptive parents who report dissatisfaction with adoption is likely to be directly related to the proportion of families with children in this age group.

Notes

1. The authors thank Karie Frasch, Cassandra Simmel, Barbara Needell, Jill Duerr Berrick, and Joan Allen for their contributions to this study. The study was supported by the Hutto Patterson Chair and grants from the U.S. DHHS, Administration on Children and Families, Children's Bureau to the Abandoned Infants Assistance Resource Center, and the Berkeley Child Welfare Research Center.

References

Adoption and Safe Families Act of 1997, 42 U.S.C. §§ 670 et seq.

Albert, V. N. & Barth, R. P. (1996). Predicting growth in child abuse and neglect reports in urban, suburban, and rural counties. *Social Service Review, 70,* 59–82.

Baker, P. C. & Mott, F. L. (1989). *National longitudinal survey of youth: Handbook.* Columbia, OH: Ohio State University for Human Resource Research.

Barth, R. P. (1998). The odds of adoption vs. remaining in foster care. Child Welfare Research Center, School of Social Welfare, University of California at Berkeley. Unpublished manuscript available from the author.

Barth, R. P. (1991a). Adoption of drug-exposed children. *Children and Youth Services Review, 13*, 323–342.

Barth, R. P. (1991b). Educational implications of prenatally drug-exposed children. *Social Work In Education, 13*, 130–136.

Barth, R. P. & Berry, M. (1988). *Adoption and disruption: Rates, risks, and responses.* New York: Aldine De Gruyter.

Barth, R. P., Courtney, M., Berrick, J., & Albert, V. (1994). *From child abuse to permanency planning: Pathways of children through child welfare services.* New York: Aldine De Gruyter.

Barth, R. P. & Needell, B. (1996). Outcomes for drug-exposed children four years after adoption. *Children and Youth Services Review, 18*, 37–55.

Berrick, J. D., Barth, R. P., Needell, B., & Jonson-Reid, M. (1997). Group care and young children. *Social Service Review, 71*(2), 257–273.

Blakeslee, S. (1990, May 19). Parents fear for future of infants born on drugs. *New York Times*, pp. A1, A8–A9.

Boyne, J. (1983). *The shadow of success: A statistical analysis of the outcomes of adoption of hard-to-place children.* Westfield, NJ: Spaulding for Children.

Brodzinsky, D. (1993). Long-term outcomes in adoption. *The Future of Children, 2*(1), 153–166.

Brooks, D. & Barth, R. P. (1998). Characteristics and outcomes of drug-exposed children in kinship and non-relative foster care. *Children and Youth Service Review 20*(6), 475–501.

Chasnoff, I.J., Anson, A. R., & Moss Iaukea, K. A. (1998). *Understanding the drug-exposed child: Approaches to behavior and learning.* Chicago: Imprint Publications.

Dumaret, A. (1985). IQ, scholarship performance, and behavior of siblings raised in contrasting environments. *Child Psychology, 26*, 553–580.

Gittler, J. & McPherson, M. (1990). Prenatal substance abuse. *Children Today, 19*(4), 3–7.

Goerge, R. M. & Harden, A. (1993). The impact of substance-affected infants on child protection services and substitute care caseloads:

1985–1992. Chicago: Chapin Hall Center for Children at the University of Chicago.

Graham, K., Feigenbaum, A., Pastuszak, A. Nulman, I., Weksberg, R., Einarson, T., Goldberg, S., Ashby, S., & Koren, G. (1992). Pregnancy outcomes and infant development following gestational cocaine use by social cocaine users in Toronto, Canada. *Clinical Investigations in Medicine, 15*, 384–394.

Griffith, D. R., Azuma, S. D., & Chasnoff, I. J. (1994). Three-year outcome of children exposed prenatally to drugs. *Journal of the American Academy of Child and Adolescent Psychiatry, 33*, 20–27.

Groze, V. & Rosenthal, J. A. (1993). Attachment theory and the adoption of children with special needs. *Social Work Research & Abstracts, 29*(2), 5–13.

Harris, J. (1998). *The nurture assumption: Why children turn out the way they do.* New York: Free Press.

Hodges, J. & Tizard, B. (1989a). IQ and behavioral adjustment of ex-institutional adolescents. *Journal of Child Psychology and Psychiatry and Allied Disciplines, 30*(1), 53–75.

Hodges, J. & Tizard, B. (1989b). Social and family relationships of ex-institutional adolescents. *Journal of Child Psychology and Psychiatry, 30*, 77–97.

Howard, J. (Winter 1990). The addicted children: Summary of Judy Howard's presentation. *Adopttalk*, pp. 4–5.

Howard, J., Beckwith, L., Espinosa, M., & Tyler, R. (1995). Development of infants born to cocaine-abusing women: Biologic/maternal influences. *Neurotoxicology and Teratology, 17*, 403–411.

Johnson, D. & Fein, E. (1991). The concept of attachment: Applications to adoption. *Children and Youth Services Review, 13*(5–6), 397–412.

Koren, G., Nulman, I., Rovet, J., Greenbaum, R., Loebstein, M., & Einarson, T. (1998). Long-term neurodevelopmental risks in children exposed in utero to cocaine: The Toronto Study. *Annals of The New York Academy of Science, 846*, 306–313.

Lester, B. M., LaGasse, L. L., & Seifer, R. (1998). Cocaine exposure and children: The meaning of subtle effects. *Science, 282*, 633–634.

Moore, P. & Camarda, T. (1993). Drug-exposed children: Fresh reasons for concern. *Leake and Watts Newsletter, 4*(1), 1–4.

Nelson, K. A. (1985). *On the frontier of adoption: A study of special needs adoptive families*. Washington, DC: Child Welfare League of America.

Nulman, I., Rovet, J., Altmann, D., Bradley, C., Einarson, T., & Koren, G. (1994). Neurodevelopment of adopted children exposed in utero to cocaine. *Canadian Medical Association Journal, 151*(11), 1591–1597.

Pannor, R. & Baran, A. (1984). Open adoption as standard practice. *Child Welfare, 63*, 245–250.

Perry, B. D., Pollard, R. A., Blakley, T. L., Baker, W. L., & Vigilante, D. (1995). Childhood trauma, the neurobiology of adaptation, and use-dependent development of the brain: How states become traits. *Infant Mental Health Journal, 16*(4), 271–291.

Richardson, G. A., Conroy, M. L., & Day, N. L. (1996). Prenatal cocaine exposure: Effects on the development of school-age children. *Neurotoxicology and Teratology, 18*, 627–634.

Robins, L. N. & Mills, J. L. (1993). Effects of in utero exposure to street drugs. *American Journal of Public Health, 83*, supplement, 1–32.

Rosenthal, J. A. & Groze, V. W. (1992). *Special needs adoption: A follow-up study of intact families*. New York: Praeger.

Rutter, M., Tizard, J., & Whitmore, K. (Eds.) (1981). *Education, health, and behavior*. Huntington, NY: R. E. Krieger.

Scarr, S. & Weinberg, R. A. (1976). IQ test performance of black children adopted by white parents. *American Psychologist, 31*(10), 726–739.

Sharma, A. R., McGue, M. K., & Benson, P. L. (1998). The psychological adjustment of United States adopted adolescents and their nonadopted siblings. *Child Development, 69*, 791–802.

U.S. General Accounting Office. (1998). *Foster care: Agencies face challenges securing stable homes for children of substance abusers* (GAO/HEHS-98-182). Washington, DC: U.S. Government Printing Office.

Warren, S. B. (1992). Lower threshold for referral for psychiatric treatment for adopted adolescents. *Journal of the American Academy of Child and Adolescent Psychiatry, 31*, 512–517.

Wulczyn, F. (1994). Drug-affected children in foster care in New York City. In R. P. Barth, J. D. Berrick, & N. Gilbert (Eds.), *Child welfare research review, I*, (pp. 146–184). New York: Columbia University Press.

Wulczyn, F., Harden, A., & Goerge, R. (1997). *An update from the multistate foster care data archive: Foster care dynamics (1983–1994)*. Chicago: Chapin Hall Center for Children.

3

African American Kin Caregivers And Child Welfare Issues: Research Implications

Robert B. Hill

A major mechanism for the survival and advancement of African Americans from slavery to present times has been the extended family. One of the most vital functions of this strong kinship network is "surrogate parenting" or the "informal adoption" of children [Hill 1972, 1977]. During slavery, thousands of children of parents who had been sold as chattel were reared by adult relatives who served as a major source of stability for many African American families.

Even today, thousands of African American children are still being reared at various stages of their lives by grandparents, aunts and uncles, cousins, and other relatives. Kin caregivers are able to provide children with family identity, family history, self-esteem, social status, and continuity of family relationships. About 2,000,000 African American children live in the households of relatives—and 1,000,000 of them live with their relatives without the presence of either biological parent [U.S. Bureau of the Census 1996; Hill 1997].

Yet, despite the long history of informal adoption in the African American community, child welfare agencies have traditionally placed foster children with nonrelatives. By the late 1970s, the number of children in foster care who were placed with relatives was still negligible. This number of kin foster parents began to increase, in part as a result of a series of lawsuits that followed the major 1979 Supreme Court decision in the Illinois case, Miller v. Youakim, which prohibited agencies from denying relatives the same foster care board rates as nonrelatives [Gleeson 1996]. The number of children with related foster parents has increased to such an extent that a new term, "kinship care," has been coined to refer to children in foster care who are placed with relatives by public agencies. Between 150,000-200,000 (or about 30%) of children of all races in foster care are currently in kinship care. Yet, since historically the child welfare system has relied on nonrelatives as foster parents, it has been very slow to modify its practices and policies to accommodate kin caregivers.

The growth in the number of children placed with kin was prompted in part by the crack cocaine and HIV/AIDS epidemics in inner-city areas that began in 1986. Prior to the mid-1980s, the number of children in foster care had been steadily declining, falling from 326,000 children in 1970 to 270,000 children in 1985 [Tatara 1993; U.S. Children's Bureau n.d.]. By 1995, however, the foster care population had soared to 500,000 [National Committee to Prevent Child Abuse 1997]. The growth in foster care was fueled by the spiraling numbers of "boarder" babies—newly-born infants who had been abandoned—and by increasing numbers of young children removed from drug-addicted mothers and placed in foster care. Because of the unavailability of nonrelatives who were willing to care for drug-exposed or HIV/AIDS-infected children, these children were placed increasingly with relatives.

Because disproportionate numbers of pregnant mothers who were screened for prenatal drug use were African Americans, drug screening practice contributed to the disparate rise of kinship care families among African Americans. Yet, one should not conclude that the issue of prenatal drug exposure was or continues to be solely a "African American" problem. As Minkler and Roe [1993, p. 12] observe, several studies suggest that cocaine and other drugs are used as extensively among pregnant Caucasian women:

> ....the use of this drug continues to cut across class and ethnic group lines. A recent hospital-based study in Florida...showed identical levels of the use of cocaine and other drugs among black and white pregnant women. Yet as this study also demonstrated, African American women were 10 times more likely to be reported to health authori-

ties for substance abuse than were white women, and poor women were similarly more likely to be reported than their wealthier counterparts.

Studies also show that African American women are far more likely than Caucasian women to be reported to the child welfare system [Chasnoff, Landress & Barrett 1980]. As a result, there has been a dramatic increase in the number of African American children entering foster care, with a resulting overrepresention of African American children in the child welfare system [Goerge et al. 1995].

With the growth in kinship care for these children, many of whom have been affected by prenatal drug exposure, the quality of kinship care has become a critical issue. Research is vitally needed to address such questions as: Do children fare better with kin caregivers than with nonrelatives? Are kin caregivers able to respond more effectively to the special emotional, physical, psychological and cultural needs of these children than nonrelatives? How adequate are the financial aid and supportive services that are provided to kin caregivers compared to nonrelative caregivers?

This chapter will focus on identifying research issues that are related to kin caregivers of children, with an emphasis on children who are prenatally exposed to cocaine and other harmful drugs. Research on the role of African American extended families in providing vital foster care and adoption services may open new vistas not only in foster care and adoption, but in the field of child welfare in general. Studies of kin caregivers may help to identify a larger pool of families who may be recruited as foster or adoptive parents. Such studies may also contribute to the development of culturally sensitive practices that expedite the adoptions of "hard-to-place" children. And, research on kin caregivers may help to develop foster care and adoption policies that lead to more stable and permanent living arrangements for waiting children. Most importantly, studies of kin caregiving may contribute to the nation's knowledge of the various cultural manifestations of surrogate parenting among people of color.

For the purpose of this chapter, four types of situations in which children are reared by kin will be distinguished: "informal adoptive" families, in which children are placed with kin by extended family members and not by child welfare agencies; "kinship care" families, in which children are placed by child welfare agencies, but who are not licensed or "approved" as formal foster parents; "relative foster" families, in which children are placed by child welfare agencies and are licensed as foster parents; and "relative adoptive" families, in which children are formally adopted by relatives. Research on these four types of relative caregivers will enhance the quality of research on foster care and adoption—both informal and formal.

This chapter will attempt to address the following questions:

- What are the characteristics of children who are reared in various situations by relatives? How different are children who are drug-exposed from those who are not drug-exposed?
- Which kinds of relatives are more likely to rear kin, and why are they willing to take children into their families? What is their marital status, age, and economic status compared to nonrelative foster parents?
- How is kin caregiving related to child abuse and neglect, length of time in care, family preservation, and reunification, and are these rates lower or higher among kin caregivers than nonrelative foster parents?
- Are the emotional, educational and behavioral outcomes of children reared by kin more or less positive than the outcomes for children reared by nonrelatives?
- What is the potential for converting kin caregiving to formal adoptions? How interested are African Americans in formal adoption?
- What implications does kin caregiving have for future research on foster care and adoption?

Studies of Kin Caregiving

There have not been many studies of kin caregiving. The research on which we rely in this discussion are:

- The study by Beth McLean and Rebecca Thomas [1996] of 165 children in 60 kin families in Philadelphia, which focuses on "informal adoptive" families in which children with kin were not placed by child welfare authorities;

- The Oakland, California study by Meredith Minkler and Kathleen Roe [1993], an in-depth examinations of the issues facing African American grandparents who are caring for drug-exposed children in informal adoptive and kinship care families;
- The Westat study for the U.S. Children's Bureau [1996], a comprehensive survey of children receiving child welfare services between 1977 and 1994 that contains national data on kinship care and nonrelative foster families by race and ethnic group;
- The research of Devon Brooks and Richard Barth [1998], one of the few studies designed to assess the separate effects on child outcomes of kinship care and nonrelative foster care among drug-exposed and non-drug-exposed children; and
- The study by Hill [1977], one of the first nationwide studies of informal kin caregiving among African Americans, which draws on a nationally representative public use sample from the 1970 U.S. Census of families.

The African Legacy

In order to understand the contemporary significance of informal adoption or kin caregiving among African American families, it is important to understand the African heritage of this pervasive child-rearing pattern. The most enduring cultural strength that African American Americans brought with them from the African continent was the extended family and its strong kinship networks. African societies are child-centered and place high value on children. Andrew Miller [1993, p. 280] identified the African legacy of informal adoption or "child fosterage" among African Americans in the United States:

> Studies of extended, multihousehold African American families over the last twenty years have all hinted at African origins for these practices, but have not been able

to build historical links. They also have not emphasized the role of child fosterage in these families, though all of their work includes clear and prominent evidence of child fosterage among African Americans in both rural and urban areas...Whether the African heritage in America manifests itself in survivals, reinterpretations, syncretisms, or any type of combination thereof, it is still present as a history and an influence...That fosterage remains a significant family choice in contemporary Africa as well as in the United States, however, even with Africa's extremely different social structures, points to reasons for fosterage that transcend the coping strategies or survival tactics of African Americans. The reasons lie in its African heritage.

Characteristics of Children Reared by Kin

What are the characteristics of children who are reared by kin? Children of color are over-represented among families with relative caregivers. Of the 5.4 million children living with relatives in 1994, over half were either African American (35%) or Hispanic (19%) [U.S. Bureau of the Census 1996]. African Americans (17%) were three times more likely to be informally reared by kin than Caucasian (6%) children [U.S. Bureau of the Census 1996]. The U.S. Children's Bureau [1997] study found that African American children (29%) were twice as likely as Caucasian children (14%) to be placed in kinship care.

How many African American children are being reared by relatives? In 1994, 2,000,000 African American children lived in households headed by kin. Over 50% of these children were reared by their grandparents, with the remainder reared by other relatives. Forty-seven percent of children living with kin had no parent present, and the remaining 53% lived in three kinds of kin households: those with only their mothers present (46%), those with only fathers present (2%), and those with both parents present (5%) [U.S. Bureau of the Census 1996].

With regard to age, children who enter kinship care tend to be younger at the time they enter care than children placed with nonrelatives. The mean age at which children placed with relatives enter foster care is five years, as compared to a mean age of seven years for children placed with nonrelatives [U.S. Children's Bureau 1997]. Research by Dubowitz and colleagues [1993] and the National Black Child Development Institute [Walker 1994] likewise report mean ages of about five years for children entering kinship care.

As would be expected from the earlier mean age of entry into kinship care, children in kinship care are younger than children with nonrelative foster parents. According to the Children's Bureau [1997], the mean age of children in kinship care was 7.7 years, as compared to a mean age of 9.7 years for children in nonrelative foster care. The Brooks and Barth study [1998], however, found that children in kinship care (8.0 years) and those in non-related foster care (7.7 years) had comparable mean ages. Yet, that study also revealed that among both kinship care and nonrelative families, drug-exposed children were much younger than children who were not exposed to drugs. Among kinship care families, drug-exposed children (6.6 years) were about three years younger than non-drug-exposed children (9.1 years). Similarly, among nonrelative families, drug-exposed children (5.7 years) were about four years younger than non-drug-exposed children (9.5 years).

Moreover, children with kin caregivers are much more likely than children placed with nonrelatives to be part of a sibling group or to be placed with several children. The McLean and Thomas study [1996] found that kinship care families average 2.7 informally adopted children, with over half (52%) of the families rearing three or more kin children. The study by Berrick, Barth and Needell [1994] revealed that among families with more than one foster child, at least two of the children were siblings in 95% of the kinship care homes, compared to only 52% of the foster homes. That study also found that four or more siblings were placed together in 19% of the kinship care homes, compared to only 7% of the unrelated foster homes. Finally, Minkler and Roe [1993] found that 60% of the kin families they studied were caring for two or more children under the age of five. These studies indicate that a high percentage of relative caregivers, many of whom already have children of their own, assume responsibility for other children in their families, suggesting that extended family members are vital resources for sibling groups of children.

Another major role that African American extended families have played is the informal adoption of infants who are born to single mothers, most often adolescents who continue to live with their children. In Hill's study [1977], 45% of the children living with only their mothers in the households of grandparents had never-married mothers. Similarly, in her study of kinship patterns of low-income African Americans in the Midwest, Carol Stack [1974] found that children of single parents were often reared by grandparents and other extended family members.

Characteristics of Kin Caregivers

An important cultural manifestation of African American extended families is that they extend beyond "blood" relatives to include "fictive kin," nonrelated friends who are bonded more closely with children and adults than blood relatives. Many informally adopted children, for example, are reared by surrogate parents who are not their biological grandparents or other relatives. Furthermore, many of these nonrelatives have been selected by parents as godparents to care for their children if they are unable to assume that responsibility [Stack 1974; Mann 1997; Jarrett 1995].

What are the social and economic characteristics of relative caregivers? Traditionally, adoption agencies have placed high priority on middle-aged, middle-income, two-parent families without children. Based on those criteria, most relatives who rear kin would be screened out as adoptive parents, since they tend to be older persons, single parents, low-income, with children of their own. However, more and more progressive child welfare agencies are placing children in suitable families that have nontraditional characteristics such as those associated with relative caregivers.

The majority of families with kin caregivers are headed by unmarried females. Only 22% of the kin caregivers in the McLean and Thomas [1996] study were currently married, and 22% were never married. Although the proportion of caregivers in the Children's Bureau study [1997] who were married was similar in kinship care (33%) and nonrelative foster care (34%), half of the kin caregivers (52%) were never married, compared to only 33% of the nonrelative foster parents. Similarly, 52% of the kinship caregivers in the

Berrick, Barth and Needell study [1994] were single parents, compared to only 24% of the nonrelative foster parents.

How old are kin caregivers? Because the majority of kin caregivers are grandparents, it is popularly assumed that most are elderly. Most studies however, have found that kin caregivers are between 40 and 55 years of age. The average age of the informal kin caregivers in the McLean and Thomas [1996] study was 50 years, with only 10% over 60 years old. The median age of kin caregivers in the study of Dubowitz and associates [1993] was 48 years, with only 20% being 60 or more years old. The median age of the grandparents in the Minkler and Roe [1993] study was 53 years.

The sizable numbers of older, female-headed caregivers in kin families has been correlated with high levels of poverty. Hill [1977] found that although about 33% of all African American families were poor, almost half (47%) of the kin families were below poverty. According to the McLean and Thomas study [1996], about half (48%) of kin caregivers had annual incomes less than $10,000.

Reasons for Kinship Parenting

Why do disproportionate numbers of relatives among African Americans become parents to their dependent kin? Minkler and Roe [1993] found two major reasons for caregiving by grandmothers and other relatives: negotiations with their children to take responsibility for their grandchildren or nieces and nephews, including situations in which the parent has experienced repeated drug relapses; and a sudden and unanticipated thrust into the caregiving role prompted by such events as parental illness, incarceration, or children welfare agency involvement because of abuse or neglect. Specific situations that are likely to lead to kin caregiving include the birth of a child outside of marriage, particularly to adolescents, since the majority of African American children who are born out-of-wedlock remain with one or both birth parents or are reared by extended family members; the death or illness of one or both parents; parental unemployment; and homelessness. In addition, parents often send their children to live with relatives to escape "bad" environments or to have access to "better" schools or neighborhoods.

Child Abuse and Neglect

What effect does kin caregiving have on the level of child abuse and neglect? Studies consistently have shown that extended family networks are strongly correlated with low levels of child abuse. Cazenave and Straus [1979, p. 292] found a direct correlation between child abuse and the proximity of relatives:

> For African American parents, there is a definite difference in child abuse between those who do and those who do not have relatives living nearby. The highest rates of child abuse occur among African American parents whose husbands have no relatives (35%) or wives who have no relatives (20%) living within one hour away. This type of social isolation appears to have adverse consequences for these African American respondents.

Hill [1997] found that most African American families have relatives who live in the same city, but not in the same household. Similarly, the National Survey of Black Americans (NSBA) found that 53% of the respondents reported that more than half of their kin lived within the same city [Hatchett et al. 1991]. In terms of contact, 38% said that they had contact with their relatives daily, and 28% had contact at least once a week [Hatchett et al. 1991]. It is this close proximity of kin and frequency of contact that has been associated with relatively low rates of child abuse among African American families. Relatives play a vital role in protecting their kin, as they are the most frequent source of official reports of abuse and neglect, serving as a buffer against child maltreatment. Similarly, relatives provide safe environments for children, as demonstrated by the lower levels of child abuse and neglect among children reared by relatives than among children reared by their biological parents or by nonrelatives [Hampton et al. 1998].

Although African American families are overrepresented in the official statistics on child abuse and neglect, national surveys have consistently revealed lower rates of child abuse than child neglect among African Americans and similar rates of child abuse and neglect between African Americans and Caucasians. The National Incidence Surveys of 1979-80, 1986, and 1993 found no significant racial differences in abuse and neglect between African Americans and Caucasians [Resource Center on Child Abuse and Neglect 1981; Sedlak & Broadhurst 1996]. Data on child abuse and neglect rates, however, must be viewed in relation to the soaring rates of crack cocaine in inner cities, a factor that has contributed significantly to increasing rates of abuse and neglect for both African American and Caucasian children. It is estimated that some level of drug or alcohol use is involved in between 50% and 80% of all confirmed child abuse cases and 75% of the child fatalities at the hands of parents known to the child welfare system [Office for Substance Abuse Prevention (OSAP) 1992]. Data further shows that the younger the child, the higher the risk posed by parental substance abuse [OSAP 1992]. It is in many of these cases in which parental substance abuse poses risks to children that kin, particularly grandparents, negotiate with their children to assume responsibility for children [Minkler & Roe 1993].

Number of Placements and Length of Stay in Care

How long do children remain in households headed by relatives? Many studies reveal that there is greater stability for children in relative care than for children reared by nonrelatives. Children in the care of relatives have fewer changes in living arrangements than foster children reared by nonrelatives. The Westat study for the U.S. Children's Bureau [1997], which focused on children receiving child welfare services in 1994, found that children in kinship care experience an average of only one move, while children in foster care may average between five and ten placements. Their study also found that 33% of the children in nonrelative foster care had two or more different placements, compared to only 10% of the children in kinship foster care. A study by Dubowitz and associates [1993] found that 76% of children in kinship care had only one move, while the remaining 24% had two or more moves.

It has been suggested that children in kinship care remain in care longer than children placed with nonrelatives, and that the increase in the length of time that African American children remain in foster care is associated with the growth in kinship care families [U.S. Children's Bureau 1997]. In order to systematically test this thesis, Westat researchers compared the length of placement of children in kinship care with those in nonrelative foster care. They found no significant differences in the median length of time that African American children were in kinship care (32.9 months) and the length of time African American children were in nonrelative foster care (27.2 months) [Children's Bureau 1997].

Nevertheless, research suggests that children whose parents abuse alcohol or drugs tend to remain in foster care longer than non-drug-exposed children and have a greater number of placements. According to the study by Walker [1994], 72% of children of substance-abusing parents were still in foster care 26 months after entry into care, compared to 49% of the children of parents who did not abuse drugs. In another study, it was found that 60% of drug-exposed infants discharged to foster care from hospitals in New York City in 1986 were still in care three years later [Walker 1994]. With regard to the number of placements experienced by substance-exposed children, a recent survey of foster care service agencies showed that the vast majority (87%) of these agencies had found that children prenatally exposed to alcohol or drugs were more likely to require multiple placements than other children [Hampton et al. 1998].

Financial Support

In most states, kin caregivers who receive public funds to care for their children fall within two categories: "kinship care" families who are not licensed foster parents and who receive welfare aid (Aid to Families with Dependent Children [AFDC] in the past, now Temporary Assistance to Needy Families [TANF]); and "relative foster care" families who are licensed or approved as foster families and who receive standard foster care payments. Following the 1979 Supreme Court decision in Miller v. Youakim, several states, including Illinois and New York, began providing similar financial support to relative foster parents and nonrelative foster parents, even when the kin parents did not meet the licensing standards for foster parents. Despite this expansion of benefits for kin caregivers in some states, it is important to note that the bulk of kin caregivers fall into a third category—"informally adoptive families"—who do not receive either welfare assistance or foster care stipends, and who are largely dependent on private sources of funds.

The study by Minkler and Roe [1993] provides extensive documentation about the increased economic hardships faced by grandparents who care for their drug-exposed kin. Their study found that grandmothers often were required to leave their jobs, reduce their work hours, or obtain multiple jobs in order to properly care for their kin. Others were not able to continue to work because of the lack of affordable child care. Minkler and Roe [1993, p. 83] observed:

> The vast majority of respondents (87%) reported significant financial difficulty since assuming full-time caregiving, often saying that they were "spending down to the last penny" or "getting by each month on prayer alone." Half of the sample said that they were "not doing very well" financially now, and 35% said that they were doing poorly.

The study, which involved interviews with grandparents in California, found that most of the grandmothers were distressed that they could receive only California's lower welfare payments (about $326 per child) on behalf of their kin children and were not eligible for the higher AFDC-Foster Care rates ($345 or more, which increased with the age of the child). Ineligibility for the higher benefit rate was usually related to the fact that the children were informally placed by family members and not by court order, or to the fact that the children had not lived with welfare-receiving parents or relatives at least six months prior to placement with the grandparents. The researchers found it ironic that the more needy grandparents received less financial aid, while the less needy nonrelative foster families received greater assistance. The research of Brooks and Barth [1998] likewise confirms the more limited incomes of kin caregivers. A lower mean family income was found for kin caregivers with drug-exposed children ($32,477) and without drug-exposed children ($32,499) in their homes than nonrelative caregivers with ($54,318) and without ($49,407) drug-exposed children.

Some states have attempted to correct the inequities in financial support for grandparents and other relatives who provide long-term care for children. Illinois and Maryland, for example, have obtained federal waivers in order to test five-year demonstration programs that provide higher levels of subsidies to relatives who assume guardianship for their kin. Studies are needed to determine the levels of economic support that are needed by kin caregivers in order to promote positive outcomes for children, especially children with special needs and including those affected by prenatal alcohol and drug exposure.

Service Needs

What are some of the service needs of kin caregivers? The McLean and Thomas [1996] study of informal adoptive families found that families identified the following needs as priority concerns: legal services, medical care, day care, educational services, family counseling, housing, mental health counseling, and respite care. Despite the high level of service needs, kin caregivers receive markedly fewer needed services than nonrelative foster parents [McLean & Thomas 1996]. Kin who care for children affected by prenatal substance exposure experience the same service deficiencies. They often receive less specialized training than nonrelatives in how to care for drug-exposed children [Hampton et al. 1998; OSAP 1992; McLean & Thomas 1996]. Dubowitz and colleagues [1993] also report marked discrepancies between the level of services that kin caregivers say that they need and caseworkers' perceptions of the service needs of kin. This disparity may be attributable to the lower level of contact that social workers have with kinship care providers as compared to the level of contact with foster parents [Brooks & Barth 1998; Berrick, Barth & Needell 1994; Minkler & Roe 1993].

Child Outcomes

Are the outcomes for children reared by kin more positive than the outcomes for children reared by nonrelatives? A comprehensive study by Dubowitz and associates [1993] revealed that children in kinship care had serious problems in the areas of physical health, mental health, educational performance, and antisocial behavior. The national study of child welfare services by Westat, however, which compared children in kinship care and children placed with nonrelatives on dimensions related to emotional problems, school problems, physical health problems, and truancy, found that such problems occur less frequently among children in kinship care than among children in nonrelative care [U.S. Children's Bureau 1997]. The study also found that there was a statistically significant difference between the two groups of children on child maltreatment indicators [U.S. Children's Bureau 1997].

Brooks and Barth [1998] conducted an in-depth analysis of outcomes for children in the homes of kin and nonkin caregivers, specifically taking into account outcomes for children who were prenatally exposed to drugs. They found no major differences between drug-exposed and non-drug-exposed children in kin and nonkin homes regarding overall grades, but there were differences in frequency of grade repetition. Non-drug-exposed children in kinship care (19%) were the least likely to repeat a grade as compared to drug-exposed children in kinship care (30%), and children in nonrelative care whether they were drug-exposed (35%) or not (28%). Among both kin and nonkin caregivers, drug-exposed children were more likely to be placed in special education than children who were not exposed to drugs. After conducting logistic regression analysis, the researchers concluded that: "Drug-exposed children placed with kin or nonrelatives were more than three times as likely, and non-drug-exposed children placed with nonrelatives were more than twice as likely, to exhibit problem behavior compared with non-drug-exposed children placed with kin" [Brooks & Barth 1998, p. 494]. The authors, however, cautioned against assuming that the emotional, educational, and behavior problems observed among drug-exposed children with kin caregivers were mainly due to their kinship status and not to a prior dysfunctional environment or to the inadequate services received by them.

Family Preservation and Reunification

A major role of relative caregivers is to preserve the bonds of children within their extended families by caring for their kin until one or both of their birth parents are able to assume parental responsibilities. African American extended families view the caring for minor kin as family preservation, not as child placement, a perspective that differs from that of many child welfare agencies. Family preservation from this vantage point occurs most frequently in informally adoptive families in which children are placed by extended family members. To some extent, child welfare agencies are embracing this form of family preservation by providing welfare assistance and other support to relative caregivers and thereby preventing the need to place children in foster care as wards of the state.

While support is provided to relative caregivers, child welfare agencies are obligated to provide birth parents with intensive family preservation and other services to facilitate reunification with their children. A major void in services to parents of drug-exposed children, however, exists because of the lack of drug treatment services. There is an insufficient number of drug treatment programs for most addicts, both men and women, who seek help; most drug programs serve men rather than women; and few programs have adequate services for pregnant and parenting women. A major reason for the many delays in developing appropriate permanency plans for drug-exposed children is the inordinate amount of time needed to find adequate drug treatment services for parents.

Just as many birth parents do not receive family preservation or other support services to facilitate reunification with their children [Maluccio & Whittaker 1988; Fein & Staff 1991], research also indicates that kin families, whether they rear children inside or outside the foster care system, often receive few family preservation services. A comprehensive survey by Danzy and Jackson [1997] found that very few states used funds under the 1993 Family Preservation and Support Services Act to target their services to kin caregivers. Because of inadequate family-based services, kinship care may not lead to reunification with biological parents, despite the fact that children in kin families often have more contact with their birth parents than children who are placed with nonrelated foster parents [Berrick, Barth & Needell 1994; Gleeson & Craig 1994]. According to the Westat study, children in kinship care (39%) were less likely to have a plan of reunification than children in nonrelative care (49%) [U.S. Children's Bureau 1997].

Formal Adoption

Conventional wisdom holds that because African Americans are heavily involved in informal adoption, they have little interest in formally adopting children. Yet many studies strongly contradict this belief. A nationally representative African American Pulse Survey conducted by the National Urban League's Research Department revealed that one-third of African American household heads said that they were interested in formally adopting a African American child [Hill 1997]. Furthermore, national surveys have revealed that African Americans are just as likely as Caucasians to adopt children [U.S. National Center for Health Statistics 1990]. Moreover, several studies have concluded that when one controls for social class, African Americans actually formally adopt at higher rates than comparable Caucasian families [Dodson 1998].

To what extent do kin caregivers formally adopt? In Illinois, between 8% and 12% of the kinship care families have formally adopted their relative children [Gleeson & Craig 1994]. Such adoptions are more likely to occur when biological parents have died, abandoned their children, or otherwise have little or no contact with the children or extended family members. The study by Brooks and Barth [1998] found that kinship caregivers (43%) were about as likely as nonrelatives (49%) to be willing to adopt the children for whom they were caring if freed for adoption. And, interestingly, they found that among kin and nonkin, caregivers of drug-exposed children were more receptive to adoption than caregivers of non-drug-exposed children. In one of the few studies of formal adoption by kin, Magruder [1994] found that adoptive kin parents were more likely to be single parents, older, of lower income, and with fewer years of education than nonrelated adoptive parents. Unfortunately, the study also revealed that despite greater disadvantages in relation to income and education, adoptive kin parents received fewer postadoption services and supports than nonrelated foster parents.

Implications for Practice

As the studies of the needs of kinship families indicate, kin are largely underserved by child welfare agencies in terms of preparation and support services. Studies have shown that kin receive far less prepa-ration than nonrelatives in the care of children prenatally exposed to drugs and alcohol and receive far fewer support services. Because kin are often involved in rearing children affected by prenatal substance exposure, there is a critical need to develop services to prepare them to meet the short- and longer-term needs of these children and to provide them with ongoing support services, includ-ing family counseling, day care, mental health services, and respite care. Because children affected by prenatal substance exposure have been shown to have a higher need for special education services and to exhibit more problem behavior often as a result of prior problem-atic home environments, kin families need assistance in accessing specialized services and may require advocacy support to ensure that the children for whom they are caring receive the services that they need and that they are entitled to under a variety of programs. Finally, because many kin provide long-term care for their kin children—through ongoing informal caregiving, adoption, or guard-ianship—services need to be in place to support them in the same way that postadoption services support nonrelated families who adopt children affected by prenatal substance exposure.

Implications for Research

What research agenda is needed to increase knowledge about kin caregiving and about kin caregivers that may lead to their serving as guardians or formal adoptive parents for children? As a starting point, research should build on the recommendations advanced by other scholars [Barth 1994; Dubowitz 1994; Berrick et al. 1994; Brooks & Barth 1998] and focus on the four types of kin families: informal adoption, kinship care, relative foster care, and relative adoption.

Informal Adoption

Studies are urgently needed on relatives who rear children who were not placed with them by public child welfare agencies. As Dubowitz [1994] observed, this group of relatives is the least studied group of kin caregivers because they are not in the public domain. Yet, these more than 800,000 families may be a major resource as foster parents or formal adoptive parents. It is important to understand the type of support systems these kin families rely upon that make it possible for them to avoid dependence on public supports such as welfare benefits. It is also important to identify the protective factors among these families that prevent their kin children from entering the foster care system. Research should build on the work on McLean and Thomas [1996], which found that by providing intensive services to informal adoptive families, the great majority of families (over 80%) did not have to seek public assistance. Finally, more surveys are needed to determine the willingness of informal adoptive families to formally adopt their kin or other children in foster care, including kin children affected by prenatal drug exposure.

Kinship Care.

Most of the current studies on kin caregivers focus on kinship care, that is, families in which children are placed by child welfare agencies, but are not formally approved as foster parents. Because most studies suggest that these families are underserved by child welfare agencies, additional research is needed to systematically document the type of services that kinship care families need and the extent to which these services are provided. Moreover, if vital services are not provided to kin caregivers, research is needed to determine which practices or policies serve as barriers to prevent receipt of these services. Inquiry is also needed into the level of financial support required by kin caregivers to adequately provide for the high-risk children that they are rearing. More demonstration research is needed to determine the quality of child rearing that could be provided by kinship care families if they were provided financial support at the same level as formally approved foster parents.

Relative Foster Care

Many of the current studies of kinship care families compare these families to nonrelative foster parents. Yet, there are few studies of kin caregivers that are licensed as foster parents because of their small numbers. Relative foster children, for example, accounted for 30% of the 5,000 foster children who were in kin families in Maryland in 1997 [Dubowitz et al. 1993]. More studies are needed that compare kinship care families with relative foster families on such issues as the socioeconomic characteristics of children and caregivers, length of child placement, financial support, services needed, services provided, child outcomes, and permanency plans. Research should examine the practices and policies that are needed to convert kinship care or relative foster care to formal adoption, including the effects of various levels of adoption subsidies.

Relative Adoptions

There have also been few studies of formal adoptions by relatives, as they comprise a small portion of all adoptions. Building on such pioneering work as Magruder [1994], research should examine the various services, including postadoption services, that are needed by relatives who adopt. Research should compare children adopted by relatives with children adopted by nonrelatives, with special attention to children with special needs, including children who are affected by prenatal substance exposure. Research should also be conducted on the factors that are associated with the successful adoption strategies of culturally sensitive agencies in placing "hard-to-place" children of color with kin and nonrelatives [McRoy et al. 1997; Danzy & Jackson 1997].

Conclusion

In sum, longitudinal studies should be conducted that compare the relative outcomes for the four types of kin caregiving: informal adoption, kinship care, relative foster care, and relative adoptions. There is an important need for more ethnographic and case studies that closely examine the cultural processes of kin caregiving among various ethnic groups and the effects of kin caregiving on various child outcomes for permanence, as legal custodians, guardians, or as formally adoptive parents.

References

Barth, R. P. (1994). Adoption research: Building blocks for the next decade. *Child Welfare, 73*, 625–638.

Berrick, J., Barth R. P., & Needell, B. (1994). Comparison of kinship foster homes and foster family homes. *Children and Youth Services Review, 16* (1–2), 33–64.

Brooks, D. & Barth R. P. (1998). Characteristics and outcomes of drug-exposed and non-drug-exposed children in kinship and non-relative foster care. *Children and Youth Services Review, 20*(6), 475–501.

Cazenave, N. & Straus, M. (1979). Race, class, network embeddedness and family violence. *Journal of Comparative Family Studies, 10*(3), 281–300.

Chasnoff, I., Landress, H., & Barrett, M. (1980). The prevalence of illicit drug or alcohol use during pregnancy and discrepancies in mandatory reporting. *New England Journal of Medicine, 322,* 1202–1206.

Danzy, J. & Jackson S. (1997). Family preservation and support services: A missed opportunity for kinship care. *Child Welfare, 76,* 31–44.

Dodson, D. (1998). *Finding families for waiting kids: The challenge of special needs adoption in the 90s and beyond.* Washington, DC: Family Impact Seminar.

Dubowitz, H. (1994). Kinship care: Suggestions for future research. *Child Welfare, 73,* 553–564.

Dubowitz, H., Feigelman, S., Harrington, D., Starr, R., Zuravin, S., & Sawyer, R. (1993). Children in kinship care: How do they fare? *Children and Youth Services Review, 16*(1–2), 85–106.

Fein, E. & Staff, I. (1991). Implementing reunification services. *Families in Society, 72*(6), 335–343.

Gleeson, J. P. (1996). Kinship care as a child welfare service: The policy rebate in an era of welfare reform. *Child Welfare, 75,* 419–450.

Gleeson, J. P. & Craig, L. (1994). Kinship care in child welfare: An analysis of states' policies. *Children and Youth Services Review, 16*(1–2), 7–32.

Goerge, R. M., Wulczyn, F. H., & Harden, A. W. (1995). *Foster care dynamics, 1983–1993: California, Illinois, Michigan, New York and Texas—An update from the multistate foster care data archive.* Chicago: Chapin Hall Center for Children, University of Chicago.

Hatchett, S., Cochran, D. L., & Jackson, J. S. (1991). Family Life. In J. Jackson (Ed.), *Life in black America* (pp. 46–83). Newbury Park, CA: Sage Publications.

Hampton, R. L., Senatore, V., & Gullotta, T. P. (1998). *Substance abuse, family violence, and child welfare*. Thousands Oaks, CA: Sage Publications.

Hill, R. B. (1997). *The strengths of African American families: Twenty-five years later*. Washington, DC: R & B Publishers.

Hill, R. B. (1977). *Informal adoption among black families*. Washington, DC: National Urban League.

Hill, R. B. (1972). *The strengths of black families*. New York: Emerson Hall Publishers.

Jarrett, R. L. (1995). Growing up poor: The family experiences of socially mobile youth in low-income African American neighborhoods. *Journal of Adolescent Research, 10* (1), 111–135.

Magruder, J. (1994). Characteristics of relative and non-relative adoptions by California public adoption agencies. *Children and Youth Services Review, 16*(1–2), 123–132.

Maluccio, A. N. & Whittaker, J. K. (1988). Helping the biological families of children in out-of-home placement. In E. W. Nunnally, C. S. Chilman, & F. M. Cox (Eds.), *Troubled relationships* (pp. 205–217). Newbury Park, CA: Sage Publications.

Mann, W. (1997). Supportive roles of significant others in black families. In H. P. McAdoo (Ed.), *Black families* (pp. 198–213). Beverly Hills, CA: Sage Publications.

McLean, B. & Thomas, R. (1996). Informal and formal kinship care populations: A study in contrasts. *Child Welfare, 75,* 489–508.

McRoy, R. G., Oglesby, Z., & Grape, H. (1997). Achieving same-race adoptive placements for African American children. *Child Welfare, 76,* 85–104.

Miller, A. T. (1993). Social science, social policy, and the heritage of African-American families. In M. B. Katz (Ed.), *The "underclass" debate* (pp. 254–289). Princeton, NJ: Princeton University Press.

Minkler, M. & Roe K. (1993). *Grandmothers as caregivers: Raising children of the crack cocaine epidemic*. Newbury Park, CA: Sage Publications.

National Center on Child Abuse and Neglect. (1981). *Study findings: National study of the incidence and severity of child abuse and neglect*. Washington, DC: National Center on Child Abuse and Neglect (DHHS), Clearinghouse on Child Abuse and Neglect Information.

National Committee to Prevent Child Abuse. (1995). *Current trends in child abuse reporting and fatalities: The results of the 1996 annual fifth state survey.* Chicago: National Committee to Prevent Child Abuse.

Office for Substance Abuse Prevention. (1992). *Identifying the needs of drug-affected children.* Washington, DC: U.S. Department of Health and Human Services, Public Health Service.

Sedlak, A. & Broadhurst D. (1996). *Executive summary of the third national incidence study of child abuse and neglect.* Washington, DC: U.S. Department of Health and Human Services.

Stack, C. B. (1974). *All our kin.* New York: Harper and Row.

Tatara, T. (1993). *Characteristics of children in substitute and adoptive care.* Washington, DC: American Public Welfare Association.

U.S. Bureau of the Census. (1996). Marital status and living arrangements: March 1994. *Current Population Reports, Series P-20-484.* Washington, DC: U.S. Government Printing Office.

U.S. Children's Bureau. (n.d.). *Research note no. 8.* Washington, DC: Children's Bureau, U.S. Department of Health and Human Services.

U.S. Children's Bureau. (1997). *National study of protective preventive and reunification services delivered to children and families.* Washington, DC: U.S. Department of Health and Human Services.

U.S. National Center for Health Statistics. (1990). Adoption in the 1980's. *Advance Data 181*[5 January]. Washington, DC: U.S. Government Printing Office.

Walker, C. D. (1994). African American children in foster care. In D. Besharov (Ed.), *When drug addicts have children* (pp. 145–152). Washington, DC: Child Welfare League of America and American Enterprise Institute.

4

Fetal Alcohol Exposure and Adult Psychopathology: Evidence from an Adoption Study

Remi J. Cadoret & Kristin Riggins-Caspers

In utero exposure to alcohol has been recognized as a teratogen for nearly a century [Sullivan 1899]. It is not until the recent two decades, however, that researchers have begun studying the detrimental and enduring effects of fetal alcohol exposure on intellectual and behavioral functioning [Famy et al. 1998; Kerns et al. 1997; LaDue et al. 1992; Mattson & Riley, 1998; Olson et al. 1997; Steinhausen et al. 1993; Steinhausen et al. 1994; Streissguth et al. 1991; Weinberg 1997]. In these studies, birth parents' genetic factors have been confounded with the environments created by these parents, including the fetal alcohol exposure. In some studies, separation of offspring from birth parents followed by foster home or institutional placement may have occurred [Aronson & Hagberg 1998; Spohr et al. 1994; Steinhausen & Spohr 1998; Steinhausen et al. 1993; Steinhausen et al. 1994; Streissguth et al. 1991] allowing one to separate the genetic factors from some of the environmental confounds. However, none of the studies cited above has tried to distinguish fetal alcohol effects from potentially genetically mediated effects, and only one has evaluated the differences associated with postnatal environmental conditions, such as out-of-home placement [Steinhausen et al. 1994]. That latter study found that institutionally placed individuals with fetal alcohol syndrome had more severe psychological deficits than those persons who remained with their birth parents or who were placed in adoptive or foster care families. However, determination as to whether or not the higher rates of psychiatric disturbance preceded placement or resulted from placement in an institution was not reported. Studies of adoptees who have been separated from their birth parents at birth and placed with nonrelatives allow for the isolation of the effects of genetics versus environment. Furthermore, an adoption paradigm allows the effects of the prenatal environment to be separated from the effects of the postnatal environment, which in this case is created by the adoptive family. In doing so, adoption studies can provide useful information to clinicians interested in designing intervention programs designed to address the consequences of fetal alcohol exposure. Specifically, adoption studies can provide important information on what aspects of the home, independent of the parent, are important in determining the ultimate impact of fetal alcohol exposure on development.

Yates and associates [1998b] presented the first adoption study to examine the additive effects of both the genetic and prenatal exposure to alcohol on substance abuse. The researchers found that, after controlling for the effects of birth parent alcoholism and antisocial personality, in utero exposure to alcohol significantly predicted substance abuse problems in adopted offspring, even when controlling for additional adoptive home environmental factors. The present study expands on the findings of Yates and associates [1998b] and examines whether fetal alcohol exposure is predictive of other types of adult psychopathology, such as personality disorder, depression, and anxiety.

Advantages of Adoption Paradigm

The adoption design has been used for decades to examine genetic and environmental predictors of human behavior [Cadoret 1986]. However, the advantages of an adoption design can be useful to other areas of interest, in that the effects of different environmental conditions can be separated. For example, a serious confound in the research examining extreme groups of individuals with fetal alcohol syndrome is the continued exposure of the individual to poor family conditions or to institutional placement. With groups of lesser extreme such as fetal alcohol effects (FAE), continued residence with birth parents can result in confounding between birth parent characteristics and additional environmental factors that would be correlated with these characteristics, a process known to behavioral geneticists as passive gene-environment correlation [Plomin et al. 1977; Scarr & McCartney 1983]. For example, an alcoholic mother may also be aggressive and incorporate aggressive behaviors in her handling of the child. Placement in an adoptive home allows separation of these effects into those that are purely genetic, such as birth parent characteristics, and those that are purely environmental, such as prenatal exposure or characteristics of the adoptive home [Plomin et al. 1990].

In the study to be presented, birth parent characteristics of alcoholism and antisocial personality were included as estimates of genetic effects thought to contribute to maladaptive behavior by the adoptee. Within the adoption paradigm, a genetic effect is estimated by correlating a characteristic of the birth parent, such as symptoms of antisocial personality, with a characteristic of the adopted offspring, such as symptoms of child conduct disorder. If the child was separated from his or her birth parents at an early age, then the only mechanism that would contribute to their being similar on a specified trait such as conduct disorder is shared genetic makeup. Genetic factors are included in the model, so that any biological predisposition to psychopathology can be separated from the effects of exposure to alcohol in utero.

Environmental effects can be estimated in much the same way as genetic effects except that characteristics of the adoptive home are used as predictors of adoptee behaviors [Cadoret 1986], while controlling for genetic factors. If characteristics of the adoptee are associated with characteristics of the adoptive home, then the only mechanism that could produce this similarity is the common environment. Not included in the present study's estimation of environmental effects are those factors unique to the adoptee, such as peers. Although the literature supports the impact of nonshared environmental effects on human development, the design of the current study does not allow separation of shared and nonshared environmental effects. Consequently, environmental effects will be operationalized as any characteristic of the adoptive home that is unassociated with any characteristics of the birth parent.

Although shared and non-shared environmental effects are indistinguishable, the present study is able to compare prenatal environmental effects, such as FAE, versus those occurring postnatally, such as an adverse adoptive home. Given the use of an adoption design, these environmental effects can be separated from any biological effects, such as parental alcoholism or antisocial personality, that might contribute to increased psychopathology in the adoptee. Such a design allows a greater understanding of the contributions of fetal alcohol exposure to later psychopathology after controlling for confounding biological and environmental factors that previous works in this field have been unable to control.

Fetal Alcohol Syndrome/Exposure

The following is a brief discussion of the terminology used in the literature to describe children exposed to alcohol in utero. It is included to enable the reader to determine the extent to which our classification of adoptees as fetally exposed to alcohol is consistent with that endorsed by researchers within the field. Recently, the United States Congress mandated a study of alcohol exposure and its developmental consequences [Stratton et al. 1996]. The appointed committee included as one of its goals the development of diagnostic criteria for the full syndrome as well as for subsyndromal conditions. Three categories of Fetal Alcohol Syndrome (FAS) were derived: 1) FAS with confirmed maternal alcohol exposure, 2) FAS without confirmed maternal alcohol exposure, and 3) partial FAS with confirmed maternal alcohol exposure. Maternal exposure to alcohol was defined as alcohol use in which alcohol intake was excessive, frequent, and social or personal problems were a direct result of alcohol use.

In the first category, FAS with confirmed maternal alcohol exposure, the child must present specific physical characteristics. Confirmed syndromic features of facial malformations must be evident, as well as low birth weight, small head circumference, or disproportionate weight to height ratio [Stratton et al. 1996]. Finally, the child or individual must present symptoms consistent with central nervous system (CNS) neurological abnormalities which would include small cranial size; structural abnormalities such as microcephaly, partial or complete agenesis of corpus callosum, and cerebellar hyoplasia; or neurological hard or soft signs such as impaired fine motor skills, neurosensory hearing loss, poor tandem gait, and poor eye-hand coordination [Stratton et al 1996: 17]. In the second group, maternal alcohol exposure to alcohol is not confirmed, but the child demonstrates all other characteristics discussed above. Finally, the third category, partial FAS with confirmed maternal alcohol exposure, refers to children who were known to be exposed to alcohol in utero, but for whom only some of the dysmorphic characteristics are present. Furthermore, growth retardation is present in only one of the three areas—birth weight, decreased weight over time, or disproportionate weight to height; or only a single CNS abnormality is present; or behavioral or cognitive developmental delays not otherwise accounted for by genetics or environmental conditions are present [Stratton et al. 1996).

Two additional categories of fetal alcohol effects were derived for individuals demonstrating outcomes previously linked to maternal ingestion of alcohol, but for whom a diagnosis of FAS cannot be made: 1) alcohol-related birth defects (ARBD) and 2) alcohol-related neuro-developmental disorder (ARND) [Stratton et al. 1996]. For both categories, maternal alcohol exposure is a necessary condition. The classification of ARBD refers to congenital anomalies in the cardiac, skeletal, renal, ocular, and auditory systems. The classification of ARND refers to the CNS abnormalities or behavioral and cognitive delays described earlier. The category of ARND best describes the sample of adoptees included in the present study, in that maternal exposure to alcohol is confirmed, but the presence of dysmorphic facial features is not.

Recent Findings on Fetal Alcohol Syndrome/Exposure

To date, the majority of research on the effects of fetal alcohol exposure has focused on cognitive and attention deficits in infants and young children [Jacobson & Jacobson 1994; Streissguth et al. 1981; Streissguth et al. 1994b]. These effects exist for individuals diagnosed with the full syndrome [Jacobson & Jacobson 1994] and for persons exhibiting characteristics of ARND and/or ARBD [Jacobson et al. 1994; Streissguth et al. 1994a, 1994b]. Fewer studies have examined the effects of fetal alcohol exposure on psychiatric problems and even fewer have studied these effects in older children and adults [Connor & Streissguth 1996; Famy et al. 1998; Kerns et al. 1997; LaDue et al. 1992; Olson et al. 1997; see review in Steinhausen et al 1993a; Steinhausen & Sphor 1998; Streissguth 1998; Streissguth et al. 1991; Streissguth, et al. 1994a]. Those who have begun investigating the behavioral and psychiatric sequelae of fetal alcohol exposure have confirmed its negative impact. For example, Olson and associates [1997] examined differences in levels of adolescent, parent, and interviewer ratings on behavior problems. Using partial least squares analyses, the researchers found adolescents exposed to alcohol in utero were rated significantly lower by interviewers in terms of how the adolescent presented herself. Furthermore, alcohol-exposed adolescents reported more engagement in misconduct and delinquent activities. More recently, Famy and associates [1998] found that 92% of adults with diagnosed FAS (n = 25) had at least one Axis I diagnosis, with 60% of these individuals having a substance abuse/dependence problem. Forty percent of the sample was diagnosed with a personality disorder, and 72% of the sample received some psychiatric treatment.

Although negative findings do exist [Abel & Hannigan 1995; Mattson & Riley 1998; Olsen 1994], the preponderance of significant results outweigh the negative findings and suggest the spectrum of potential outcomes should be expanded. This study is unique in that the inherent confound between the prenatal and postnatal environments of alcohol-exposed individuals can be disentangled by complete separation of the two environments. With an adoption paradigm, adoptive families are typically middle class and have been carefully evaluated for the absence of such adverse factors as parental psychopathology, low socioeconomic status, and marital problems at the time of placement [Cadoret 1986]. Consequently, an adoption design allows the researcher to examine the enduring effects of fetal exposure, independent from any negative postnatal environmental conditions associated with alcoholism in the birth mother. Furthermore, the effects of any negative environmental conditions such as marital problems and psychopathology that might develop in the adoptive home can also be controlled. The following sections outline the methods used and the findings examining long-term consequences of fetal alcohol exposure.

Methodology

Sample

Data collection for this adoption study was funded by the National Institute of Drug Abuse and was collected between 1989 and 1992. Specific details about the study are presented in Cadoret, Yates, Troughton, Woodworth, and Stewart [1995]. The data collection procedure was typical of an adoptee study method in which the starting point of sample identification is the birth parent [Yates et al. 1998a]. Two groups of birth parents were included: an index group (n = 95) and a comparison group (n = 102). The index group consisted of birth parents with documented psychiatric problems such as alcoholism, antisocial personality, and drug abuse, whereas the comparison group consisted of birth parents who lacked any such identification. Index and comparison adoptees were matched on age and sex of the adoptee and by age of the birth mother at the time of the adoptee's birth.

The process of sample identification began with social service agencies identifying all adoptees between the ages of 17 and 45 at the beginning of the study. All adoptees were placed by their birth parent at the time of birth, with some infants placed in temporary foster care prior to final adoption. The names of both birth parents of these adoptees (n = 11,700) were circulated through the following institutions: State of Iowa Mental Health Institutions, University of Iowa Hospitals and Clinics, and the Iowa Department of Corrections [see Cadoret et. al 1995). Anonymity of the birth parent was maintained, while at the same time coded to allow matching with the adoptees. Following collection of institutional information, three psychiatrists independently diagnosed the birth parent from birth parent records using criteria from the DSM-III-R. The kappa values for diagnosing antisocial personality and alcoholism were adequate (range: .67 - .90). Differences in diagnoses were resolved through conference with unresolved differences in case identification resulting in the case being discarded. To be included in the index group, only those adoptive families having an adoptee with a birth parent diagnosed as antisocial and as a drug or alcohol abuser were contacted for participation (n = 238). Of those 238 index adoptive families, 95 agreed to participate in the study. The process of selecting comparison families was similar, resulting in a pool of 249 potential families. Of those, 102 comparison adoptive families agreed to participate. Reasons for not participating included lack of interest, confidentiality concerns, and not wanting to upset the adoptee. Analyses showed that the refusal rate was not correlated with birth parent status [Cadoret et al. 1995]. The protocol of this study was approved by the Institutional Review Board of the University of Iowa College of Medicine.

Adoptees and their adoptive parents were interviewed in person by a research assistant who was blind to the diagnosis of the birth parents. The adoptive parent interview assessed the adoptive child's physical health, temperament, school achievement, and social adjustment from infancy to the present. Questions about emotional and psychiatric problems within the adoptive family were included, as well as other family disturbances such as separations, divorce, and legal problems. In addition, adoptive parents were administered the Diagnostic Interview Schedule Screening Instrument, as well as a computerized version of the Diagnostic Interview Schedule (DIS). Adoptees and their adoptive parents were interviewed separately.

The adoptee interview consisted of administration of the DIS (III-R) developed by Robins and colleagues [1989]. The DIS allows lay interviewers to assess current and lifetime prevalence of psychiatric illness by DSM-III-R criteria and Research Diagnostic Criteria, as well as Feighner criteria. Prior to data collection, the research assistants responsible for the interviewing attended a weeklong DIS instruction course offered by Washington University in St. Louis, Missouri.

Grade school, high school, and medical records also were collected to verify treatment and diagnosis of psychiatric conditions or substance abuse. Agency records containing information on the prenatal course of the birth mother, including labor and delivery, and the adoptee neonatal course were abstracted.

Measures

Prenatal Fetal Alcohol Exposure.   Adoption agency, hospital, and prison records were reviewed for determination of fetal alcohol exposure (for descriptions of individual cases, see Table 1). If a record indicated that drinking had occurred at the time of conception or around the time of pregnancy, then fetal exposure was coded as possible (n = 12). If drinking was stated to occur during pregnancy or if the adoptee was arrested on drinking-related charges, then fetal exposure was coded as definite (n = 9). Due to small numbers, the possible and definite fetal alcohol exposure groups are combined for these analyses, as well as males (n = 15) and females (n = 6) who were in the FAE group

Birth Parent Psychopathology. Identification of alcoholism and antisocial personality in a birth parent is described in detail in the sample section. The absence of either alcoholism or antisocial personality was coded as zero, whereas the presence of these disorders was coded as one. Twenty-three percent of the birth parents, either mother or father, were diagnosed with either an alcohol problem or displayed significant antisocial behaviors; 10% were diagnosed with both alcohol and antisocial problems; and only 52% were not identified as demonstrating any alcohol or antisocial behaviors [Cutrona et al. 1994].

Postnatal Adverse Adoptive Home Factors. The factors that comprise the composite adverse adoptive home factors are listed in Table 2. Previous research conducted by this group has shown marital and psychiatric problems in the adoptive parents to be associated with poor behavioral outcomes by the adoptee [Cadoret et al. 1986]. Both the adoptee and the adoptive parent interviews were used to determine the presence of the factors. The possible range of adverse adoptive home factors was from zero to six.

Adoptee Self-Reported Behaviors. This measure was obtained through the use of a structured diagnostic interview at the

Table 4-1. Evidence from Records Suggesting FAE

	FAE	_Sex_
Case 1: Biological mother was 17 at time of adoptee birth in 1969. When mother was 37, report from mental hospitalization indicated she had used marijuana and alcohol since age 17.	Possible	M
Case 2: Adoption agency record states mother used alcohol "moderately" during pregnancy. Child born in 1947.	Definite	M
Case 3: Biological mother heavy drinker from 1938 to 1947 when she was psychiatrically hospitalized until January 1948. She left hsopital, became pregnant, and delivered adoptee late in 1948. She returned to hospital about 4 weeks after adoptee birth because of drinking.	Possible	F
Case 4: Biological mother arrested for intoxication in February 1953, when she was 2 months pregnant. Adoptee born later in fall of 1953. The hospital record states biological mother is epileptic, alcoholic, and has been treated for syphilis, but does not mention drinking during pregnancy.	Definite	M
Case 5: Biological mother separated from husband in June 1957 and then would frequent taverns when baby was conceived around August 1957. Adoptee born in 1958.	Possible	F
Cases 6 and 7: Biological mother placed in mental hospital October 1957, when 3–4 months pregnant. According to her husband, she had begun drinking heavily 6 months before and had become worse in preceding 6 weeks. Twin babies born in 1958.	Definite	M
Case 8: Biological mother reported to be drinking to intoxication (and writing bad checks) at the time of first month of pregnancy (August 1958). Adoptee born in spring of 1959.	Possible	M
Case 9: Biological mother admitted to prison March 1960 for writing bad checks, and Department of Corrections record indicates she was using alcohol and tobacco prior to prison admission (while pregnant) Adoptee born spring of 1960	Possible	M

Table 4-1. Continued.

	FAE	Sex
Case 10: Biological mother reported by adoption agency to be using a "large" amount of alcohol during pregnancy. Adoptee born in spring of 1960.	Definite	M
Case 11: Biological mother reported by adoption agency to be using a "large" amount of alcohol during pregnancy. Adoptee born in summer of 1960.	Definite	M
Case 12: Biological mother using drugs and alcohol since age 15 until hospitalization in June 1970. Adoptee born in spring of 1969.	Possible	M
Case 13: Biological mother admitted problem with alcohol shortly after birth of adoptee in spring of 1968. Drinks to intoxication some of time.	Possible	M
Case 14: Biological mother admits to "1–2 drinks" a night on weekends during the years 1968–1974. Adoptee born in spring of 1971.	Possible	F
Case 15: Biological mother reported by adoption agency to drink "moderately" during pregnancy.	Definite	M
Case 16: Biologiccal mother reported to drink a lot and being promiscuous from ages 14 to 20. Adoptee born (when mother was 18) in 1967.	Possible	M
Case 17: Biological mother reported to be involved in "drinking parties and sexual promiscuity" prior to birth of adoptee in summer 1967.	Possible	M
Case 18: Birth of adoptee in summer 1969, when biological mother was 21 years old. Records indicate drinking was occurring during period of pregnancy.	Possible	M
Case 19: Biological mother reported to have used a "small" amount of alcohol during pregnancy.	Definite	F
Case 20: Biological mother reported to be drinking and promiscuous from age 18 to age 30. Adoptee born in 1970 during time the mother was 20 years old.	Possible	F
Case 21: Biological mother reported to be drinking and promiscuous during pregnancy. Adoptee born in fall of 1964.	Definite	M

Table adapted from Yates, et al., [1998].

Table 4-2. Adverse Adoptive Family Factors by Fetal Alcohol Exposure (n = 21)

Adoptive Home Characteristics	FAE Absent (n = 176)	FAE Present (n = 21)
Alcoholic	31 (18%)	4 (19%)
Anxious	61 (35%)	10 (48%)
Legal Problems	5 (03%)	1 (5%)
Depression	64 (36%)	11 (52%)
Drug Use	3 (2%)	1 (5%)
Family Marital Problems[a]	33 (19%)	9 (43%)
Parental Psychological Problems	46 (26%)	7 (33%)
Divorced Adoptive Parents	15 (9%)	1 (5%)

[a] One-tailed Fisher's Exact Test, p < .05.

time the DIS-III-R was administered and the use of a Structured Interview of Deviant Personality- Revised (SIDP-R).

1. The Diagnostic Interview Schedule - III - R. The adoptee participated in a structured interview, at which time the DIS-III-R was administered. All adult psychiatric symptom counts were derived from this interview. Symptom counts for the following disorders demonstrated adequate distributional properties and were included in the analyses: tobacco abuse/dependence, somatization disorder, generalized anxiety disorder, any phobia, social phobia, simple phobia, panic disorder, posttraumatic stress disorder (PTSD), major depression, dysthymia, mania, gambling, alcohol abuse/dependence, any substance abuse/dependence, cannabis abuse/dependence, amphetamine abuse/dependence, cocaine abuse/dependence, and antisocial personality disorder. Means and standard deviations for the above disorders are presented in Table 4. Log-transformation was used to normalize the following outcomes: somatization, all phobias, panic, PTSD, gambling, and all substance abuse variables.

2. SIDP-R. The Structured Interview of Deviant Personality-Revised [SIDP-R; Pfohl et al. 1989] was used to assess symptoms of

the following DSM-III-R Axis II Personality Disorders: Paranoid, Schizoid, Schizotypal, Obsessive-Compulsive, Histrionic, Dependent, Antisocial, Narcissistic, Avoidant, Borderline, Passive-Aggressive, Sadistic, Self-defeating, Mixed. A count score of all endorsed personality disorder symptoms was used. A log-transformation of this total symptom count score [log10(variable + 1)] was used for analyses to help normalize the distribution. The mean number of personality disorder symptoms for the whole sample was 9.44.

3. Psychiatric Comorbidity. In order to examine comorbidity, the co-occurrence of independently diagnosed psychiatric disorders, of psychiatric disorders, the total number of diagnoses was counted to create a comorbidity variable. The following diagnoses were included: dysthymia, major depression, posttraumatic stress disorder, alcoholism, drug abuse/dependence, antisocial personality, social phobia, simple phobia, tobacco dependence, and any personality disorder. The range of the psychiatric comorbidity score was 6 (min, max = 0, 6).

Statistical Analyses and Preliminary Analyses

Environmental Risk

Upon preliminary examination, it was discovered that fetal alcohol exposure and adverse adoptive home factors were completely confounded, in that all adoptees identified as being exposed to alcohol prenatally resided in adoptive homes with one or more adverse factors (see Table 2). In order to disentangle the effects of fetal alcohol exposure from adverse environmental effects, the number of adverse adoptive home factors was held constant across the two groups of adoptees: those who were or were not exposed to alcohol in utero. A three-level environmental-risk variable was created having the following categories: 1) no environmental risk, 2) postnatal environmental risk present (one or more adverse adoptive home factor), and 3) both prenatal and postnatal environmental-risk factors present (fetal alcohol exposure and at least one adverse adoptive home factor). The prenatal effect of fetal alcohol exposure, above and beyond that of the postnatal effect of adverse adoptive home factors, is confirmed by significant differences between the latter two groups.

A one-way analysis of variance, with the total number of adverse adoptive home factors as the dependent variable and the environmental-risk variable as the predictor variable, was conducted to ensure comparability of postnatal environment across the latter two environmental- risk groups. The results showed the two environmental-risk groups had significantly more adoptive home factors (M postnatal and prenatal = 2.00) than the no-environmental-risk group (M = .00), but did not differ significantly from each other. The lack of difference in number of adverse adoptive home factors between the two environmental risks demonstrates comparable postnatal environments, allowing the effects of fetal alcohol exposure to be examined independent of an adverse adoptive home environment.

Association Between Environmental Risk Factor and Genetic Risk

Table 3 shows the distribution of the environmental risk factor by birth parent alcoholism and antisocial personality. As shown in the table, adoptees having a biological risk for alcoholism or antisocial personality were included in all of the environmental risk groups (see Table 3). Furthermore, adoptees with an alcoholic birth parent were more likely to be assigned to the prenatal plus postnatal environmental risk group, whereas adoptees without biological alcoholism were more likely to be classified as having no environmental risk. Including biological risk as a factor in the analyses of variance allowed examination of the impact of prenatal alcohol exposure on later psychopathology beyond any biological contributions.

Analyses of Variance

Symptom counts of both Axis I and Axis II psychiatric disorders were analyzed for significant effects of fetal alcohol exposure, using a 2 (Gender) x 2 (Biological Alcohol) x 2 (Biological Antisocial Personality) x 3 (Pre/Postnatal Environmental risk) Analysis of Variance. In addition to fetal alcohol exposure, gender of the adoptee and birth parent alcoholism and antisocial personality were entered as main effects. Due to small cell sizes, interactions were limited to the following: 1) two-way interactions between adoptee gender and birth parent characteristics, such as alcoholism and antisocial per-

Table 4-3. Distribution of Biologic Risk by Environmental Risk

	Biologic ASP[a]		Biologic Alcohol[b]	
	Absent	Present	Absent	Present
No Environmental Risk	43	15	44	14
Postnatal Environmental risk	88	30	77	41
Prenatal and Postnatal Environmental Risk	11	10	6	15

Note. Bolded cells were significantly higher than expected by chance. ASP = antisocial personality

[a] Chi-square: 4.54, d.f. = 2, p > .05
[b] Chi-square: 15.13, d.f. = 2, p < .001.

sonality, and 2) two-way interactions between fetal alcohol exposure and birth parent characteristics. If the main effect for fetal alcohol exposure was significant, then Tukey post-hoc comparisons were computed to determine whether fetal exposure predicted the outcome beyond that of an adverse adoptive home.

Initially, measures of gestational age, birth weight, and age adopted were intended to be included as co-variates in the ANOVA. Birth weight and gestational age were chosen as co-variates due to their identification as significant outcomes of fetal alcohol exposure and subsequent association with later developmental and psychological decrement, and because non-FAE factors, such as maternal illness during pregnancy, are also associated with these variables. Age adopted was included due to the high-risk nature of late adoptions. However, inclusion of these variables in the analyses resulted in the loss of a third of the FAE cases. Comparison of the findings with and without these variables showed minimal differences; consequently, the findings for analyses without gestational age, birth weight, and age adopted as co-variates are presented.

Results

The findings will be organized with respect to the first two diagnostic axes identified in DSM-IV-Axis I (Substance Abuse Disorders, Mood Disorders) and Axis II (Personality Disorders, Antisocial Personality) and then in relation to psychiatric comorbidity.

Axis I Symptoms

The findings for the analyses of variance for the three environmental risk groups just described showed significant main effects on symptom counts for fetal alcohol exposure (see Table 4, final column). The main effect for pre/postnatal environmental risk remained after controlling for gender and birth parent characteristics for the following symptom counts: tobacco abuse/dependence, drug abuse/dependence, cannabis and amphetamine abuse/dependence, any phobia, simple and social phobia, PTSD, panic disorder, and dysthymia. Tukey post-hoc comparisons showed adoptees exposed to alcohol in utero were significantly different from adoptees in the no-environmental-risk group and from adoptees in the adverse postnatal environment group. The significant difference between the adverse postnatal environment group and the FAE/adverse postnatal environment group provides evidence for the deleterious effects of fetal alcohol exposure, in addition to the effects of adverse adoptive home environment factors.

Figure 1 shows the observed mean differences in symptom levels for all substance abuse/dependence problems and the striking effect of FAE. Adoptees who were exposed to alcohol in utero report two to three times more substance abuse symptoms than adoptees who have been exposed only to adverse experiences in the adoptive home, or adoptees who were without any environmental risk. Again, the findings from the post-hoc comparisons suggest that the higher symptoms of substance abuse/dependence in the pre/postnatal environmental risk group is due solely to FAE or some other unmeasured factor such as the birth mother having smoked or taken drugs during pregnancy. Similar patterns of results are found for the remaining Axis I diagnoses in that FAE contributes significantly to higher levels of symptoms for all disorders (see Figure 2).

Axis II Symptoms

Analysis of the total number of personality disorder symptoms and adult antisocial personality disorder also showed a significant main effect for environmental risk after controlling for gender and birth parent characteristics of alcoholism and antisocial personality (see Table 4). Post-hoc comparisons again showed significant increases

Figure 4-1. Axis I Substance Abuse/Dependence Symptoms by Pre- and Post-natal Environmental Risk Status

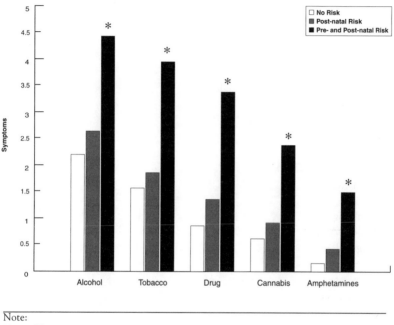

Note:

Vertical bars represent 95% confidence interval.

* Denotes significant difference between prenatal/postnatal environmental risk group from the postnatal and no environmental risk groups.

in number of symptoms by adoptees that were exposed to alcohol in utero, versus adoptees without any environmental risk, or those exposed only to adverse adoptive home experiences (see Figure 3 and 4).

Psychiatric Comorbidity

In order to demonstrate the clinical significance of the above findings, the rate of diagnosed psychiatric and personality disorders within each environmental risk group was examined (see Figures 5 and 6). As with symptom counts, the proportion of adoptees with

Table 4-4. Results for 2 (Gender) x 2 (Bio ALC) x 2 (Bio ASP) x 3 (Environmental Risk) Analyses of Variance Examining Psychiatric Symptoms

Symptoms	M	SD	Gender	Bio Alcohol	Bio ASP	FAE
				Main Effects		
Axis I Disorders						
Tobacco	2.00	2.11	+	+	+	+
Somatization[†1]	1.29	1.65	+	-	-	+
Generalized Anxiety[†]	2.50	3.80	-	-	-	-
Any Phobia[†]	1.61	1.99	-	+	-	+
Simple Phobia[†, ††]	1.00	1.26	-	+	-	+
Social Phobia[†, †††]	.46	.81	-	-	-	+
Panic[†]	.72	2.20	-	-	-	+
Posttraumatic Stress[†]	2.16	3.85	-	-	-	+
Major Depression (MD)	2.76	2.53	-	-	-	-
Dysthymia	1.92	1.98	-	-	-	+
Mania	1.08	1.58	+	-	-	-
Gambling[†]	.25	.94	+	-	-	-
Alcohol Abuse/ Dependence	2.71	2.50	+	-	-	-
Any Substance Abuse/ Dependence[†]	1.43	2.45	+	+	-	+
Cannabis[†]	.99	1.92	+	+	-	+
Amphetamine[†]	.47	1.43	+	+	-	+
Cocaine[†]	.60	1.79	+	-	+	-
Axis II Disorder						
Antisocial Personality	.15	.36	+	+	-	+
Any Personality Disorder	9.44	8.86	+	+	+	+

Note. ASP = antisocial personality, ALC = alcoholism.
[†] Log Transformed = [Lg10(variable + 1)]. [††] Gender x Bio Alc Interaction Significant. [†††] Gender x Bio ASP Interaction

diagnoses was substantially higher if fetal exposure to alcohol was documented. Examining the rates of comorbidity by environmental-risk group showed a substantial effect of fetal alcohol exposure. A

Figure4-2. Axis I Psychiatric Disorder Symptoms by Pre- and Post-natal Environmental Risk Status

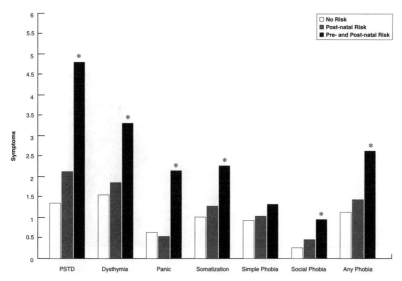

Note:
Vertical bars represent 95% confidence interval.
*Denotes significant difference between prenatal/postnatal environmental risk group
   from the postnatal and no environmental risk groups.

one-way analysis of variance was used to examine differences by environmental risk group. Post-hoc comparisons showed the pre/postnatal environmental risk group (M = 5.58) to have significantly more diagnoses than the other two groups. The difference in number of total diagnoses for the no-environmental-risk group and the postnatal environmental-risk group (M = 1.90 and M = 2.55, respectively) was non-significant. The minimum, maximum, and median for number of diagnoses for each environmental risk group were as follows: no environmental risk (min, max = 0, 6; median = 1); postnatal environmental risk (min, max = 0, 9; median = 1), and pre- and postnatal environmental risk (min, max = 3, 10; median = 4). These numbers show that 100% of adoptees exposed to alcohol

Figure 4-3. Axis II Personality Disorder Symptoms by Pre- and Post-natal Environmental Risk Status

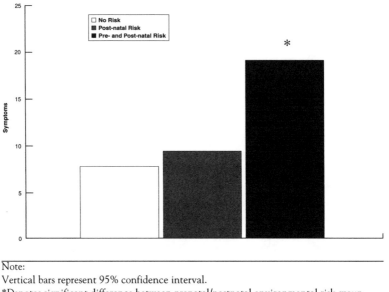

Note:
Vertical bars represent 95% confidence interval.
*Denotes significant difference between prenatal/postnatal environmental risk group
  from the postnatal and no environmental risk groups.

prenatally had three or more psychiatric diagnoses, making this a very high-risk sample [Famy et al. 1998].

Discussion

The present paper presents findings from analyses examining the adult psychopathological correlates of exposure to alcohol in utero. This study represents one of the first studies to examine adult psychiatric outcomes as they are related to fetal alcohol exposure [Famy et al. 1998; Yates et al. 1998b] and further confirms the enduring effects of prenatal exposure to alcohol on future behavior [Connor & Streissguth 1996; Famy et al. 1998; Kerns et al. 1997; LaDue et al. 1992; Olson et al 1997; see review in Steinhausen et al 1993a; Steinhausen & Sphor 1998; Streissguth 1998; Streissguth et

Figure 4-4. Axis II Antisocial Personality Disorder Symptoms by Pre- and Post-natal Environmental Risk Status

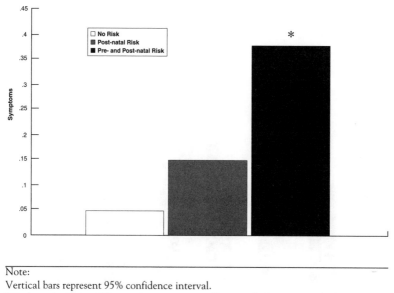

Note:

Vertical bars represent 95% confidence interval.

*Denotes significant difference between prenatal/postnatal environmental risk group
  from the postnatal and no environmental risk groups.

al. 1991; Streissguth et al. 1994a, 1994b]. Specifically, this study examines a group of adoptees for whom FAS could not be diagnosed, but for whom documentation did exist with regard to maternal ingestion of alcohol during pregnancy [Stratton et al. 1996].

Unique to this study is the use of an adoption paradigm, which allowed the separation of prenatal alcohol exposure and later post-natal environmental factors typically correlated with alcohol abuse by the birth mother. To our knowledge, only one other study has utilized information afforded by the adoption paradigm to study the effects of fetal alcohol exposure on adult psychiatric conditions [Yates et al. 1998b]. The study conducted by Yates and associates [1998b] used the same data as the study presented in this paper; however, the range of outcomes in this study extended beyond those examined in the previous research. Both studies were able to evalu-

Figure 4-5. Percentage of Subjects with Substance Abuse/Dependence DSM-III-R Lifetime Diagnoses for Three Environmental Risk Groups

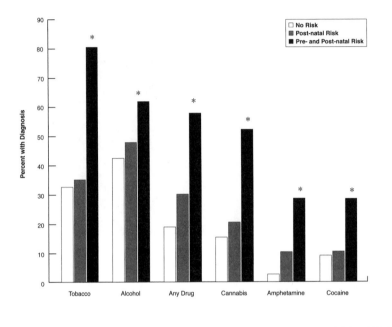

*Denotes significant difference between prenatal/postnatal environmental risk group
from the postnatal and no environmental risk groups.

ate the relative importance of the prenatal and postnatal environment for the development of psychiatric disorders in adulthood.

Another important distinction between this study and that of
Yates and associates [1998b] is the distinction between prenatal and
postnatal environmental risk. In this study we distinguish between
adoptees who were exposed to alcohol in utero and resided in
adoptive homes characterized by the presence of parental psychopathology or marital stress, from adoptees who only resided in high-risk
adoptive homes. This comparison allowed further examination of
the unique contribution of prenatal environmental effects and
postnatal environment effects, effects that tend to be confounded in

Figure 4-6. Percentage of Subjects with Axis I and II DSM-III-R Lifetime of Psychiatric and Personality Disorder Diagnoses for Three Environmental Risk Groups

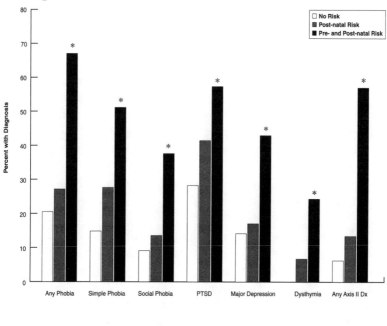

*Denotes significant difference between pre-natal/post-natal risk group from the post-natal and no environmental risk groups.

previous research. The findings confirmed this to be a significant distinction. Adoptees residing in adverse adoptive homes showed increases in psychiatric symptoms only if they were exposed to alcohol in utero. The absence of a significant interaction between birth parent alcoholism, antisocial personality and pre/postnatal environmental risk further suggests that the effect of fetal alcohol exposure is not due to any genetic predisposition that might have been inherited. In other words, exposure to alcohol in utero contributed to the development of adult psychiatric problems even after exposure to postnatal environmental risk factors and genetic predispositions had been taken into account. The following discussion will focus on the findings for both symptoms of psychiatric diagnoses, as well as the presence or absence of the specific diagnosis.

As stated above, the findings showed that adoptees who were exposed both to adverse adoptive home factors and to alcohol in utero reported two to three times the number of psychiatric symptoms, as compared to adoptees who were never exposed to any environmental risk factors or who were exposed only to adverse adoptive home factors. These effects were found for symptoms of substance abuse and adult antisocial personality, as well as for other psychiatric disorders, including anxiety conditions, depression, and personality disorder. Clearly, exposure to alcohol in utero contributes to the development of psychiatric illness beyond those factors most commonly associated with parental alcoholism. These further confirm the findings of Yates and associates [1998b], who also found fetal alcohol exposure contributed significantly to substance abuse beyond that of association with bad peers and poor adoptive environment.

With regard to psychiatric diagnoses, the proportion of adoptees with diagnosable psychiatric illness ranged from 15% to 80%, depending on the disorder examined (refer to Figures 5 and 6). Again, these findings emerged for diagnoses of substance abuse/dependence, as well as the additional psychiatric disorders mentioned above. Analyses of the current data showed a substantially higher number of diagnosed psychiatric illnesses in the fetal alcohol group (Mean = 5). Comorbidity of psychiatric illness was high as well, with 100% of adoptees exposed to alcohol prenatally diagnosed with three or more psychiatric illnesses. The rates of comorbidity are slightly higher in this group of adoptees than in the sample reported on by Famy and associates [1998], in which 92% of a sample of adults exposed to moderate alcohol in utero had at least one psychiatric diagnosis. This difference (100% vs. 92%) could represent the higher environmental risk status of this group of adoptees or this group of individuals in general. However, the rates of comorbidity in this study are identical to those presented by Streissguth and associates [1991], in which all individuals with diagnosed FAS or FAE demonstrated moderate to severe maladaptive behaviors such as dependency, stubbornness, poor concentration and attention, teasing or bullying, social with-drawal, and anxiety. It must be noted that the analysis of comorbidity did not take into account adoptee gender or other biological factors that might increase the environmental risk of psychiatric illness.

As with all studies, limitations of the present study must be recognized and discussed. First, and most relevant, are questions regarding the dose, duration, and timing of in utero alcohol exposure. In the current study, the process of identifying adoptees as fetally exposed to alcohol relied on adoption agency, hospital, and prison records. In most cases, alcohol use during pregnancy was deduced from time frames noted in institutional records and the time in which the adoptee was born. Despite the potential inaccurate documenta-tion of the timing of exposure, the CNS is developing throughout pregnancy, and any exposure to alcohol during the nine months of pregnancy could result in CNS damage. The psychiatric symptoms shown to be affected by fetal alcohol exposure are consistent with the ARND category described in the introduction, which further con-firms the validity of these findings.

A second potential confound is the lack of measurement of other potentially teratogenic factors such as other drug use, smoking, other medications, and/or nutritional deficits. These factors were not clearly indicated in the records, and thus, determination of their presence could not be made. Previous work has shown some effect of tobacco, cocaine, and marijuana on fetal development and later learning and behavioral development [Day & Richardson 1994]. Future research must further examine the unique and additive effects of each drug on fetal and child development.

A third limitation is the disregard of the potential teratogenic effects of paternal alcohol use on fetal and child development through a mechanism of direct effects of alcohol in causing delete-rious changes in genes. Current animal research is beginning to show the presence of detrimental effects of paternal ingestion of alcohol on genomic imprinting, as well as the physical and psychological health of offspring sired by alcohol-exposed fathers [Cicero 1994; Durcan & Goldman 1993]. The extent and nature of this effect in isolation as well as concurrent with maternal alcohol ingestion during pregnancy requires further research and confirmation in humans.

A fourth limitation of the present study is that the effects of fetal alcohol exposure could not be examined separately for males and females due to small numbers (N = 15 vs. 6, respectively). Although there are no anticipated sex differences in environmental risk for alcohol exposure, rates of exposure are higher in males, raising the question of why fewer females were exposed to alcohol in utero. Possible explanations could be a differential effect of fetal alcohol exposure on the viability of a fetus or differential susceptibility of male and female fetuses to alcohol [Abel & Hannigan 1995].

Finally, the study showed that fetal alcohol exposure contributed beyond that of adverse environmental conditions. The data, however, were such that the effect of fetal alcohol exposure in the absence of these environmental factors could not be evaluated. For this sample, the presence of two or more adverse adoptive home factors did not increase the adoptees' environmental risk of developing psychiatric conditions in adulthood. This finding provides some evidence for the effects of fetal alcohol exposure regardless of environment. Manipulation of the postnatal environment by way of well-designed interventions, however, could help determine the mutability of the deleterious effects of exposure to alcohol during gestation [Coles & Platzman 1992; Weiner & Morse 1994]. Furthermore, the findings here suggest that interventions consisting of both cognitive and behavioral components should be employed. Specifically, teaching children who are prenatally exposed to alcohol about the consequences of their actions and strategies for learning and memory could improve their prognosis [Weiner & Morse 1994]. Parents and teachers should be included in intervention programs, emphasizing ways to increase consistency in the environment and the reduction of overstimulation. Finally, the environment should be constructed so that the alcohol-exposed child can succeed both academically and behaviorally. Parents and teachers should break down difficult tasks into achievable components and provide the child with clear and consistent direction.

In conclusion, the findings from this study raise many questions. First, the apparent nonspecificity of the effects of fetal alcohol exposure brings into question the neurological substrates affected.

Do the outcomes represent a general condition contributing to much of the psychiatric disorders examined, or do the findings reflect confounds associated with the exposed adoptee providing information for all disorders? The fact that there were some negative findings—the presence of major depression, generalized anxiety disorder, mania, gambling, alcohol abuse/dependence, and cocaine abuse—suggests that adoptee response bias does not completely account for the findings. However, this conclusion must be tempered by the small number of adoptees who were exposed to alcohol in utero. Second, and perhaps more importantly, are questions pertaining to the relevance of these findings for practitioners who place children affected by fetal alcohol exposure and persons who accept parenting responsibility for these children. Should adoption agencies and other social service agencies that place children with foster and adoptive families incorporate more stringent evaluation procedures for alcohol consumption as well as other potential teratogenic substances during pregnancy? Procedures such as testing the birth mother's hair samples or obtaining more complete histories of maternal health behaviors from the mother herself and from multiple independent sources may yield more valid knowledge of maternal prenatal care and possible exposure of the fetus to teratogens, thereby allowing more immediate implementation of intervention services.

Should adoption agencies offer or refer adoptive families to services that address prevention or treatment of psychiatric and behavioral problems in children with histories of fetal alcohol exposure? In view of the increased risk for severe and life-long problems caused by fetal alcohol exposure, a more accurate assessment of factors such as exposure to alcohol and other potential teratogens is warranted. Such policies would probably be welcomed by those who face the difficult task of making out-of-home placement decisions for children exposed to alcohol in utero.

Notes

1.   Presented as a paper at the 1997 conference, Adoption and Prenatal Drug Exposure, sponsored by the Evan B. Donaldson Adoption Institute. The studies

cited in this paper were supported in part by a grant from NIDA (R01DA05821) to the first author and by a National Research Scientist Award (T32MH14620) to the second author.

References

Abel, E. L. & Hannigan, J. H. (1995). J-shaped relationship between drinking, pregnancy, and birth weight: Reanalysis of prospective epidemiological data. *Alcohol and Alcoholism, 30,* 345– 355.

Aronson, M. & Hagberg, B. (1998). Neuropsychological disorders in children exposed to alcohol during pregnancy: A follow-up study of 24 children to alcoholic mothers in Goteberg, Sweden. *Alcoholism: Clinical and Experimental Research, 22,* 321–324.

Cadoret, R. J. (1986). Adoption studies: Historical and methodological critique. *Psychiatric Developments, 1,* 45–64.

Cadoret, R. J., Troughton, E., O'Gorman, T. W., Heywood, E. (1986). An adoption study of genetic and environmental factors in drug abuse. *Archives of General Psychiatry, 43,* 1131–1136.

Cadoret R. J., Yates W., Troughton E., Woodworth G., & Stewart M. (1995). Adoption study demonstrating two genetic pathways to drug abuse. *Archives of General Psychiatry, 52,* 42–52.

Cicero, T. J. (1994). Effects of paternal exposure to alcohol on offspring development. *Alcohol Health and Research World, 18,* 37–41.

Coles, C. D. & Platzman, K. A. (1992). Fetal alcohol effects in preschool children: Research, prevention, and intervention. In *OSAP Prevention Monograph – 11: Identifying the Needs of Drug-Affected Children: Public Policy Issues.* Rockville, MD: U.S. Department of Health and Human Services, Office of Substance Abuse Prevention.

Connor, P. D. & Streissguth, A. P. (1996). Effects of prenatal exposure to alcohol across the life span. *Alcohol Health and Research World, 20,* 170–174.

Cutrona, C. E., Cadoret, R. J., Suhr, J. A., Richards, C. C., Troughton, E., Schutte, K., & Woodworth, G. (1994). Interpersonal variables in the prediction of alcoholism among adoptees: Evidence for gene-environment interactions. *Comprehensive Psychiatry, 35,* 171–179.

Durcan, M. J. & Goldman, D. (1993). Genomic imprinting: Implications for behavioral genetics. *Behavior Genetics, 23,* 137–143.

Famy, C., Streissguth, A., & Unis, A. (1998). Mental illness in adults with fetal alcohol syndrome or fetal alcohol effects. *American Journal of Psychiatry, 155*, 552–554.

Hollingshead, B. (1965). *Two-Factor Index of Social Position*. New Haven, Connecticut: Yale Station.

Jacobson, J. L. & Jacobson, S.W. (1994). Prenatal alcohol exposure and neurobehavioral development: Where is the threshold? *Alcohol Health and Research World, 18*, 30–36.

Jacobson, J. L., Jacobson, S. W., Sokol, R. J., Martier, S. S., Ager, K. W., & Shankaran, S. (1994). Effects of alcohol use, smoking, and illicit drug use on fetal growth in black infants. *Journal of Pediatrics, 124*, 757–764.

Kerns, K., Don, A., Mateer, C. A., & Streissguth, A. P. (1997). Cognitive deficits in non-retarded adults with fetal alcohol syndrome. *Journal of Learning Disabilities, 30*, 685–693.

LaDue, R. A., Streissguth, A. P., & Randels, S. P. (1992). Clinical considerations pertaining to adolescents and adults with fetal alcohol syndrome. In T. Sonderegger (Ed.), *Perinatal Substance Abuse: Research Findings and Clinical Implications* (pp. 104–132). Baltimore: Johns Hopkins University Press.

Mattson, S. N. & Riley, E. P. (1998). A review of the neurobehavioral deficits in children with Fetal Alcohol Syndrome or prenatal exposure to alcohol. *Alcoholism: Clinical and Experimental Research, 22*, 279–294.

Olsen, J. (1994). Effects of moderate alcohol consumption during pregnancy on child development at 18 and 42 months. *Alcoholism: Clinical and Experimental Research, 18*, 1109–1113.

Olson, H. C., Streissguth, A., Sampson, P. D., Barr, H. M., Bookstein, F. L., & Thiede, K. (1997). Association of prenatal alcohol exposure with behavioral and learning problems in early adolescence. *Journal of the American Academy of Child and Adolescent Psychiatry, 36*, 1187–1194.

Pfohl, B., Blum, N., Zimmerman, M., & Stangl, D. (1989). *Structured Interview for DSM-III-R Personality SIDP-R*. Iowa City:University of Iowa.

Plomin, R., DeFries, J. C., & Loehlin, J. C., (1977). Genotype-environment interaction and correlation in the analysis of human behavior. *Psychological Bulletin, 84*, 309–322.

Plomin, R., DeFries, J. C., McClearn, G. E., & Rutter, M. (1990). *Behavioral Genetics: A Primer*. New York: W. H. Freeman and Company.

Robins, L., Helzer, J., Cottler, L., Goldring, E. (1989). *NIMH Diagnostic Interview Schedule, Version 3, Revised (DIS-III-R)*. St. Louis, MO: Washington University School of Medicine.

Scarr, S. & McCartney, K. (1983). How people make their own environments: A theory of genotype environment effects. *Child Development, 54*, 424–435.

Spohr, H. L., Willms, J., & Steinhausen, H. C. (1994). The fetal alcohol syndrome in adolescence. *Acta Paediatrica, 404*, 19–26.

Steinhausen, H.-C. & Spohr, H.-L. (1998). Long-term outcomes of children with fetal alcohol syndrome: Psychopathology, behavior, and intelligence. *Alcoholism: Clinical and Experimental Research, 22*, 334–338.

Steinhausen, H.-C., Willms, J., & Spohr, H-L. (1993). Long-term psychopathological and cognitive outcome of children with fetal alcohol syndrome. *Journal of the American Academy of Child and Adolescent Psychiatry, 32*, 990–994.

Steinhausen, H.-C., Willms, J., & Spohr, H.-L. (1994). Correlates of psychopathology and intelligence in children with fetal alcohol syndrome. *Journal of Child Psychology and Psychiatry, 35*, 323–331.

Stratton, K., Howe, C., & Battaglia, F. (1996). *Fetal Alcohol Syndrome: Diagnosis, Epidemiology prevention, and treatment. Summary*. Washington, DC: National Academy Press.

Streissguth, A. P., Aase, J. M., Clarren, S. K., Randels, S. P., La Due, R. A., & Smith, D. F. (1991). Fetal alcohol syndrome in adolescents and adults. *Journal of the American Medical Association, 265*, 1961–1967.

Streissguth, A.P., Barr, H.M., Olson, H.C., Sampson, P.D., Bookstein, F.L., & Burgess, D. M. (1994a). Drinking during pregnancy decreases word attack and arithmetic scores on standardized tests: Adolescent data from a population-based prospective study. *Alcoholism: Clinical and Experimental Research, 18*, 248–254.

Streissguth, A. P., Martin, D. C., Martin, J. C., & Barr, H. M. (1981). The Seattle longitudinal prospective study on alcohol and pregnancy. *Neurobehavioral Toxicology and Teratology, 3*, 223–233.

Streissguth, A., Aase, J., Clarren, S., Randels, S., LaDue, R., & Smith, D. (1991). Fetal Alcohol Syndrome in Adolescents and Adults. *Journal of the American Medical Association, (17)265*, 1961–1967.

Streissguth, A., Sampson, P. D., Olson, H. C., Bookstein, F. L., Barr, H. M., Scott, M., Feldman, J., & Mirsky, A. F. (1994b). Maternal drinking during pregnancy: Attention and short-term memory in 14-year-old offspring—A longitudinal prospective study. *Alcoholism: Clinical and Experimental Research, 18,* 202–218.

Sullivan, W. C. (1899). A note on the influence of maternal inebriety on the offspring. *The Journal of Mental Science, 45,* 489–503.

Weinberg, N. Z. (1997). Cognitive and behavioral deficits associated with parental alcohol use. *Journal of the American Academy of Child and Adolescent Psychiatry, 36,* 1177–1186.

Weiner, L., & Morse, B. A. (1994). Intervention and the child with FAS. *Alcohol Health & Research World, 18,* 67–72.

Yates, W. R., Cadoret, R. J., & Troughton, E. (1998a). The Iowa Adoption Studies: Methods and Results. In M. C. LaBuda and E. L. Grigorenko (Eds.), *Current Methodological Issues in Behavioral Genetics* (pp. 95–125). Commack, NY: Nova Science Publishers.

Yates, W. R., Cadoret, R. J., Troughton, E. P., Stewart, M., & Giunta, T. S. (1998b). Effect of fetal alcohol exposure on adult symptoms of nicotine, alcohol, and drug dependence. *Alcoholism: Clinical and Experimental Research, 22,* 914–920.

5

T.I.E.S. for Adoption: Supporting the Adoption of Children Who Were Prenatally Substance Exposed[1]

Susan B. Edelstein, Jill Waterman,
Dorli Burge, Carolyn McCarty, and Joseph Prusak

Many children affected by...drugs will place additional burdens on a system currently strained and with diminishing resources, but there is every reason to expect and demand services that ensure that all children will live every day of their life in the care of a family that is passionately committed to their welfare. [Groze et al. 1994: 81]

The T.I.E.S. for Adoption (Training, Intervention, Education, and Services) program goals are to reduce barriers to the adoption of children in foster care with prenatal substance exposure; optimize their health, growth, and development; and help ensure children's successful adoptive placements, thereby providing legal permanence. The project achieves these goals in three ways. The first is by carefully preparing and educating prospective adoptive parents. The second is by supporting children, foster families, and adoptive families with an array of services before, during, and following the children's transition from foster care into adoptive placement. The third is by providing training and consultation to professionals working with the children and families.

The project is a collaboration between the Los Angeles County Department of Children and Family Services (DCFS), Adoptions

Division, the UCLA Center for Healthier Children, Families and Communities, and the UCLA Psychology Department. Thus far, the TIES project has been successful in a variety of ways. It has developed and successfully demonstrated a pioneering curriculum of three sessions to prepare prospective adoptive families for parenting this group of children. It has implemented a support and service delivery model during the transition to and following adoptive placement, a model that has been evaluated by the families themselves as critically helpful. Finally, it has been credited by social workers with the Adoption Division for making possible many placements that would not have taken place and/or would not have succeeded without this project. This chapter describes the need for and basis of the project, the key components of the model, and the program's current and future directions.

Need for the Project

The number of children living outside their homes has increased significantly since the mid-1980s [Tatara 1993, 1994]. The dramatic increase in the number of substance-affected families with children and the large number of children born with prenatal drug exposure have contributed greatly to the growing population of children who are in out-of-home care nationwide [Feig 1990; Tatara 1993; Cole et al.1996], as well as to the growing numbers of those children for whom adoptive placement needs to be considered as the most appropriate long-term plan.

It is estimated that 80% to 90% of child abuse and neglect cases involve parental substance abuse [Feig 1990]. A substantially smaller but still significant percentage involves children prenatally exposed to substances. A recent national study of over 70,000 children receiving child welfare services under the age of one year found that 28% had a positive drug toxicology, 7% had a positive alcohol toxicology, and 2% were HIV positive [U.S. Department of Health and Human Services 1997]. Many children who do not have a positive toxicology screen are also prenatally substance-exposed but are not identified as such. Difficulties in identifying children who are substance-exposed are related to the limitations on toxicology screens themselves and the lack of a consistent and informed assessment process of children for the effects of prenatal substance exposure. Many children not identified at birth as substance-exposed are discharged to substance-abusing parents and later enter the child protective services system because of abuse or neglect. Health data from the Los Angeles County Department of Children and Family Services, Adoption Division, indicate that 38% of children placed for adoption by that agency in fiscal year 1992 had positive toxicology screens at birth, and most of the remainder had histories consistent with prenatal substance exposure. On this basis, staff of the Adoption Division informs prospective adoptive parents that to maximize their opportunities for placement of a child, they need to be willing to consider a child with prenatal substance exposure.

A variety of pediatric medical and developmental complications and problems have been associated with maternal substance abuse. The sequelae of prenatal substance exposure may include low birthweight; premature birth and resultant complications; withdrawal symptoms; congenital anomalies (primarily associated with alcohol); cerebrovascular effects; growth retardation; developmental delays; impairments in fine motor skills and expressive language; exposure to sexually transmitted diseases and HIV; and difficulties with behavior, self-regulation, learning and social interaction, and adaptation [Jones & Smith 1973; Streissguth et al.1990; Zuckerman & Bresnahan 1991; Azuma & Chasnoff 1993; Robin & Mills 1993; Brooks-Gunn et al. 1994; Young 1997].

Perhaps as important as the possible biological insult of prenatal substance exposure is the consistent finding that children who are placed in out-of-home care because of parental substance abuse stay in care longer, have more frequent changes in placement, are less likely to return to their birth parents, and have lower rates of adoption than children placed for reasons other than parental substance abuse [Walker et al. 1991; Tracy & Farkas 1994]. A significant number of the children are moved from home to home because of their parents' and their own problems, and the lack of preparedness and supports for relative caregivers, foster parents, and adoptive parents. These multiple placements compound children's existing problems and losses. Children with prenatal substance exposure are often intense and highly sensitive children, characteristics that heighten the impact of the pain associated with moves from one family to another. Children may blame themselves for the moves, and often exhibit even more troublesome, impulsive, self-defeating behavior, putting in full force a downward spiral. What we often see is biological risk exacerbated by these repeated traumatic losses of family, friends, teachers, and neighborhoods, and the plummeting of the children's self-esteem.

There is much evidence that many of the possible physiological and developmental effects can be mitigated if addressed early and comprehensively, and that the postnatal environment for these children is critical in influencing outcomes [Brooks-Gunn et al. 1992; Edelstein et al. 1995]. Children who cannot be reunified with their birth parents are in desperate need of stable and consistent nurturing, and prepared and supported adoptive families at the earliest possible point. Services must be available before, during, and after adoptive placement because of the challenges of building a family by adoption, combined with the challenges that some of these children present. The assurance and availability of this guidance and support is essential to ensuring that families will be willing and able to make the commitment involved in adopting children who are prenatally exposed to alcohol and/or other drugs. Lack of accessible support can serve as a great disincentive for adoption, as well as heighten the risks of an emotional and financial drain on families.

Obstacles to Permanent Placement. There are significant obstacles to permanence for children who are prenatally exposed to alcohol or other drugs. The general public, prospective adoptive parents, and foster parents, as well as professionals in the fields of child welfare, law, health, and mental health, are often ambivalent about the "adoptability" and future prospects of children who were prenatally exposed to alcohol and/or other drugs. Many prospective adoptive parents are frightened by the uncertainties regarding the long-term outcomes for substance-exposed children; worry about the possibility that children may exhibit at some point in the future a variety of negative and alarming behaviors; and express concerns that the necessary resources to meet their children's needs will not be available [Groze et al. 1994; Edelstein et al.1995].

Some of the myths and stereotypes derive from the fact that the media rarely portrays the risks and potentials of this group of children in a realistic, balanced fashion. They have generally presented contradictory and confusing information, predicting either that prenatally drug-exposed children are "doomed" or will be "just fine." In addition, researchers disagree among themselves regarding the effects of prenatal substance exposure. Thus, it is not surprising that prospective adoptive parents have difficulty making informed decisions about the benefits and challenges involved in building a family by adopting a child with prenatal substance exposure [Edelstein et al. 1995].

The second obstacle is the lack of educational programs to guide adoptive parents and professionals regarding the special issues involved in the adoption of children who were prenatally exposed. Foster parents and prospective adoptive parents often make decisions not to adopt these children based on inadequate, inaccurate, and incomplete information [Edelstein et al.1995]. Time and again, research has shown that the better the preparation, the more satisfied foster and adoptive parents are with placements [Barth & Berry 1988; Rosenthal & Groze 1992]. By providing potential adoptive parent(s) with accurate and complete information, strategies, and anticipatory guidance, adoptive parents are helped to play an active role and make thoughtful decisions. Often, adoptive parents are better prepared for major impairments than minor, less visible ones, such as learning disabilities or short attention spans, because the major impairments are more readily noticed and diagnosed, while minor problems may catch unprepared adoptive parents unaware [Rosenthal & Groze 1992]. Minor impairments, such as difficulties with processing auditory or visual information and short attention spans, are common among children with prenatal substance exposure, and as a result, thorough and realistic preparation of adoptive applicants is even more crucial [Edelstein et al. 1995].

The third obstacle to permanence for substance-exposed children is that background information about individual children and their functioning is often episodic and fragmented. Assessments conducted in order to formulate plans for a child are too often poorly done, are not interdisciplinary in nature, and are not integrated with the child's history. Children may be evaluated immediately following a move, when they may be most vulnerable and their behavior the most disorganized; they may be prescribed psychotropic medications which are not indicated; or they may be given inappropriate psychiatric labels and diagnoses without supporting evidence, which become part of their permanent records. Such background information may discourage and misinform prospective adoptive parents, such as in cases referred to our program in which two-year-olds have been assessed shortly after moves to new foster homes and diagnosed as "defiant and oppositional" and "mean." Children who are prenatally substance exposed need coordinated and highly skilled assessments because they present with complex health, mental health, educational and developmental needs [Halfon et al. 1995; Rosenfeld et al. 1997], which must be understood within the context of their all-too-frequently traumatic and chaotic histories.

The fourth obstacle to permanence is the lack of integrated, available services prior to the placement, during the child's transition from foster care to adoption, and following the adoptive placement. Anticipatory guidance, ongoing support and counseling, interventions, and advocacy for children and adoptive families should be available on an as-needed basis because of the range of needs of children with prenatal substance exposure; children's varying backgrounds, strengths and vulnerabilities; the different stages of the placement process; the individual interests, differences, needs and receptivity to services of their foster, prospective, or current adoptive parents; and the plans of the child welfare and legal systems [Edelstein et al. 1995].

The fifth obstacle is a lack of timeliness in the court system to terminate parental rights of birth parents who have not been successful in reunification services. All too frequently, lengthy periods of time have been allowed to pass in order to determine with assurance whether parental problems will resolve. As a result, in many instances, the permanency needs of the young child have been compromised with a significant negative impact on the child [Wald

1994; Edelstein 1995]. This project addresses the first four of these obstacles. The last obstacle was recently addressed by California and federal legislation.

Description of the Model

The T.I.E.S. for Adoption Program offers an array of training, educational, and service components to help families and the professionals working with them move through the adoption process as smoothly as possible. Program services are facilitated by an interdisciplinary, interagency staff team to assure a comprehensive, coordinated, consistent approach to serving children and families. Staff includes professionals from the UCLA Center for Healthier Children, Families and Communities, the UCLA Psychology Department and the DCFS Adoption Division. The collaboration provides credibility, expertise, access, and resources to the families served and to each partner that would not be possible separately.

The staff is comprised of professionals from multiple disciplines. The project director from UCLA and the liaison from the Adoption Division are both experienced social workers. Another social worker with expertise in chemical dependency, cultural issues, and working with groups is part of the training team for prospective adoptive parents as well as for professionals. A pediatrician, licensed clinical psychologists, and an educational consultant with a masters degree in special education are key program staff in working with children and families, as well as in training professionals. An adoptive mother of three children who has a masters degree in early childhood education functions as the project's adoptive parent consultant, as well as a trainer for prospective adoptive parents and one of the cofacilitators of the support groups.

In addition, clinical psychology advanced doctoral students provide counseling to children and parents under the supervision of the licensed psychologists. These trainees not only provide skilled and cost effective services, but also develop expertise which helps build a community of clinicians and researchers attuned to the issues, strengths, and needs of adoptive families of children with prenatal substance exposure. Because of the complex histories of so many of the children and their experiences with loss, only interns who can make long-term commitments are utilized.

The program targets children from birth through eight years of age who were identified by toxicology screens as prenatally substance exposed or whose case history shows that it was probable that the child's mother used alcohol and/or other drugs during pregnancy. Staff work with a few older children if they are under eight years at the time of referral or are part of a sibling group in which services are being provided to a younger child. All children are dependent children of the Juvenile Court at the time of referral, although many children have their adoptions legalized during the course of their participation in the project.

During the program's initial two-year period, over one hundred prospective adoptive parents completed the nine-hour preparation sessions, and 65 children received clinical services. Priority for services was given to children who were being adopted by parents who took part in the preparation training. Twenty-seven of the children were female and 38 were male. Approximately 50% of the children were African American; 32% were Latino; and 18% were Caucasian. Seven children were under the age of two; 27 were between ages two and three; 29 were between four and nine; and two were between ages 12 and 13.

Components of the Model

The components of the T.I.E.S. model, which work in unison to promote healthy and secure adoptions for children with prenatal substance exposure, are: 1) educational workshops to help prepare prospective adoptive parents; 2) medical, psychological, and educational consultation for prospective adoptive parents; 3) parent support groups prior to and during the adoptive placement; 4) parent counseling; 5) individual play therapy for the children; and 6) consultations and training for professionals, including children's social workers and attorneys.

Preparation of Foster and Adoptive Parents

Prospective adoptive parents are invited by the liaison from the DCFS, Adoption Division, to voluntarily attend nine hours of training. These sessions, divided into three sessions of three hours each and offered one evening a week on consecutive weeks, were developed specifically to address the issues of parenting and providing permanency to children with prenatal substance exposure. While parents are completing the Model Approaches to Partnerships in Parenting-Group Preparation and Selection (MAPP-GPS) [Child Welfare Institute 1992] training as part of their adoption home study, they are encouraged by the facilitators to take part in the additional nine-hour training. One T.I.E.S. training series each year is specifically for foster parents who are providing permanence by adopting children who were already in their care.

Each session is facilitated by two trainers, both of whom have extensive clinical experience with prenatally substance-exposed children. The project director and Adoptions Division liaison are present at every session to respond to any questions about the T.I.E.S. project or about the functioning and policies of the DCFS. A balanced, objective, realistic, and practical approach is vital in this highly charged area. An interdisciplinary team models the range and roles of professionals who may be helpful later to the families. Videotapes and slides are used, as well as a variety of exercises and role-plays. The groups are small, usually no more than 15 people, to allow for exploration and discussion. An extensive packet with outlines and readings corresponding for each session is provided to each participant.

Session One. Parental substance abuse and the adoption connection. This session introduces the series and the topics of parental substance abuse and prenatal substance exposure. Participants are asked to identify what they believe will be their biggest challenge related to the birth parents of a child they may adopt. Participants view a video of a mother talking about her drug use during pregnancy and how her continued substance abuse affected her parenting when her son was an infant and toddler. Participants are encouraged to express their attitudes, feelings, and fears about parental substance abuse and women who use drugs during pregnancy. They explore the ways these attitudes can impact children and the child-parent relationship. Information is provided about the nature of substance abuse—its etiology, prevalence, dynamics, treatment, and impact on parenting. Participants learn that although there appears to be a genetic element in alcohol and possibly other drug abuse, environment plays a role in either increasing or decreasing the risk [Bays 1990; Cadoret 1990]. Participants then role-play talking to the child of the mother in the video about his mother, with each participant taking turns playing the role of the adoptive parent and of the child. They practice communicating to the child the information that they have learned in the session with sensitivity, empathy and honesty, appropriate to the child's developmental level and background.

Session Two. Infants and children with prenatal substance exposure. In this session, a pediatrician explains what is known and not known about the short- and long-term effects of prenatal substance exposure, the difficulties in predicting outcomes for individual children, and the methodological problems and limitations in existing research. The pediatrician describes the evaluation process for prenatal substance exposure; provides guidance as to how to assess a child's birth and medical history; and reviews typical recommendations for medical and developmental follow-up services. In addition, the adoptive parent consultant discusses the joys and the struggles of her parenting experience and provides practical caregiving and behavioral strategies and interventions.

Session Three. Special considerations in adopting children with prenatal substance exposure. In this session, participants explore issues related to parenting of children with prenatal substance exposure and how they can sensitively and constructively respond to these issues. Topics include living with and coming to terms with uncertainties about the long-term impact of prenatal substance exposure, including how to deal with exaggerated and contradictory media reports; developing lifelong substance abuse prevention strategies for children; building empathy for and answering questions about substance-abusing birth parents; advocating for services for children whose needs often "fall between the cracks"; deciding whether and whom to tell about the child's prenatal substance exposure; and evaluating the appropriateness of maintaining contact with members of the child's birth family when there is a history of substance abuse. At the conclusion of this session, additional T.I.E.S. services are explained. T.I.E.S. team members may be introduced and respond to questions.

Families evaluating these sessions have rated them very highly, reporting that the preparation program eased their fears, answered their questions, and empowered them to proceed with adoption. As a result of the training, an unusually large number of participating families accepted sibling groups into their homes, many of whom had waited for long periods of time for adoptive homes. A comment repeated over and over again was that "this training should be added for all adoptive families, very important."

Consultation with Foster and Prospective Adoptive Parents

Following participation in the three educational sessions, prospective adoptive parents who desire additional guidance and consultation may meet with project staff about a child who is in their home as a foster child or a child who has been identified for them as a prospective adoptive child. Staff review all relevant medical, psychological, developmental, and educational reports, explain and interpret the information, and make recommendations. The consultations assist potential adoptive parents in making informed decisions about adoption and optimizing the child's transition from foster care to adoption.

A case example shows the importance of the preparation and educational sessions, as well as the individualized consultations. A prospective adoptive father attended the initial three sessions because he was interested in learning more about children with prenatal substance exposure, but had many fears and doubts about parenting children with these histories. After completing the sessions, he decided to pursue adoption and met with the T.I.E.S. pediatrician, psychologist, and social worker to discuss two brothers, ages seven and four. The team members interpreted the medical and psychological information on both boys, including the developmental and neurological problems of the seven-year-old, and made recommendations about referrals and services, much of which could be provided by the T.I.E.S. team. With this assistance, he made plans to adopt the two brothers. He is clear that he would not have considered adoption of these children without the T.I.E.S. project.

Parent Support Groups

Parent support groups allow new parents to share their concerns and experiences with other new parents in a supportive atmosphere. Prospective parents who have participated in the preparation sessions and have indicated an interest in a support group are invited to join, once a child has been identified for placement with them. Allowing group members to begin attending the support group prior to placement and, whenever possible, prior to visitation has been invaluable to parents as they embark on what is often a very emotional and sometimes difficult process of helping a new child enter their home. Other parents in the group share their experiences, help normalize the new parent's feelings, and provide helpful practical pointers and techniques that aid in smoothing the transition for their families.

Structure of the parent support groups. In the project's initial two years, two support groups for adoptive parents were started. Both groups are now entering their third year. The first group serves newly forming families, that is, parents who attended the preparation sessions and subsequently had children placed with them or parents in the planning stages for a placement. The second group serves foster parents who adopt children in their homes. Both groups meet for two hours, once a month, in the evening. Usually eight to twelve parents participate, and the groups include single, married, and gay parents. Groups are open-ended so that parents can enter an ongoing group if there is an opening. In the group for newly forming families, the majority of the parents have chosen to continue. For a few families, especially those at great geographical distance, attendance becomes less frequent after six months, as many of the major transition issues have been resolved at that point. The group has a yearly holiday party, to which former members are invited to come and renew friendships. In the group for foster parents, four original members still participate. Child care is provided during the parent support groups for newly formed families, with at least one staff member and several volunteers in each group. Volunteers (usually university graduate students from psychology, law, and medicine) play with the children, facilitate their use of play materials, provide snacks and videos, and contribute useful observations of the children's play.

Group process. In general, parent support groups have little formal structure. Parents have preferred the flexibility to discuss whatever issues are most pressing and have actively resisted a more formal structure with guest speakers. Group leaders serve mainly as facilitators, ensuring that everyone has a chance to participate, identifying nonverbal messages, and encouraging sharing in a trusting atmosphere. In each session, leaders ensure that the topics of transition, grief and loss, and difficult child behavior are raised and discussed, as appropriate.

When parents first join, they are often reluctant to discuss issues that might reflect negatively on their parental competence, which is almost always fragile in the first months of placement. As parents get to know one another, the level of self-disclosure increases greatly. Parents who have been in the support group develop trust and model vulnerability for newer parents. For example, one parent disclosed that she told her partner, "How could you do this to us? The child is ruining our lives!" Another said, "I knew I shouldn't have told Sara to go ahead when she said she was going to leave and go back to her foster mother, but I did." Tearfully, another new mother admitted, "I haven't a clue what to do with him—I think I'm screwing him up by demanding perfect behavior."

Issues related to placement, transition, and loss. Three issues related to placement consistently arise in the support groups. The first issue is how to relate to the child's past caregivers during and after transition. Adoptive parents are assisted in understanding that foster parents may grieve the loss of the child, and that their grief may affect their ability to help the child transition to adoption. In the course of group work, several adoptive parents have shared feelings of significant emotional turmoil at the time of placement as a result of foster parents' grief at the loss of the child. One adoptive parent, for example, shared her distress when her child's foster mother threw herself on the floor and sobbed as the child left with the new adoptive parents.

A second issue involves adoptive parents' needs to help children deal with feelings of loss and grief about their previous caregivers. Parents may find it threatening to allow children to express feelings of loss about their earlier caregivers. They may require a great deal of support from group leaders and other parents to allow the child to express those feelings and to fully accept the child's feelings. Parents may need help in learning how to respond to children's comments about former foster parents. For example, instead of saying, "You're our little boy now, and you're going to live with us forever," say, "I know you miss your foster mom very much." The third issue involves helping adoptive parents understand attachment as an interactional process that takes place over time. Strategies for facilitating attachment are discussed, with more experienced adoptive parents sharing their experiences with new parents going through the process.

Issues related to prenatal substance exposure. Participants in the support groups frequently deal with issues related to prenatal substance exposure that mirror issues covered in the three preparatory sessions. With a particular child in the home, parents view these issues from a new perspective. These issues include:

- Developing empathy for the substance-abusing birth parent. Parents vary greatly in their understanding of and tolerance for birth parents who are involved with drugs or alcohol. When parents have difficulty managing the behavior of the child, they may blame the birth parent. In the words of one parent, "I'd like to wring her neck—she took drugs and screwed up John, and I'm dealing with the consequences."
- Dealing with emotional reactions to information about birth parents. As a consequence of drug or alcohol abuse, many birth

parents have been homeless, incarcerated, or involved with prostitution. For adoptive parents whose lives have not involved such experiences prior to adopting their child, efforts to assimilate this information may be difficult. A related issue involves whether to have contact with the birth parent. Some parents want to meet their child's birth parents to have a sense of their child's background, while others worry about any level of involvement with the birth family.

- Deciding what to tell or not tell friends, family, or strangers about the child's history of prenatal substance exposure. Parents report that many people, including strangers in public places such as the grocery stores, ask if their child was exposed to drugs. The tolerance for sharing information varies greatly. One father, for example, was incensed when anyone asked if his child who was of a different ethnicity was adopted, feeling it was no one's business, while another father felt compelled to educate anyone who asked if the child had been exposed to drugs by saying that research showed that most children do well.

- Deciding what and when to tell the child about his or her birth parents and their substance involvement. Parents are encouraged to share information about their child's birth parents when their child is ready to hear it, gradually sharing more information as the child matures. Parents are helped to become comfortable with background information so that they can share it in an empathic way with their children.

- Dealing with fears about the child's own drug use. In a preliminary survey, the T.I.E.S. team found that 86% of the parents were at least somewhat concerned regarding their child's potential for substance abuse in the future, particularly in adolescence and adulthood. Group leaders stress the importance of early and continuous education about substance abuse prevention.

- Dealing with fears about the effect of prenatal substance exposure on the child's development. Parents express fears about how prenatal substance exposure may affect various aspects of their child's development. Parents are usually most concerned about the child's cognitive development, especially language development, and behavior issues, particularly with regard to attention and impulse control.

Handling difficult child behaviors. Parents often discuss children's behavior problems, but if they do not raise problems in this area, group leaders inquire about difficult child behaviors. Parents share ideas as to how to handle behaviors and offer examples of similar situations they have encountered. Problematic child behaviors most often discussed are:

- Temper tantrums, which can be particularly intense in the postplacement period and especially for children with multiple placements. Parents are helped to understand that tantrums are encountered by every parent, irrespective of the fact of adoption or prenatal substance exposure.
- Aggressive behavior, including hitting, kicking, and biting. One mother, for example, came in particularly distraught, with a huge cut and bruise where her child had bitten her while in a rage.
- Regressive behavior, including wanting a bottle, using baby talk, and toilet training difficulties. Parents are strongly encouraged to allow regressive behavior immediately after placement and not require more mature functioning.
- Sexualized behavior, including masturbation and discussion of sexual body parts. These behaviors may be of particular concern for adoptive parents who may not be aware of a child's sexual abuse history.
- Limit testing. Techniques for dealing with limit-testing behaviors are shared by group leaders, with particular emphasis on strategies for dealing with children who are active, intense, and slow-adapting.

Challenges with systems. Parents frequently identify challenges they are experiencing with the legal and social services systems. Because group leaders are not part of the formal systems, parents feel free to discuss their concerns without fear of consequences. The most common issues involve court proceedings, delays in termination of parental rights, and difficulties getting timely

responses from overworked caseworkers. Parents share and empa-
thize with each other's experiences and also provide concrete help,
such as sharing lawyers' phone numbers, recommending child advocates, or encouraging families to call supervisors.

Parent support groups have been a valuable resource for parents
throughout the placement process and beyond. The groups offer the
advantages of providing support during the crucial transition phase,
allowing families to stay connected to each other, reducing isolation
in their new roles, and facilitating the provision of needed resources.

Parent Counseling

Parents are offered individual parenting counseling on a weekly basis
if they need assistance in addition to the support group. Parent
counseling may be provided in conjunction with play therapy for the
child. In these cases, children generally have their own therapist who
works in close cooperation with the parents' therapist, although in
some cases the same therapist sees the child and parent. Counseling,
provided in T.I.E.S. offices or at the home, may be conducted over
a period of a few weeks to more than a year. Individual parent
counseling may assist with the following issues:

Dealing with grief of foster parents. Program staff make
home visits to foster parents in volatile transition situations. By
providing foster parents with an opportunity to talk about their
feelings about losing the child and express grief and anger, staff
support them in making the transition as smooth as possible. Once
foster parents feel heard about their feelings and reactions, they may
be able to help the child view their new home in a positive way and
symbolically bless the new family [Edelstein, Burge & Waterman in
preparation].

Dealing with attachment and loss. The issue of attachment
and loss is a frequent theme in work with new adoptive parents and
their child. Adoptive parents are primarily future oriented, focused
on forming a new family unit including the child, while the child is
often preoccupied with past losses, including longing for former
foster parents. With support and an opportunity to air feelings of
anger and rejection, parents can be helped to understand and accept

the normalcy of the child's reactions. As the therapist listens empathetically to the parents' concern, she models acceptance of complex emotions. Parents are helped to understand that by being empathetic with the child's loss and grief, they are building the foundation of a healthy and close relationship in the future [Fahlberg 1991].

Parents whose child is older or who has had multiple placements need special support in learning to understand that attachment takes time to develop and is the result of multiple interactions. Attachment develops as the parent is available to the child in distress, the parent and child engage in pleasurable and positive interactions, and the parent "claims" the child by including him or her in family rituals and history [Fahlberg 1991]. The therapist plays a crucial role in interpreting the child's reticence in forming a relationship or acting out, explaining that the child may not trust that the placement is truly permanent or may feel unworthy of love. The therapist helps parents contain the pain of being rejected by the child and also alerts them to small signs that the child is becoming closer, signs that may be difficult to see if they are hoping for the big "break-through."

During counseling, parents are alerted that attachment and loss issues will be revisited as the child becomes older and enters different developmental phases. Fears of abandonment and loss may be reactivated by vacations, the death of a pet, or the moving away of a friend or relative. Parents are helped to analyze the events that may reactivate the child's fears and concerns.

Learning to understand children's behavior. Many adoptive parents have little experience with children and are not aware of the range of normal behaviors of young children. The therapist empathizes with parents about how difficult parenting can be and what complex emotions it elicits. When appropriate, parents are reassured about the normalcy of the child's behavior and helped to see behavior in a developmental and psychosocial context. Children's behavior may be most difficult during the transition phase once the "honeymoon" is over. Parents may interpret these behaviors as evidence of damage associated with prenatal drug exposure and may feel helpless and powerless to change the behavior. The therapist helps parents understand that even if certain behavioral difficulties are associated with the biological vulnerability of prenatal substance exposure, they are amenable to management through skillful parenting.

The therapist helps adoptive parents to understand children's behavior by encouraging them to observe the child's temperamental qualities and then discussing with them the wide range of normalcy within temperamental dimensions. The therapist also describes how particular constellations of temperamental characteristics can make a child more challenging without being pathological [Kurcinka 1991; Chess & Thomas 1986]. Parents complete questionnaires and receive a written profile of the child's temperament and parenting strategies suitable to the child's temperament. [Preventive Ounce 1996; Cameron et al. 1994]. Parents are helped to reflect on how their own temperaments match that of their child and to identify areas in which they may have inappropriate expectations. Normalizing and reinterpreting the child's responses in the light of temperamental characteristics makes the behavior more understandable and manageable. Parents are also helped to develop strategies for handling transitions, introducing new routines, and anticipating situations that might be difficult for the child, such as vacations, visiting relatives, or entering a new school.

Dealing with the parenting role. Individual counseling sessions also deal with the parents' discomfort with and lack of confidence in their new role. Parents may feel scrutinized by the adoption agency and may harbor fears that their child will be removed from their home if they do not handle problem behaviors perfectly. The therapist clarifies that striving for perfection in parenting is not realistic, as parenting is a constant learning process. The therapist also creates an environment in which the parent can safely vent feelings, including anger toward their child and fantasies of returning the child to the agency. Parents come to understand that these feelings are normal and not evidence that they are unfit for parenting.

Dealing with children's behavior problems. Children often have behavior problems that require more intensive assistance to parents than the support group can provide. In individual sessions, the therapist encourages parents to target one behavior that is of most concern rather than a number of troublesome behaviors. Parents are encouraged to become careful behavioral observers and to take notes on the sequencing of events before, during, and after a difficult episode. Home visits by T.I.E.S. staff can be useful in observing the child's behavior in his environment. Based on careful behavioral observations, the staff develops, in cooperation with the parents, specific strategies to deal with the child's behavior, strategies that may include preventive interventions tailored to the temperamental characteristics of the child, techniques to stop the behavior, and strategies to reward the child for decreasing negative behavior and for engaging in positive behavior.

Dealing with children with traumatic backgrounds. Parents of children with traumatic backgrounds involving sexual or physical abuse require special supports as they encounter the sequelae of these experiences. With the therapist's support, parents become therapeutic agents in the child's recovery. In one case, for example, a little girl who had been abused in her previous foster home had occasional, intense tantrums which were highly distressing for the adoptive mother. The therapist helped the mother, who felt inadequate and helpless because she was unable to comfort the child, understand the episodes as symptoms of post traumatic stress, and she coached her as to how to handle the episodes. The adoptive mother, who was sensitive and responsive, was able to implement the suggestions, and the episodes rapidly decreased in frequency. In another case, the child, who had been molested, had prolonged screaming spells before falling asleep every night. Her mother, who was exhausted in the evening and needed rest, felt that the child simply did not like going to sleep and wanted to play. The therapist reinterpreted the screaming as indicative of fearfulness about what might happen at night. The reconceptualization enabled the mother to talk with her child about how she would keep her safe at night and remain close by. She initiated a routine of cuddling with the child, providing safe body contact every night before bedtime. The screaming spells became shorter and disappeared after about two months.

Play Therapy

The child therapy component of the program is designed to provide a forum for expression of the child's feelings and reactions as he or she progresses through the placement process. Prospective adoptive parents are encouraged to bring the child for therapy early in the adoption process. Beginning therapy at the point that the parents decide to proceed with the adoption has the advantage of creating a closer bond between the child and therapist. It also provides the therapist with a better sense of the difficulties the child is experiencing as they occur and allows the therapist to intervene before problems escalate.

The therapy follows the tenets of play therapy, using play as the vehicle for communication between the child and therapist. In play therapy, children can either directly converse with the therapist or can act out fantasies through games and use of toys, clay, and drawings. The therapist's role is to perceive the world as it is from the child's perspective, while making reflective and interpretive comments that have meaning both in the play scenario and in the child's real life. These "double meaning" comments convey a sense of empathy, understanding, and reassurance to the child [Esman 1983; Mills & Crowley 1986]. Play therapy provides a permissive environment for expression and elaboration of the child's feelings, conflicts, and coping patterns. The child's relationship with a therapist who is responsive, caring, and nonjudgmental forms the cornerstone for the therapeutic work.

The therapist also takes an active role in understanding and helping the child adjust to the new environment. They conduct school visits, attend Individual Educational Plan meetings, coordinate with other service providers and interdisciplinary team members, and observe in-home interactions between parents and children. When appropriate, they are present during significant transitions and visits with foster parents and birth siblings. There are six guiding themes that recur in therapy with children.

Moving and transitions. Many children have moved from one home to the next, often with little preparation for or understanding of the move. As they come into therapy, they often play out these moves by creating scenarios in which the characters move from home to home. David, a five-year-old who had been in five different homes, including a recently failed adoptive placement, used transportation vehicles in his play extensively for the first two months, repeatedly making groups of people travel from car to plane to boat. His therapist used the moving theme as a way to talk about his real-life experiences, remaining within the metaphor of the play: "It seems like the people are always moving around. It's hard to move so many times; they didn't even get a chance to say goodbye."

Creating a life history book can be a useful activity in therapy to help children process and understand the various moves that they have made. Typically, the therapist introduces the idea of constructing a book that includes all the child's families (birth, foster, adoptive, and group home), but follows the child's lead for the details of how it will be made (such as going backward from the present time or forward from the time of the child's birth). The child's feelings and memories are explored as the child or therapist draws or paints each family member.

Dealing with grief and loss. Because these children have experienced loss, the relationships they have had with their previous caregivers and families will surface throughout the transition to adoption. The therapist's role is to look for play material in which loss becomes relevant and to validate the child's feelings. Anna, age seven, created birthing scenes in her play, in which she would pretend to have a baby and tell the therapist to take it away. She would require the therapist to go to court with her and then would ask the judge to decide who should keep the baby. The therapist reflected on how confusing this was for the baby, and how the baby loved and missed her mother. As Anna's therapy progressed, her play changed so that she would include the therapist as another amicable parent who could look after and care for the baby. There was no longer an antagonistic relationship between the birth and adoptive parent in her play, and the baby could express love toward both of them. The therapeutic processes involved in Anna's case included expressing grief about losing her birth mother and resolving her feelings about being adopted by other members of her family.

For particularly strong attachment figures, the loss will be felt very deeply. In such cases, the therapist may want to consider additional techniques to help the child work through the loss, such as writing a letter to the missed caregiver or making a picture for them. For children who are dealing with loss, the therapist's own vacations or changes in scheduling may bring about fears of abandonment. It is important that the therapist be sensitive to such issues and give the child adequate preparation for any absences, and especially termination.

Coping with previous trauma and abuse. Many children have experienced abusive situations that led to their placement in foster care, and some children in care—between 2% and 7% of children placed outside their homes—are maltreated by their caregivers [Bolton et al. 1981; Ryan et al. 1987]. As children are allowed to play freely in therapy, it is not unusual for material related to traumatic or abusive experiences to surface. Some children will reenact painful experiences, often playing out the role of the perpetrator in order to gain mastery and control over the situation. For example, Angie, a three-year-old child with a suspected sexual abuse history, would undress a doll family and have a lion repeatedly attack the family members. Initially, the therapist focused on what the child would be feeling in such a situation: "She must be so scared; the lion is very powerful and cruel." As treatment progressed, the therapist helped the child to find a more acceptable resolution to the play, by asking questions such as, "What can they do when the lion is being mean like that?" and helping the child to problem-solve in the situation. This type of reparative approach allows children to process the traumatic events they have experienced in such a way that the events can be understood and tolerated [James 1989].

Becoming a family. Another issue for a child as he or she transitions into the adoptive family is becoming a part of a family. Past experience has taught many children to be uncertain about permanency. Despite having been told that they will be a "forever family," many children believe that if they behave badly, they will be sent elsewhere. In the course of play therapy, the therapist explores the child's perception of the new family and the nature of the move.

One approach uses family drawings and paintings on which the therapist may comment as to who is included and the way the family is organized. For example, a therapist may say, "I notice that you and your brother are over here, and Lisa and Pedro [the birth children of the adoptive family] are on the other side of the house." An interesting clinical phenomena observed in some children in transition is the tendency to include the therapist in drawings of the family, perhaps because therapy often begins at the same time as the child's move to the adoptive family. The therapist deals with this distortion by reflecting the fantasy—"Sometimes you wish I was part of your family, too"—and by talking about the difference between family and close people in the child's life.

The child's sense of self and self-esteem. Many children have experienced or perceived rejection from their birth parents. Play therapy provides an opportunity for success and acceptance, presumed to increase children's self-esteem. In one case, a therapist made a life book with a child who had been in multiple homes. When asked about his birth, the child drew a baby with a large, lopsided head and a few, random black marks on the face. When asked what those were, he replied that he "was born bruised and ugly," which was his way of understanding why his mother abandoned him. Therapists correct cognitive distortions that children create about themselves and emphasize their positive attributes.

Relationship with the therapist. The relationship between the child and therapist usually parallels the attachment process that occurs between the parent and child. Some children initially approach the therapist with enthusiasm but may have only a superficial attachment, approaching other adults indiscriminately as well. Other children may be slow to "warm up," even reticent about seeing the therapist. They may have more difficulty in the adoptive placement at first, but adjust gradually. Behaviors that may convey the nature of the child's attachment include how close she sits to the therapist, how enthusiastically the child goes with the therapist, whether the therapist is included in the play, and how the child responds to the therapist's limit-setting.

The relationship with the therapist can also be used to discuss the child's wishes and desires in the family. Juan was a five-year-old boy who was removed from a foster home where he was close to his foster mother and placed with an adoptive father. In therapy, he played out various scenarios in which he was a puppy and the therapist was the mommy dog, bringing his dinner and cleaning his doghouse. As the therapy continued, Juan eventually revealed to the therapist that sometimes he wished the therapist was his mommy. The therapist reflected that the child really missed having a mom. Other children express a desire to find out about the therapist's own family. If the therapist is comfortable with self-disclosure, sharing information can be a valuable way to connect with the child around the topic of family. For example, when asked if she had a mommy, one therapist replied, "Mommies are important. You want to find out about whether I have someone to take care of me, too. I don't have a mommy, but there are other adults who look out for me and help take care of me."

Case Consultations and Training

The T.I.Ex.S. program has conducted sixteen interdisciplinary case conferences in which the DCFS liaison identified a challenging situation. These consultations, which result in written recommendations for resolving the challenges presented by the case, also serve as a training opportunity for participating professionals. Professionals are exposed to interdisciplinary problem solving and case management that takes into account the special needs of prenatally substance exposed children, normal child development, and issues of children's physical and mental health and educational needs.

In one case, as an example, the child's social worker reported her concern about a two-year-old whose foster mother thought was autistic. The consultation began with a home visit to better understand the quality of interaction between the child and foster mother. T.I.E.S. staff learned that the foster mother believed that children with prenatal substance exposure are overstimulated by touching and hugging and, as a result, she had emotionally withdrawn from the child, leaving her alone in her crib many hours each day. Testing revealed that the child was developmentally delayed, but not autistic. The foster placement was ended, and the child was placed with a preadoptive family with whom she thrived. In another case, the

T.I.E.S. educational consultant made a visit to a preschool with the social worker to assess whether the preschool was suited to the needs of a very active and intense child. The consultant determined that the school was not appropriate for the child, which the social worker already had suspected. The joint visit, however, provided the social worker with the consultant's expertise and support, and she was then able to explain to the adoptive mother why the school was not a good choice and what would constitute a more beneficial setting.

Four times a year, T.I.E.S. staff selects key issues, based on lessons learned from the project, for presentation to the DCFS Adoption Division social workers and to attorneys representing children. The issues have included the latest research on the impact of prenatal substance exposure on children; what information can be gained from a developmental/ psychological evaluation; helping intense children transition from foster care to adoptive placements; and strategies for working with schools regarding children with prenatal substance exposure in adoptive placement.

Present and Future Directions

The California legislature as well as the United States Congress recently passed critical legislation to address the lack of timeliness in termination of parental rights, laws which emphasize children's needs for permanency at the earliest possible juncture. In cases that involve parents with extensive and chronic histories of drug or alcohol abuse, these laws allow for shortening of the service period and revise the requirements for filing a petition to terminate parental rights. As these laws are implemented, even greater numbers of children with prenatal substance exposure will be referred for adoption planning and at younger ages. The impact of these new reforms, however, may be only minimally positive or actually potentially harmful if the resources for training, preparation, and services are not available to effect and support these children's adoptions [Child Welfare League of America 1997]. These laws increase the need for the services provided by programs such as T.I.E.S.

In the case of T.I.E.S., continuing and augmented funding is now in place, ensuring that larger number of children and families will be served yearly by the project. T.I.E.S. also has added direct and consultative services of a psychiatrist to more comprehensively serve the needs of children and has expanded the role of the pediatrician. For older children, ages six through eight, the program has begun more formal children's support groups to help children learn about and express feelings, often using adoption-specific activities. Finally, the program has implemented a component to strengthen and preserve adoptive families of children with prenatal substance exposure whose adoptions are already legalized or near legalization. Together, these services form the beginnings of a seamless model of continuity of services for children with prenatal substance exposure, for whom adoption planning with unrelated caregivers is a strong possibility or a reality.

There are a number of directions in which the T.I.E.S. program hopes to move in the future: expanding, replicating and tailoring the project in order to be more accessible to a larger number of families countywide; providing services to children older than nine; involving trainees from the disciplines of pediatric medicine, psychiatry, social welfare, law and education; and institutionalizing the program's services through statewide replication, a step that will be facilitated by a new California law. The T.I.E.S. for Adoption program provides a strong model for reducing the barriers to adoption for children in foster care with prenatal substance exposure. The program provides other communities with a highly effective approach to supporting children and their foster and adoptive families.

Notes

1. TIES for Adoption began as a model demonstration project funded from 1995 through 1997 by the Children's Bureau, Administration for Children, Youth, and Families, Health and Human Services, Adoption Opportunities Program (# 90-CO-0743). In 1998, the Stuart Foundation began funding this project in order to reach a larger number of children and families and work toward institutionalizing these critical services.

Acknowledgments

The authors thank Peter G. Digre, director, Los Angeles Department of Children and Family Services, and Neal Halfon, M.D., M.P.H., UCLA professor of pediatrics and public health and the project's UCLA Principal Investigator, for their steadfast advocacy on behalf the project. We also want to thank Rose Corona, M.A., Kristine Santoro, Lisa Suarez, M.A., MaryAnn Skelton, M.A., Claudia Wang, M.D., Marci Schoenbaum, M.A., and Rose Monteiro, M.S.W., L.C.S.W., for their invaluable contributions to the project. Our heartfelt appreciation goes to the parents and children who shared their lives, struggles, and joys with us.

This chapter is dedicated to the memory of Sara E. Berman, M.S.W. Ms. Berman was chief of the adoption division of Los Angeles County DCFS and principal investigator of TIES for Adoption. Her leadership and belief in this project continue to be an inspiration.

References

Associated Press. (1997, September 25). First Lady pushes easier adoptions. *Los Angeles Daily News*, p. 4.

Azuma, S. & Chasnoff, I. (1993). Outcomes of children prenatally exposed to cocaine and other drugs: A path analysis of three-year data. *Pediatrics, 92*, 396–402.

American Public Welfare Association. (1991). *Guiding principles for working with substance abusing families and drug-exposed children: The child welfare response*. Recommendations of the National Association of Public Welfare Administrators, approved by the Executive Committee of the National Council of State Human Services Administrators. Washington, DC: American Public Welfare Association.

Barth, R. P. & Berry, M. (1988). *Adoption and disruption: Rates, risks and response*. Hawthorne, NY: Aldine de Gruyter.

Bays, J. (1990). Substance abuse and child abuse: Impact of addiction on the child. *Pediatric Clinics of North America, 37*, 881–904.

Bolton, F., Laner, R., & Gai, D. (1981). For better or worse? Foster parents and children in an officially reported child maltreatment population. *Children and Youth Services Review, 3*, 37–53.

Brooks-Gunn, J., Liaw, F., & Klebanov, P. K. (1992). Effects of early intervention on cognitive function of low birthweight preterm infants. *Journal of Pediatrics, 120*, 350–359.

Brooks-Gunn, J., McCarton, C. , & Hawley, T. (1994, January). Effects of in utero drug exposure on children's development: Review and recommendations. *Archives of Pediatric and Adolescent Medicine 148*, 33–39.

Cadoret, R. J. (1990). Biologic perspectives of adoptee adjustment. In D.M. Brodzinsky &, M.D. Schechter (Eds.), *The psychology of adoption.* (2nd Ed.) (pp.25–41). New York: Oxford University Press.

Cameron, J. (1994). *Preventive Ounce: Toddler and preschool advice sheets.* Unpublished manuscript. Oakland, CA: Preventive Ounce.

Cameron, J. R., Rice, D. C., Hansen, R., & Rosen, D. (1994). Developing temperament guidance programs within pediatric practice. In W.B. Carey & S.C. McDevitt (Eds.) *Prevention and early intervention: Individual differences as risk factors for the mental health of children: A Festschrift for Stella Chess and Alexander Thomas* (pp. 226–234). New York: Brunner/Mazel.

Chess, S. & Thomas, A. (1986). *Temperament in clinical practice.* New York: Guilford.

Child Welfare Institute (1992). *Model Approaches to Partnerships in Parenting Group Preparation and Selection (Revised).* Atlanta, GA: Child Welfare Institute.

Cole, E., Barth, R.P., Crocker, A.C., & Moss, K. G. (1996). *Time to decide: Policy and practice challenges in serving infants and young children whose parents abuse drugs and alcohol.* Boston, MA: Report on the Family Builders Network Conferences, SAFS and the Family Builders Network.

Edelstein, S.B., Howard, J., Tyler, R., Waldinger, G., & Moore, A. (1995). *Children with prenatal alcohol and/or other drug exposure: Weighing the risks for adoption.* Washington, DC: Child Welfare League of America.

Edelstein, S. B., Burge, D., & Waterman, J. M. (In press). Helping foster parents cope with separation, loss, and grief. *Child Welfare.*

Esman, A. H. (1983). Psychoanalytic play therapy. In C. E. Schaefer & K. J. O'Connor (Eds.), *Handbook of play therapy* (pp.11–20). New York: John Wiley & Sons.

Fahlberg, V. (1991). *A child's journey through placement.* Indianapolis, IN: Perspectives Press.

Fanshel, D. (1975, June). Prenatal failure and consequences for children: The drug-abusing mother whose children are in foster care. *American Journal of Public Health*, 604–612.

Feig, L. (1990). *Drug-exposed infants and children: Service needs and policy questions.* Washington, DC: U.S. Department of Health and Human Services, Office of the Assistant Secretary for Planning and Evaluation.

Gil, E. (1991). *The healing power of play: working with abused children.* New York: Guilford Press.

Groze, V., Haines-Simeon, M., & Barth, R. (1994). Barriers in permanency planning for medically fragile children: Drug affected children and HIV infected children. *Child and Adolescent Social Work Journal, 11,* 63–85.

Halfon N., Mendonca, A., & Berkowitz, G. (1995). Health status of children in foster care. *Archives of Pediatric Adolescent Medicine, 149,* 386–392.

James, B. (1989). *Treating traumatized children: New insights and creative interventions.* Lexington, MA: D.C. Heath and Company.

Jones, K. L. & Smith, S. W. (1973). Recognition of the fetal alcohol syndrome in early infancy. *Lancet, 2,* 999–1001.

Kurcinka, M. S. (1991). *Raising your spirited child.* New York: Harper Collins.

Mills, J. C. & Crowley, R. J. (1986). *Therapeutic metaphors for children and the child within.* New York: Brunner/Mazel.

Robin, L. E. & Mills, J. L. (1993). Effects of in utero exposure to street drugs. *American Journal of Public Health, 83,* 1–32.

Rosenfeld, A. A., Pilowsky, D. J., & Nickman, S. (1997) Foster care: an update. *Journal of the American Academy of Child and Adolescent Psychiatry, 36,* 448–457.

Rosenthal, J. A. & Groze, V. K. (1992). *Special needs adoption: A study of intact families.* New York: Praeger Publishers.

Ryan, P., McFaden, E., & Wiencek, P. (1987). *Analyzing abuse in family foster care: Final report to the National Center on Child Abuse and Neglect.* Ypsilanti, MI: Institute for the Study of Children and Families.

Streissguth, A. P., Sampson, P. D., & Barr, H. M.(1990). Moderate prenatal alcohol exposure: Effects on child IQ and learning problems at age 7 1/2 years. *Alcoholism: Clinical and Experimental Research, 14,* 662–669.

Tatara, T. (1990). *Children of substance abusing /alcoholic parents referred to the public child welfare system: Summaries of key statistical data obtained from states.* Washington, DC: American Public Welfare Association.

Tatara, T. (1993). *Characteristics of children in substitute and adoptive care: A statistical summary of the VCIS National Child Welfare Data Base, based on FY82 through FY90 data.* Washington, DC: American Public Welfare Association.

Tatara, T. (1994). *Child substitute care flow data for FY1993.* Washington, DC: American Public Welfare Association, Voluntary Cooperative Information System.

Thomas, A., Chess, S., & Birch, G. (1968). *Temperament and behavior disorders in children.* New York: New York University Press.

Tracy, E. M. & Farkas, K.(1994). Preparing practitioners for child welfare practice with substance abusing families. *Child Welfare, 73,* 57–68.

U.S. Department of Health and Human Services, Children's Bureau. *National Study of Protective, Preventive and Reunification Services Delivered to Children and Their Families.* Washington, DC: U.S. Government Printing Office, 1997.

Wald, M. S. (1994). Termination of parental rights. In D. J. Besharov (Ed.), *When drug addicts have children: Reorienting child welfare's response* (pp.195–210). Washington, DC: Child Welfare League of America.

Walker, C., Zangrillo, P., & Smith, J. (1991). *Parental drug abuse and African American children in foster care: Issues and study findings.* Washington, DC: National Black Child Development Institute.

Young, N. (1997). Effects of alcohol and other drugs on children. *Journal of Psychoactive Drugs, 29*(1), 23–42.

Zuckerman, B. & Bresnahan, K. (1991). Developmental and behavioral consequences of prenatal drug and alcohol exposure. *Pediatric Clinics of North America, 38,* 1387–1406.

6

Alcohol-Related Disorders and Children Adopted from Abroad

Jane Ellen Aronson

This chapter focuses on prenatal alcohol exposure and children who are adopted internationally. It provides a review of the impact of prenatal alcohol exposure on children's growth and development and the disorders associated with fetal alcohol exposure. Primary focus is on the effects of prenatal alcohol exposure on children adopted from the Former Soviet Union where the incidence of alcoholism is particularly high. Two illustrative case examples are offered, of children adopted from the Former Soviet Union who were diagnosed with the classic form of Fetal Alcohol Syndrome (FAS). Issues related to the long-term outcomes associated with alcohol-related disorders are discussed, with a brief review of other health conditions that affect children adopted internationally.

Introduction

Family formation through international or intercultural adoption has been a longstanding practice. Throughout history, children have been abandoned and/or institutionalized as a result of war, disease, poor economic conditions, and religious, political, and social philosophies. Historically, some children who have lost their families have joined new families outside of their native countries through adoption. The Korean conflict of the 1950s and the Vietnam War in the 1960s and 1970s prompted the adoption of a number of foreign-born children by United States citizens. In the 1990s, many urban, socially-conscious Americans adopted Chinese girls who had been

147

abandoned and placed in orphanages as a result of that country's "one-child family policy" and the preference for male heirs [Johnson 1993; Johnson 1996; Scott 1997].

International adoptions have increased over the past decade as a result of several factors. First, there has been a significant decrease in the number of children in the United States who are available for adoption since the 1970s as a result of the legalization of abortion following Roe vs. Wade and greater access to birth control measures [Mansnerus 1998; Fein 1998]. These decreases have occurred simultaneously with an increase in the number of individuals diagnosed with infertility [Abma et al. 1997]. Even with the rapid development of new reproductive technologies, the expense of infertility treatment coupled with the lack of health insurance coverage for such services has resulted in the consideration of adoption by greater numbers of individuals [National Center for Health Statistics 1997]. For those who wish to adopt, highly publicized media reports of contested adoption cases (such as "Baby Jessica") have raised concerns that domestic adoption may be "risky." Some families have been uncomfortable with the developing practice of open adoption, which encourages ongoing relationships between birth families and children. These factors have combined to prompt greater interest in international adoption. In the U.S., international adoptions have increased by more than 50% over the past decade: 15,774 children were adopted from abroad in 1998, compared to 9,120 in 1988 [Immigration and Naturalization Service & the U.S. Department of State 1998].

Throughout the world, children face health concerns and medical conditions that may be unique to the countries in which they live, or at least are more prevalent than in other countries. The health problems experienced by children in their home countries will be influenced by such factors as economic conditions, social practices, the availability of health education, and the adequacy of medical facilities. When children are adopted internationally, the health issues are likely to be even more complex. Children may suffer from the psychological and physical effects of abandonment and institutionalization, in addition to physical health problems and conditions that exist in their native countries. In general, children adopted from outside the U.S. may be at risk of infectious diseases such as HIV, tuberculosis, hepatitis B and C, and syphilis; conditions associated with undernourishment such as anemia and rickets; intestinal parasites due to contaminated water; iodine deficiency and hypothyroidism; and complications attributed to lack of prenatal care [Barnett & Miller 1996; Frank et al. 1996; Hostetter & Johnson 1996; Miller et al. 1995; Mitchell & Jenista 1997]. Disorders related to prenatal alcohol exposure, including Fetal Alcohol Syndrome, also occur at a relatively high rate, particularly among children adopted from the Former Soviet Union (FSU) and other countries in Eastern Europe.

The impact of prenatal alcohol exposure on children adopted from the FSU has been a key health issue in international adoption. The number of children adopted from the FSU has grown substantially [Immigration and Naturalization Service & the U.S. Department of State 1998] as a result of economic hardships since the dissolution of that country's communist political system. Children adopted from the FSU have been affected by the poverty and deteriorating social conditions in the country, as well as by the increase in substance abuse [Chicago Tribune 1995; Davis 1994; Garrett 1997]. Between 1992 and 1993, the number of individuals diagnosed with alcoholism in FSU clinics increased by 40.8%, and of this percentage, almost half were women [Feshbach & Prokhorov 1995]. Adolescent girls have been particularly susceptible to substance abuse. When questioned about their alcohol intake, 80% to 94% of girls between the ages of 15 and 17 reported that they drank "sometimes," and 17% reported that they drank "often" [Feshbach & Prokhorov 1995]. The significant growth in the rate of alcoholism in general, and among adolescent women in particular, has been accompanied by a marked increase in adolescent pregnancy and a lack of public health programs to educate women of childbearing age about the deleterious effects of drinking during pregnancy. The result has been a growing number of children affected by conditions associated with prenatal alcohol exposure.

The Nature and Incidence of Alcohol-related Disorders

The early work on the effects of prenatal alcohol exposure, conducted in the 1970s, found that a pattern of altered growth and development emerged among infants born to women who were chronically alcoholic during pregnancy [Jones & Smith 1973]. Researchers identified head and facial abnormalities in the form of a small head, small eye openings, extra skin folds close to the nose at the inner eyes, and a flattened appearance of the middle area of the face. They also found that these infants suffered systemically from prenatal and postnatal growth deficiency; problems with joints, kidneys, and genitals; cleft palate; and congenital heart anomalies. Jones and Smith [1973] labeled these physical effects of prenatal alcohol exposure, Fetal Alcohol Syndrome (FAS).

Subsequent work in 1980 led to the issuance of the first definitional guidelines for FAS by the Fetal Alcohol Study Group of the Research Society on Alcoholism (RSA). The guidelines were subsequently modified by Sokol and Clarren [1989]. Under these guidelines, the diagnosis of FAS may be made only when there is a documented history of maternal alcohol use during pregnancy and the child has signs of abnormality in each of three categories:

1. Prenatal and/or postnatal growth retardation (weight and/or length or height below the tenth percentile when corrected for gestational age);

2. Central nervous system involvement, including neurological abnormality, developmental delay, behavioral dysfunction or deficit, intellectual impairment and/or structural abnormalities, such as microcephaly (head circumference below the third percentile) or brain malformations found on imaging studies or autopsy; and

3. A characteristic face, currently qualitatively described as including small eye openings (palpebral fissures), an elongated midface, a long and flattened groove in the midline of the upper lip (philtrum), a thin upper lip, and flattened bones forming the upper jaw (maxilla).

Children who have only some of the characteristics of FAS are diagnosed as having Fetal Alcohol Effects (FAE) or Possible Fetal Alcohol Effects (PFAE) [Sokol & Clarren 1989; Streissguth 1997]. Some debate concerning the accuracy of these terms, however, has arisen, and other terminology has been suggested as more appropriate descriptions of the disorders that do not fit the criteria for FAS. These terms include Alcohol-related Birth Defect (ARBD) [Sokol

& Clarren 1989] and Alcohol-Related Neurodevelopmental Disorder (ARND) [Institute of Medicine et al. 1996]. For the sake of simplicity and uniformity in this chapter, a child who fits the strict guidelines for Fetal Alcohol Syndrome (FAS) will be referred to as having FAS. A child who is of normal size but has some of the classic facial features and central nervous system and behavioral manifestations of FAS will be referred to as having ARND or FAE. The term Alcohol-Related Disorder (ARD) will be used as a general description, encompassing all of the conditions associated with prenatal alcohol exposure.

The estimated incidence of FAS worldwide is 1.9 per 1,000 live births [Abel & Sokol 1987]. Incidence estimates, however, vary considerably depending on the methodology of studies and, particularly, on study sites. Nevertheless, based on an incidence rate of 1.9 per 1,000 live births, the number of children born each year with FAS can be calculated at approximately 7,600 children. In Eastern Europe and the Former Soviet Union, the use of alcohol during pregnancy is rampant and as a result, a large number of children adopted from these countries suffer some effects of prenatal alcohol exposure. In one U.S. study [Albers et al. 1997], the incidence of FAS among a group of 56 children adopted from Eastern Europe was 1.6 percent. In a retrospective chart review of 131 preadoption evaluations of children from the FSU (including videos) conducted by the author between 1994 and 1997, it was determined that 17 charts contained a documented history of maternal alcohol ingestion during pregnancy. Using the strictest FAS criteria, there were 2 children (1.53 %) with FAS. Fifteen children (11%) were exposed to alcohol and were at risk for FAE. There was a suspicion of FAS by video evaluation in 28 children (21.4 %), out of which 5 children had a documented history of maternal alcohol abuse in the medical record. Extrapolation from the number of actually diagnosed FAS cases among these Russian children results in a rate of 15 per 1,000 live births—which is 8 times the worldwide rate of 1.9 per 1,000 live births. In another study evaluating children adopted from the FSU, McGuinness [1998] found that of the 47 children whose birth mother histories were available, 43 had a history of maternal alcohol abuse. Of the children with documented histories of maternal alcohol abuse, 6 children were reported by their adoptive parents to have FAE.

The Effects of Prenatal Alcohol Exposure and Diagnostic Issues

The effect of alcohol on the growing and developing embryo and fetus is still not completely understood. The exact mechanisms by which alcohol induces malformations may be as a result of a direct toxic effect [Abel 1984; Campbell & Fantel 1983; Dreosti et al. 1981; Sreenathan et al. 1982], or the timing of alcohol exposure and the peak alcohol concentrations may work together to exert a teratogenic effect, interfering with the fetus's normal development in utero [Schenker et al. 1990]. The principal outcomes of these effects are malformations, growth deficiencies, functional deficits, and in the most extreme cases, death. While the severity of the effects of alcohol on a fetus may vary due to the genetic makeup of both the mother and the developing embryo/fetus, an estimated 25% to 45% of children born to mothers who drink during pregnancy suffer from severe alcohol-related conditions in the form of FAS [Gilliam et al. 1988; Streissguth 1997].

The actual amount of alcohol necessary to produce malformations seen in alcohol-related disorders is unknown, and it is still not clear whether one can predict particular abnormalities based on the trimesters when alcohol was consumed. It is, however, widely believed that alcohol consumed throughout pregnancy has a lasting effect on the fetus, and evidence suggests that short-lived, high concentrations of alcohol, such as in binge drinking, can be especially deleterious [Enhart et al. 1987; Lewis & Woods 1994; Schenker et al. 1990; FDA 1981], affecting the physical, behavioral, and cognitive capacities of children.

As outlined in Table 1, physical abnormalities associated with alcohol-related disorders may occur in the face, heart, skeleton, teeth, eyes, genitals, kidneys, and hearing [Stromland & Hellstrom 1996; Taylor et al. 1994]. In fact, 20% to 50% of children with FAS or FAE demonstrate such anomalies [Committee on Substance

Abuse and Committee on Children with Disabilities 1993]. In terms of the behavioral and cognitive effects of alcohol-related disorders, effects range in degree from mild to severe. The average IQ for individuals affected by prenatal exposure to alcohol is in the mental retardation range, but there is a tremendous variation as demonstrated in a recent survey of FAS case reports in which the range of IQ scores was from 20 to 120, with a mean of 65.73 [Mattson & Riley 1997]. Children with ARND or FAE appear to have higher IQ scores than children with classic FAS, but these scores likewise are generally in the mentally retarded range [Mattson & Riley 1997]. Even when IQ is within normal range, children with alcohol-related disorders may have severe and complex cognitive deficits and unusual behavioral manifestations as outlined in Table 2.

As the child grows from infancy through childhood to adolescence and adulthood, some or all of these cognitive and behavioral manifestations may become apparent. These effects, however, are difficult to diagnose, particularly early in a child's life. Cognitive and behavioral problems cannot be predicted based on the physical abnormalities of the child, and there are no tests to predict future effects. Additionally, if an alcohol-related disorder is not suspected, the child may be mislabeled and treated inappropriately [Streissguth 1997; Mattson & Riley 1997].

The diagnosis of FAS is not easy and may be completely overlooked in newborns, as many health care providers have not had training in recognition of alcohol-related disorders [Little et al. 1990]. The face of an infant will not necessarily indicate prenatal alcohol exposure, as some of the classic FAS facial features may be indistinguishable from certain ethnic characteristics. Asian and Native American children, for example, generally have epicanthal folds and a flattened midfacial area, and some Russian children have Asian characteristics due to the mixing of Russian and Asian cultures over the centuries. On the other hand, some of the classic FAS facial features are not consistent with certain facial characteristics of ethnic groups. African American children, for example, do not have the thin upper lip that is characteristic of FAS. The absence of this physical characteristic associated with FAS, however, should not be

Table 6-1. Features Observed in Fetal Alcohol Syndrome/Fetal Alcohol Effects*

Growth
   Prenatal and Postnatal growth deficiency+
   Decreased adipose tissue∫
Performance
   Mental retardation+
   Development delay
   Fine-motor dysfunction
   Infant irritability +, child hyperactivity ∫, and poor attention span
   Speech problems
   Poor coordination, hypotonia∫
   Cognitive, behavioral, and psychosocial problems
Craniofacial
   Microcephaly+
   Short palpebral fissues+
   Ptosis≈
   Retrognathia in infancy+
   Maxillary hypoplasia∫
   Hypoplastic long or smooth philtrum+
   Thin vermillion of upper lip+
   Short upturned nose∫
   Micrognathia in adolescence∫
Skeletal
   Joint alterations including camptodactyly, flexion contractures at elbows,
      congenital hip dislocations
   Foot position defects
   Radioulnar synostosis
   Tapering terminal phalanges, hypoplastic finger and toe nails®
   Cervical spine abnormalities
   Altered palm crease pattern≈
   Pectus excavatum≈
Cardiac
   Ventricular septal defect‡
   Myopia‡, strabismus≈
   Epicanthal folds≈
   Dental malocclusion
   Hearing loss, protuberant ears

Abnormal thoracic cage

Strawberry hemangiomata≈

Hypoplastic labia majora≈

Microophthalmia, blepharophimosis‡

Small teeth with faulty enamel‡

Hypospadias, small rotated kidneys, hydronephrosis‡

Hirsutism in infancy

Hernias of diaphragm, umbilicus or groin, diastasis recti‡

*From Streissguth, Clarren and Smith, and Jones. Principal (+,∫) and associated (≈, ‡) features observed in 245 affected individuals. + > 80%; ∫ > 50%; ≈ 26% to 50%; ‡ 1% to 25% of patients.

Table 6-2. Cognitive and Behavioral Effects Associated with Alcohol Related Disorders

Jitteriness

Distrubed sleepwake cycles

Hypertonia

Poor state regulation

Poor habituation

Poor fine motor control

Poor gross motor control

Hyperactivity

Poor Tandem gait

Central auditory dysfunction

Delayed or perseverative language

Attentional impairments

Learning disabilities

Poor impulse control

Poor concentration

Difficulties with abstract reasoning

Memory impairments

Difficulties with judgment

Head banging /or body rocking (self-stimulation behaviors)

Poor adaptive functioining

Poor eye-hand coordination

Poor balance

Inability to generalize from situation to situation

Difficulties with abstractions such as time, space, cause and effect used to rule out FAS [Streissguth 1997]. Finally, other syndromes such as fetal hydantoin syndrome [exposure to dilantin (phenytoin), an anticonvulsant medication during pregnancy], may result in facial features similar to FAS, which may make it difficult to determine whether an infant has FAS.

Diagnosis also may be difficult because of changes in children's appearance over time. Classic FAS features may not be apparent in early infancy, but as the muscles and bones mature, more recogniz-able symptoms of FAS may become evident. On the other hand, some children with alcohol-related disorders outgrow the classic facial features over time and gain weight at a steadier rate, although their linear growth remains limited [Streissguth 1997]. Other chil-dren are born with a normal head circumference, but as a result of slower-than-average growth velocity, microcephaly (small head size) becomes apparent by the time they are one year of age. This process is commonly documented in the preadoption growth charts of Russian children who are adopted internationally. The reasons for this late onset microcephaly are not clear, but may be a result of alcohol exposure, malnutrition and deprivation in orphanage set-tings, or intrauterine infections.

Because prospective adoptive parents generally do not meet the children they adopt from other countries prior to actual placement, they typically depend on photographs or occasional video of children provided as part of the preadoption review. It is extremely difficult to make a diagnosis of FAS from videos and photographs. Photographs are frequently of poor quality—taken too far away or at awkward angles—and they often are copied or faxed before they are presented to prospective adoptive parents. Videos, too, are often poorly produced or copied numerous times, thereby losing most of the quality and acuity. A photographic screening tool, developed by Astley and Clarren [1996], uses computer analysis of standardized photographs to make the diag-nosis of FAS. For the diagnosis of children adopted from abroad, however, this tool has limited utility. The quality of available photographs usually does not meet the stringent requirements of the computer software, and the ethnicity of these children cannot be properly taken into account with a simple, computerized photographic screening tool.

Special Problems for Children with Alcohol-related Disorders Adopted from the FSU

Difficulties in diagnosing and treating Russian children with FAS or FAE are often exacerbated, because medical care for children living in orphanages tends to be intermittent, nonexistent, or provided by inadequately trained staff. Old equipment that provides inaccurate information, such as unbalanced scales, may be the only available means for obtaining relevant medical information, and even when data is accurate, it may be only partially noted in medical charts or not recorded at all. In a chart review conducted by the author, of 93 children adopted from the FSU and other Eastern European countries, only 35 (37.6 %) of the medical abstracts had birth head circumferences recorded—a factor relevant in the diagnosis of alcohol-related disorders.

The medical records of children in orphanages in the FSU may be difficult to decipher because they often are handwritten and utilize medical terminology and abbreviations of the Russian medical system. Because of significant differences in medical training, diagnosis, and treatment in the FSU and the U.S., the terminology used by doctors in the FSU may not be helpful to U.S. physicians in understanding the actual medical status of a child. Symptoms related to prenatal alcohol exposure may not be recognized or recorded in the medical chart, or they may be recorded and incorrectly attributed to a non-alcohol-related disorder. Translations are apt to be of questionable accuracy because of the extremely limited availability of translators in the FSU, particularly those with knowledge of medical terminology. Translations often are done by individuals who do not understand the medical relevance of such data as the child's weight or head circumference measurement and may not appreciate the importance of accurate information. Translated medical reports that are sent to adoptive parents in the U.S., consequently, are often incomplete or inaccurate or contain only the vaguest information.

The impact of FAS on children who are internationally adopted is perhaps best illustrated with actual case studies. The following case histories of MPZ and PEK provide examples of the histories and medical conditions of children with FAS adopted from Russia and demonstrate the range of ongoing services that children with FAS often need following adoption.

Case Study #1: MPZ

MPZ, now 3 years old, was adopted from the FSU in April 1997 at 19 months of age. MPZ's medical history indicated congenital heart disease, though there was no specific cardiac lesion designated. There was no history of maternal alcohol abuse in the medical history, but upon review of MPZ's video and medical abstract, her primary care physician noted the possibility of facial features consistent with Fetal Alcohol Syndrome. The medical abstract indicated prematurity (a gestational age of 34 weeks), low birthweight consistent with her prematurity, and a growth curve well below the fifth percentile for all growth parameters (these have continued to be below this percentile though there has been improvement). Laboratory studies standard for a child adopted from abroad were performed when she first arrived in the U.S. and were all normal.

MPZ was evaluated for suspected Fetal Alcohol Syndrome, including a genetics/dysmorphology consultation, a hearing test, a pediatric ophthalmologic evaluation, a cardiac consultation with echocardiogram, a kidney sonogram, and a pediatric surgery evaluation for some toe abnormalities. Her heart condition was further evaluated and successfully treated.

Although the findings from many of MPZ's evaluations were normal, there were other findings consistent with FAS. Her dysmorphology evaluation revealed a thin upper lip and other physical characteristics associated with FAS. MPZ's bone age at 20 months was found to be like that of a six-month-old, consistent with severe failure-to-thrive secondary to malnutrition, institutionalization, and FAS. Her developmental assessment performed in April/May 1997 revealed significant (greater than 33%) delays in all assessed areas: gross motor, fine motor, language, personal-social, and cognitive development. MPZ is currently receiving speech, occupational, and physical therapy in her home through an early intervention program in her community. Although her vocabulary has increased, she does not combine words. Her cognitive and language skills continue to be assessed, and MPZ's parents are slowly learning to cope with her severe delays.

Case Study #2: PEK

PEK, now 5-1/2 years old, was adopted from the FSU in March 1996. He lived with alcoholic parents and three siblings until he was two years old, when his parents "were deprived of their parental rights," and he was placed in an orphanage. PEK's medical abstract, which was not reviewed by an adoption medical specialist preadoption, included a history of parental alcohol abuse. PEK's adoptive parents were aware of this history before they adopted him.

PEK's facial features are consistent with classic FAS. He has other physical anomalies that are often found in children with alcohol-related disorders, including tendon shortening of his second fingers. PEK's medical abstract on his initial examination in the U.S. indicated that he had a small birth head circumference and his height, weight, and head circumference at the time were found to be below the fifth percentile. His linear growth has improved (at 5.5 years, it is in the tenth percentile), but he is still less than the fifth percentile for weight and head circumference.

PEK was developmentally evaluated in September 1996 through his school district and was found to have significant developmental delays, including severe delays in receptive and expressive language. Initially, he could hardly be understood even after he learned English, and although he has made marked improvement, language remains a problem. His fine motor skills were also delayed, and he had difficulty using utensils, a problem exacerbated by his shortened second fingers. PEK was quite awkward and often stumbled, but now appears to have better coordination. He is currently in a special education school program, receiving occupational, speech, and physical therapy. Regular evaluations by the child study team indicate that he is doing well in school and has shown no behavioral problems in his very structured and predictable home environment.

Long-term Outcomes for Children with Alcohol-related Disorders

These case studies demonstrate that children with FAS suffer from serious effects of prenatal alcohol exposure, but that their health and development can be maximized with multiple services and interventions. Although these cases describe possible short-term gains for children with FAS, they do not provide answers to the concerns of most adoptive parents about longer-term health and developmental outcomes. Research focusing on potential long-term consequences for patients affected by prenatal alcohol exposure, however, has provided adoptive parents with some information. Streissguth and colleagues [1997], for example, studied 415 individuals, 37% of whom were diagnosed with FAS and the rest with FAE. The individuals were racially diverse (60% Caucasian, 25% Native American, 7% African American, 6% Hispanic and 2% Asian or other ethnic group) and ranged in ages from 6 to 51 years (39% were between 6 and 11 years, 39% between 12 and 20 years old, and 22% percent were between 21 and 51 years old). More than half were male.

A telephone questionnaire, or life history interview, conducted with patients' caregivers was used to assess patients' functioning and/or experiences in ten major areas: household and family environment; independent living and financial management; education; employment; physical abuse, sexual abuse, and domestic violence; physical, social, and sexual development; behavior management and mental health issues; alcohol and drug use; legal status and criminal justice involvement; and companionship and parenting. Significant percentages of the caregivers reported that patients experienced problems in each of the areas. A great majority (90%) of patients had mental health problems and 30% of the patients age 12 and over had alcohol and drug problems. Half of the patients in this age range (12 and over) had been confined for mental health or alcohol or drug treatment or had been incarcerated for a crime. More than half of all of the patients had had disrupted school experiences (60%), and 60% had been in trouble with the law. Half of these patients had engaged in inappropriate sexual behavior. Caregivers were also asked about patients' living situation and employment status when the patients were at least 21 years old. Eighty percent of those age 21 and older did not live independently and had experienced problems with employment.

The study also explored factors that were associated with more positive outcomes for patients over the age of 12 who were diagnosed as having FAS or FAE. A number of factors emerged from the researchers' analysis:

- Living in a stable and nurturing home for the majority of the patient's life,
- Being diagnosed as having FAS or FAE before the age of 6 years,
- Never having experienced personal violence,
- Remaining in each living situation for, on average, more than 2.8 years,
- Experiencing a good quality home between the ages of 8 and 12 years,
- Eligibility for disability benefits,
- Having a diagnosis of FAS, rather than FAE, and
- Having basic needs met for at least 13% of life.

The research has not clarified whether the disabilities observed in individuals diagnosed as having FAS or FAE is strictly attributable to prenatal alcohol exposure or, instead, to the combined impact of prenatal alcohol exposure and a postnatal alcoholic environment. Several studies have focused on individuals with alcohol-related disorders who were removed from alcoholic home environments and placed in foster care or adopted. Although some studies show no changes in cognitive or intellectual levels of children who are placed in more stable environments [Aronson 1984; Spohr et. al 1994], there have been reports of improvements in children's psychosocial functioning [Aronson 1984; Aronson & Olegard 1987]. Thus, findings from these studies, as well as the research of Streissguth and colleagues [1996], suggest that more positive outcomes for children with alcohol-related disorders are associated with nurturing home environments and offer some encouragement for adoptive parents of alcohol-exposed children.

Other Health Issues for Children Adopted from Abroad

In addition to alcohol-related disorders, children adopted from other countries may experience a range of other health problems. A brief review of these problems is presented here, as evaluations of children adopted internationally should include assessments for these conditions as well as the alcohol-related disorders that are the subject of this chapter. Briefly, children who are adopted internationally should be assessed for the following health conditions:

- Rickets, a disease of the bone and muscles that results from a deficiency of vitamin D and calcium [Barness & Curran 1996]. Children from orphanages may be at particular risk of rickets because of diet and lack of exposure to sunlight [Aronson 1998; Jenista 1997].
- Lead poisoning, a condition affecting particularly high numbers of children from China as a result of coal burning and the use of gasoline containing lead [Shen et al. 1996; Aronson et al. 1999].
- Anemia, which may take the form of iron deficiency anemia, which is caused primarily by malnutrition or genetic anemia found in children from a number of Asian countries [Glader & Look 1996].
- Human Immunodeficiency Disorder (HIV). An evolving issue in international adoption, there has been only limited evidence of HIV infection among children adopted internationally [Richner et al. 1997; Albers et al. 1997]. The association of HIV with drug abuse and prostitution, however, highlights the importance of testing children for HIV upon their arrival in the U.S.
- Hepatitis B, which historically has been an issue in international adoption because of its prevalence in Asia [Hostetter et al. 1991]. Recent studies have found that, as a result of transfusions of unscreened blood, children adopted from Romania may

also be at heightened risk of carrying Hepatitis B infection [Johnson et al. 1992; Miller et al. 1995; Aronson et al. 1998a].
- Hepatitis C, which is quickly becoming a worldwide problem in association with intravenous drug use and transfusion of blood [Alter 1997; CDC 1998]. There is no established epidemiology for Hepatitis C for internationally adopted children, and efforts are underway to better understand the risk factors for children adopted from abroad.
- Tuberculosis, a well understood health condition that is prevalent in many of the countries from which children are adopted [Report of the Working Group on Tuberculosis Among Foreign-Born Persons 1998].
- Syphilis, a health problem that is on the rise in Eastern Europe and the Former Soviet Union [Specter 1997]. Aggressive treatment of infants who may have been exposed to syphilis has kept prevalence rate quite low.
- Intestinal parasites, a common condition in Eastern Europe, the Former Soviet Union, Asia and Latin America as a result of contaminated water. Studies show that from 14% to 50% of all children adopted from abroad suffer from intestinal parasites [Albers et al. 1997; Hostetter et al. 1991; Johnson et al. 1992; Miller et al. 1995].
- Iodine deficiency, which currently is not epidemic worldwide, nevertheless must be monitored, particularly for children adopted from China, where it is difficult to determine the geographic regions of the country where salt is iodized. Particular attention must be given to iodine deficiency as it applies to hypothyroidism.
- Hypothyroidism, which is an embryologic defect that causes significant brain damage if not diagnosed in the first few months of life. Although reports indicate that prevalence of hypothyroidism among internationally adopted children is quite low, the current worldwide occurrence of one in every 4,000 births highlights the need for testing nonetheless.
- Malnutrition, failure to thrive, psychosocial short stature, microcephaly, and developmental delay. These conditions, already discussed in relation to alcohol-related disorders, may be

present in the absence of prenatal alcohol exposure [Miller et al. 1995; Aronson et al. 1998b; Galler & Ross 1993]. Assessments for each of these conditions may be particularly important when children have been reared in orphanages and growth has been affected by children's basic struggles to survive.

Conclusion

There are significant health issues affecting children adopted from abroad and specifically from the Former Soviet Union. In addition to the range of health conditions associated with diet, environmental factors, and blood transfusions, alcohol-related disorders present significant risks, particularly in countries such as the FSU because of the high incidence of alcoholism. The severity of the effects of prenatal alcohol exposure range from severe, as in the case of Fetal Alcohol Syndrome (FAS), to moderate or mild, as evidenced by the range of fetal alcohol effects (FAE) or alcohol-related birth defects (ARBD). Even in the case of more severe disorders, however, early diagnosis and treatment can assist in moderating the health and developmental effects of prenatal alcohol exposure. Sound pediatric assessments and care are essential to maximizing a child's health and development. In addition, as illustrated by the recent book, *Fantastic Antone Succeeds* [Kleinfeld & Wescott 1993], a nurturing home environment combined with early intervention and educational services can have a significant impact on alcohol-affected children's lives.

Endnotes

1. Postmortem findings on fetuses, infants, and children of mothers who consumed alcohol during pregnancy have shown a number of neuropathologic anomalies affecting the brain stem as well as other parts of the brain. Magnetic Resonance Imaging (MRI) has shown a high incidence of midline brain anomalies in children, adolescents, and adults with classic FAS [Swayze et al. 1997].

2. The 95% confidence limits for 15 per 1,000 live births are as follows: lower limit is 1.9 per 1,000 and the upper limit is 54.1 per 1,000. The birthrate in the Former Soviet Union is 1.4 million births per year.

With an incidence of FAS of 15 per 1,000 live births, there could potentially be 21,000 children with FAS born each year (0.015 X 1, 400,000) in the FSU.

3.   The Challenge of Fetal Alcohol Syndrome/Overcoming Secondary Disabilities, edited by Ann Streissguth and Jonathan Kanter [1997], contains articles which summarize the outcomes of prenatal alcohol exposure, with particular emphasis on long-term effects.

References

Abel, E. L. (1984). Prenatal effects of alcohol. *Drug and Alcohol Dependence, 14,* 1–10.

Abel, E. L. & Sokol, R. J. (1987). Incidence of fetal alcohol syndrome and economic impact of FAS-related anomalies. *Drug and Alcohol Dependence, 19,* 51–70.

Abma, J., Mosher, W., Peterson, L., & Piccinino, L. (1997). Fertility, family planning, and women's health: New data from the 1995 National Survey of Family Growth. *Vital Health Statistics 23*(19).

Albers, L. H., Johnson, D., Hostetter, M. K., Iverson, S., & Miller, L. C. (1997). Health of children adopted from the former Soviet Union and Eastern Europe. *Journal of the American Medical Association, 278,* 922–924.

Alter, M. J. (1997). Epidemiology of hepatitis C. *Hepatology, 26,* 62S-65S.

Aronson, J. E. (1998). Rickets in Chinese children. *Families with Children from China/San Francisco Bay Newsletter, 3,* 34–36.

Aronson, J. E., Johnson, D. E., Federici, R. S., Faber, S., Pearl, P., & Taraglia, M. (1998a). *Hepatitis B infection in a neuropsychiatric institution in Videle, Romania.* Unpublished research, November 1998.

Aronson, J. E., Melnikova, M., & Alonso, M. (1998b). Unpublished research on head circumferences in children adopted from Eastern Europe and the Former Soviet Union at the International Adoption Medical Consultation Services.   On file with author, Winthop-University Hospital, Mineola, NY.

Aronson, J. E., Johnson, D., Hostetter, M. K., Traister, M., Smith, A. M., Kothari, V., & Alonso, M. (1999). Lead poisoning in children adopted from China. Presentation at the 39th Annual Meeting of the Ambulatory Pediatric Association, Program and Abstracts, May 1–4, 1999.

Aronson, M. (1984). *Children of Alcoholic Mothers*. Unpublished doctoral dissertation, University of Goteborg, Departments of Pediatrics and Psychology, Sweden.

Aronson, M. & Olegard, R. (1987). Children of alcoholic mothers. *Pediatrician, 14*, 57–61.

Astley, S. J. & Clarren, S. K. (1996). A case definition and photographic screening tool for the facial phenotype of fetal alcohol syndrome. *Journal of Pediatrics, 129*, 33–41.

Barness, L. A. & Curran, J. S. (1996). Rickets of Vitamin D Deficiency. In Nelson, W. E., Behrman, R. E., Kliegman, R. M., & Arvin, A. M. (Eds.), *Nelson textbook of pediatrics* (pp.179–183). Philadelphia: W.B. Saunders.

Barnett, E. D. & Miller, L. C. (1996). International adoption: The pediatrician's role. *Contemporary Pediatrics, 13*, 29–46.

Campbell, M. A. & Fantel, A. G. (1983). Teratogenicity of acetaldehyde in vitro: Relevance to the fetal alcohol syndrome. *Life Science, 32*, 2641–2647.

Centers for Disease Control & Prevention, National Center for Infectious Diseases (March 15, 1999). Section on Hepatitis. [On-line]. Available on website: www.cdc.gov/ncidod/diseases/hepatitis/hepatitis.htm.

Committee on Substance Abuse and Committee on Children With Disabilities/American Academy of Pediatrics (1993). Fetal Alcohol Syndrome and Fetal Alcohol Effects. *Pediatrics, 91*, 1004–1006.

Davis, R. B. (1994). Drug and alcohol use in the former Soviet Union. *International Journal of Addiction, 29*, 303–323.

Dreosti, I. E., Ballard, F. J., Belling, G. B., Record, I. R., Manuel, S. J., & Hetzel, B. S. (1981). The effect of ethanol and acetaldehyde on DNA synthesis in growing cells and on fetal development in the rat. *Alcoholism:Clinical and Experimental Research, 5*, 357–362.

Ernhart, C. B., Sokol, R. J., Martier, S., Moron, P., Nadler, D., & Ager, J. W. (1987). Alcohol teratogenicity in the human: A detailed assessment of specificity, critical period, and threshold. *American Journal of Obstetrics and Gynecology, 156*, 33–39.

Fein, E. B. (1998, October 25). Secrecy and stigma no longer clouding adoptions. *The New York Times*, pp. 30–31.

Feshbach, M. & Prokhorov, B. (1995). *Environmental and health atlas of Russia*. Moscow, Russia: PAIMS.

Food and Drug Administration. (1981). Surgeon General's advisory on alcohol and pregnancy. *FDA Drug Bulletin, 2,* 10–16.

Frank, D. A., Klass, P. E., Earls, F., & Eisenberg, L. (1996). Infants and young children in orphanages: One view from pediatrics and child psychiatry. *Pediatrics, 97,* 569–578.

Galler, J. R. & Ross, R. N. (1993). Malnutrition and Mental Development. In R. M. Suskind & L. Lewinter-Suskind (Eds.), *Textbook of Pediatric Nutrition* (pp. 173–179). New York: Raven Press, Ltd.

Garrett, L. (1997, November 3). Crumbled empire, shattered health. *Newsday,* p. A 4.

Gilliam, D. M., Kotch, L. E., Dudek, B. C., & Riley, E. P. (1988). Ethanol teratogenesis in mice selected for differences in alcohol sensitivity. *Alcohol, 5,* 513–519.

Glader, B. E. & Look, K. A. (1996). Hematologic disorders in children from Southeast Asia. *Pediatric Clinics of North America, 43,* 665–681.

Hostetter, M. K. & Johnson, D. (1996). Medical examination of the internationally adopted child. *Postgraduate Medicine, 99,* 70–82.

Hostetter, M. K., Iverson, S., Thomas, W., McKenzie, D., Dole, K., & Johnson, D. E. (1991). Medical Evaluation of Internationally Adopted Children. *New England Journal of Medicine, 325,* 479–485.

Immigration and Naturalization Service, U.S. Department of State (February 3, 1997). [Online]. Available at: http://travel.state.gov/orphan_numbers.html.

Institute of Medicine (IOM), Stratton, K. R., Howe, C. J., & Battaglia, F. C. (Eds.). (1996). *Fetal alcohol syndrome: Diagnosis, epidemiology, prevention and treatment.* Washington, D.C: National Academy Press.

Jenista, J. A. (1997). Rickets in the 1990s. *Adoption/Medical News, 3*(6), 1–4.

Johnson, D. E., Miller, L. C., Iverson, S., Thomas, W., Franchino, B., Dole, K., Kiernan, M. T., Georgieff, M. K., & Hostetter, M. K. (1992). The health of children adopted from Romania. *Journal of the American Medical Association, 268,* 3446–3451.

Johnson, K. (1993). Chinese orphanages: Saving China's abandoned girls. *The Australian Journal of Chinese Affairs, 30,* 61–87.

Johnson, K. (1996). The politics of the revival of infant abandonment in China, with special reference to Hunan. *Population and Development Review, 22,* 77–98.

Jones, K. L. & Smith, D. W. (1973). Recognition of the fetal alcohol syndrome in early infancy. *Lancet, 2*, 999–1001.

Kleinfeld, J. & Westcott, S. (Eds.). (1993). *Fantastic Antone succeeds!: Experiences in Educating Children with Fetal Alcohol Syndrome*. Fairbanks: University of Alaska Press.

Lewis, D. D. & Woods S. E. (1994). Fetal alcohol syndrome. *American Family Physician, 50*, 1025–1032.

Little, B. B., Snell, L. M., Rosenfeld, C. R., Gilstrap, L. C., & Gant, N. F. (1990). Failure to recognize fetal alcohol syndrome in newborn infants. *American Journal of Diseases of Childhood, 144*, 1142–1146

Mansnerus, L. (1998, October 26). Market puts price tags on the priceless. *The New York Times*, p. A16–17.

Mattson, S. N. & Riley, E. P. (1997). Neurobehavioral and neuroanatomical effects of heavy prenatal exposure to alcohol. In A. P. Streissguth & J. Kanter (Eds.), *The challenge of fetal alcohol syndrome: Overcoming secondary disabilities* (pp. 3–14). Washington: University of Washington Press.

McGuinness, T. M. (1998). Risk and protective factors in children adopted from the Former Soviet Union. *The Parent Network for Post-institutionalized Children, 18*, 1–5.

Miller, L. C., Kiernan, M. T., Mathers, M. I., & Klein-Gitelman, M. (1995). Developmental and nutritional status of internationally adopted children. *Archives of Pediatric and Adolescent Medicine, 149*, 40–44.

Mitchell, M. A. & Jenista, J. A. (1997). Health care of the internationally adopted child/Part 2: Chronic care and long-term medical issues. *Journal of Pediatric Health Care, 11*, 117–126.

Report of the working group on tuberculosis among foreign-born persons (1998). *Morbidity and Mortality Weekly Report, 47*, 1–29.

Richner, B., Lauren, D., Sunnarat, Y., Bee, D., & Nadal, D. (1997). Spread of HIV-1 to children in Cambodia. *Lancet, 349*, 1451–1452.

Russians drowning their trouble in booze. (1995, November 23). *Chicago Tribune*, pp. 1, 12.

Schenker, S., Becker, H. C., Randall, C. L., Phillips, D. K., Baskin, G. S., & Henderson, G. I. (1990). Fetal alcohol syndrome: Current status of pathogenesis. *Alcoholism: Clinical and experimental research, 14*, 635–647.

Scott, J. (1997, August 19). Orphan girls of China at home in New York. *The New York Times*, p. B4.

Shen, X., Rosen, J. F., Guo, D., & Wu, S. (1996) Childhood lead poisoning in China. *The Science of the Total Environment, 181*, 101–109.

Sokol, R. J. & Clarren, S. K. (1989). Guidelines for use of terminology describing the impact of prenatal alcohol on the offspring. *Alcoholism: Clinical and experimental research, 13*, 597–598.

Specter, M., (1997, May 17). AIDS's onrush sends Russia to the edge of an epidemic. *The New York Times*, p. A1.

Spohr, H-L., Williams, J., & Steinhausen, H-C. (1994). The fetal alcohol syndrome in adolescence. *Acta Paediatrica, 83*, 19–26.

Sreenathan, R. N., Padmanabhan, R., & Singh, S. (1982). Teratogenic effects of acetaldehyde in the rat. *Drug and Alcohol Dependency, 9*, 339–350.

Streissguth, A. P. (1997). *Fetal alcohol ayndrome: A guide for families and communities*. Baltimore, MD: Paul H. Brookes Publishing.

Streissguth, A. P. & Kanter, K. (1997). *The challenge of fetal alcohol syndrome: Overcoming secondary disabilities*. Seattle: University of Washington Press.

Streissguth, A. P., Barr, H., Kogan, H., Bookstein, F. (1997). Primary and secondary disabilities in fetal alcohol syndrome. In A. Streissguth & J. Kanter (Eds.), *The challenge of fetal alcohol syndrome: Overcoming secondary disabilities* (pp. 25–39). Seattle: University of Washington Press.

Streissguth, A. P., Barr, H., Kogan, H., Bookstein, F. (1996). *Understanding the occurrence of secondary disabilities in clients with fetal alcohol syndrome (FAS) and fetal alcohol effects (FAE)*. Final Report to the Centers for Disease Control and Prevention (CDC), August, 1996 (Tech. Rep. No. 96-06). Seattle: University of Washington.

Stromland, K. & Hellstrom, A. (1996). Fetal alcohol syndrome—An ophthalmological and socioeducational prospective study. *Pediatrics, 97*, 845-850.

Swayze, V. W., Johnson, V. P., Hanson, J. W., Piven, J., Sato, Y., Giedd, J. N., Mosnik, D., & Andreasen, N. C. (1997). Magnetic resonance imaging of brain anomalies in fetal alcohol syndrome. *Pediatrics, 99*, 232–240.

Taylor, C. L., Jones, K. L., Jones, M. C., & Kaplan, G. W. (1994). Incidence of renal anomalies in children prenatally exposed to ethanol. *Pediatrics, 94*, 209-212.

7

Attachment Issues for Adopted Infants

Mary Dozier & Kathleen E. Albus

Attachment Issues for Adopted Infants

A one-year-old infant is playing contentedly at home. Suddenly she stumbles and falls, knocking her head against a chair. She cries and immediately crawls to her mother, reaching and clambering to be held. The mother picks up the child, holds and comforts her, and in a moment, the child is content to resume play.

This scenario is familiar to many parents. Indeed, this sequence of events illustrates some of our most fundamental expectations about the relationship between a parent and her infant. A child experiences distress, retreats to her parent for reassurance, and when sufficiently comforted, returns to play. The child feels confident in her parent's availability, and the parent feels confident in her ability to soothe her child.

Ideally, infants come into the world equipped to engage in this sort of social interaction. For example, infants' appearance, with large forehead and cheeks, as well as their behaviors, including crying and orienting to the human face, has been found to elicit caregiving responses in adults [Emde 1980; Fullard & Reiling 1976]. However, if a cry is shrill or the infant fails to orient to the human face, the infant may not function competently in the role of early social partner. Such interactional difficulties are more likely to be seen among infants born preterm and among infants with prenatal drug-exposure [See Allessandri et al. 1995]. In these cases, caregivers require more of their own resources if they are to provide the nurturance and care the infant needs. If they can provide sensitive, nurturing care despite the child's limitations, the child may be able to develop into a competent social partner. Sensitive parenting from birth can promote the development of secure attachment, even in children experiencing such complications. For example, some children born with difficult temperaments [Mangelsdorf et al. 1990], with Down's Syndrome [Thompson et al. 1985], and with cerebral palsy [Marvin & Pianta 1996] have been shown to develop secure attachments to sensitive caregivers.

The effects of extended exposure to inadequate parenting and/ or disruptions in care may be more difficult to remediate, even for infants born without the limitations noted above [Bowlby 1969; Tizard 1977]. Over time, infants develop expectations of their caregivers that are manifested in characteristic behavioral strategies. When the infant's history with caregivers includes maltreatment or loss, the infant may adopt behavioral strategies to help him or her cope with the problematic caregiving history. For example, infants who have become accustomed to nonresponsive caregiving may learn to deal with distress by turning away from the caregiver. These infants may cope with distress by minimizing their own negative emotions and looking "tough." Others cope by being hypervigilant to their caregivers' cues. These behavioral strategies may, in the words of Alan Sroufe [1988], be "adaptive but not competent." That is, the strategies may help the child to cope with relationship failures but may also serve to alienate subsequent caregivers, thus perpetuating the child's experience of insensitive care. Even extremely sensitive caregivers, who usually respond appropriately to the expressed needs of infants, often respond to children with attachment issues in ways that perpetuate the children's negative views of the world [Stovall & Dozier, in press]. For example, the new caregiver of an infant who turns her back on the caregiver while in distress may interpret such behavior as a lack of need, and therefore may not respond, perpetuating the child's experience of nonresponsive care.

For many adopted infants, such as those placed early in life and without significant prior trauma, the issues addressed in this chapter will be less relevant. However, for infants who are adopted at older ages, particularly for those with prenatal substance exposure, the issues addressed here are critical. We suggest that if the adoptive parent is to develop smooth, loving, and nurturing transactions with the infant, he or she may need to get beyond some infant behavioral strategies. For example, for infants who have learned to deny emotional needs as a means of coping with nonresponsive caregiving, adoptive parents need to understand and develop new ways of responding to help children develop new capacities. Similarly, for infants who have difficulty physiologically regulating subsequent to prenatal substance exposure, adoptive parents need to develop new ways of interacting with them in order to help them learn self-regulatory skills.

In this chapter, we develop our argument that many babies who are placed into adoptive care after about the age of one year will require unusually sensitive, indeed even "therapeutic" caregivers to help them acquire new expectations and behavioral strategies. We begin with an overview of attachment theory. A clear understanding of the significance of infant-parent attachment is key to the issues raised here. We then move to discuss the early caregiving contexts commonly experienced by babies who are adopted, with a particular focus on the infant-caregiver relationship, the significance of disruptions in caregiving, and the significance of fetal drug exposure. We consider these issues from the perspective of both the child and his or her caregiver. Finally, we present details regarding our attachment-based intervention for adoptive parents and our expectations regarding its effectiveness.

Fundamentals of Attachment Theory

Key to attachment theory is the assumption that the human infant's earliest relationship, that with the primary caregiver, serves as a sort of blueprint for subsequent relationships [Bowlby 1969]. Through the relationship with the caregiver, the infant develops an understanding of the world and of him or herself, and forms expectations regarding others' availability. If caregivers have been largely responsive to the infant's distress, the infant develops a sense of security—a sense that he or she can depend on the caregiver to be there when needed. Consider, for example, the child in the first vignette, whose mother was able to effectively comfort her. If this child has repeated experiences in which her parent responds with sensitivity and nurturance when she is hurt, frightened, or otherwise in need, she will likely develop an expectation of the caregiver as a dependable, reliable source of comfort and will experience a sense of confidence in her parent's availability. Alternatively, if caregivers have not been sensitive to the infant's needs, the infant develops a sense of insecurity—a sense that she cannot depend on caregivers to be there when she is in distress.

Infant Attachment

John Bowlby [1969; 1973] proposed that infant-caregiver attachment has an evolutionary basis in protecting the young of the species from predators and other dangers. Attachment behaviors, such as proximity seeking during distress, are believed to have evolved to increase the likelihood of the infant's survival. That is, such behaviors keep the infant in proximity to the caregiver at times when proximity promotes survival. Thus, attachment behaviors are most readily observed when infants are tired, hungry, frightened, or hurt—in other words, when children feel distressed.

A parent's responses during infant distress are believed to influence the infant's sense of parental availability and dependability, subsequently affecting his or her behavior and playing a critical role in the child's development [Bowlby 1969; 1973]. Based on this theory, Ainsworth and colleagues [1978] developed the Strange Situation, a laboratory assessment associated with infants' attachment to the primary caregiver within the home. As a result of formative research using the Strange Situation, three infant attachment classifications have been defined: the secure infant, who tends to approach and seek comfort from his or her parents readily and successfully when distressed; the avoidant infant, who turns away from or ignores his or her parents when distressed; and the resistant infant, who exhibits overly clingy and needy behavior, changing to resistance or anger when a parent approaches.

In Ainsworth's research, naturalistic observations revealed that secure infants had mothers who were generally sensitive to their needs. Thus, these babies had developed expectations of available caregiving as the result of repeated experiences in which they found they could count on their caregivers. In contrast, insecure infants, both avoidant and resistant types, were found to demonstrate less confidence in the mother's availability. The mothers of avoidant infants were likely to try to distract their distressed, crying infants or to tell them that they were not really hurt—essentially rejecting their avoidant infants' needs. Mothers of resistant infants tended to be inconsistent in their availability. In light of their caregivers' responses, the infants' behaviors are understandable: the avoidant infant's turning away is a strategy for coping with distress in the presence of a rejecting caregiver, and the resistant infant's hypervigilance and exaggerated signals of distress comprise a strategy for maximizing the likelihood of response from an inconsistently available caregiver [Ainsworth et al. 1978; Cassidy 1994].

During the last decade, an additional insecure attachment classification, the disorganized infant, has been defined by Main and Solomon [1990]. Disorganized infants show an apparent disorganization or disorientation when distressed and in their caregivers' presence. These infants, who appear to face the unsolvable dilemma of fear of the caregiver to whom they look for reassurance, are seen in disproportionate numbers in samples of maltreated children and among children whose caregivers have experienced an unresolved loss or trauma [van IJzendoorn 1995]. The mechanism associated with disorganized infant behavior is thought to be the caregiver's own frightened or frightening behavior, which leaves the infant "frightened without solution" [Main & Hesse 1990].

The notion that infants' attachment relationships have "special" importance for later functioning has been a source of controversy among developmental psychologists [see Fox et al. 1991; Lamb 1987]. For example, Fox and associates suggest that attachment is a measure of temperament rather than a measure of relationship security. Lamb raises concerns about the predictive validity of infant Strange Situation classifications in relation to later functioning, citing lack of clear evidence for the significance of attachment with regard to future behavioral and emotional functioning. Perhaps most compelling with regard to the significance of attachment in terms of later development are findings from the Minnesota Longitudinal Project, demonstrating that children classified as secure in infancy function more competently than children classified in infancy as avoidant, resistant, or disorganized [Carlson 1998; Elicker et al. 1992; Erickson et al. 1985; Sroufe 1983]. According to psychiatric interviews in these studies, secure infants were rated as more independent than others by their preschool teachers [Erickson et al. 1985], more socially accepted by peers in their elementary school years [Elicker et al. 1992], and better adjusted psychologically in late adolescence. [Carlson 1998]. Children who showed the most pathology were those classified as disorganized/disoriented in infancy, the group of infants that appeared to be at particularly high risk [Carlson 1998; Lyons-Ruth 1996].

Adult States of Mind with Regard to Attachment

How parents think about their own childhood attachment experiences, or their "state of mind with regard to attachment," appears to affect what they provide for their children in terms of a safe haven in times of distress. The infant categories of secure, avoidant, resistant, and disorganized are paralleled by adult state of mind categories of autonomous, dismissing, preoccupied, and unresolved [Main & Goldwyn in press]. Adult state of mind is assessed via the Adult Attachment Interview [George et al. 1985], a semistructured interview asking adults to conceptualize their early relationships with their parents.

Adults are referred to as autonomous when they speak openly and nondefensively about early attachment experiences and demonstrate clear valuing of attachment [Main & Goldwyn in press]. Autonomous adults are expected to be generally available and sensitive to their infants' attachment needs. In contrast, dismissing adults tend to demonstrate a pushing away of attachment-related concerns, as demonstrated by either a defensive idealization of childhood attachment figures, lack of memory for childhood experiences, or active derogation of attachment or attachment figures. Dismissing adults are expected to minimize their infants' attachment needs as well and, thus, to behave in ways that are experienced by the infant as rejecting. Preoccupied adults demonstrate an ongoing emotional involvement in childhood attachment experiences, either through lapses into angry speech, or passive, rambling and incoherent discourse regarding attachment figures. Preoccupied caregivers are expected to demonstrate inconsistent availability toward their infants [See Main & Goldwyn for a review]. Finally, adults may be referred to as unresolved in relation to a loss or abuse [Main & Goldwyn, in press]. Unresolved individuals demonstrate lapses in the monitoring of reasoning or discourse around loss or abuse, and may, for example, speak about a loss in ways indicating a disbelief that the loss has actually occurred or a sense of having caused the loss, such as in the case of a loved one's death. They may also deny the occurrence, frequency, or severity of abuse on the part of a caregiver at one time, while acknowledging it at another time.

Because there is a strong concordance between maternal state of mind and infant attachment [See van Ijzendoorn 1995], each of those adult "states of mind" regarding attachment affects the infant's attachment-related behavior. Even when assessed before her child is born, the mother's state of mind is predictive of her infant's attachment classification [See Fonagy et al. 1991; Ward & Carlson 1995], providing evidence for the intergenerational transmission of attachment tendencies.

Effects of Early Privation and Relationship Disruption on Children

Our discussion thus far has focused primarily on intact dyads. Findings regarding intact dyads may not inform us directly about children who experience early inadequate care before entering adoptive or foster care or those who experience disruptions in relationships with caregivers. How are these children affected by early inadequate care and/or disruptions in caregiving? How are their caregivers affected by the children's "different" behaviors? We consider these questions in this section.

Extreme conditions of privation. Children experiencing severe privation have been studied in a number of institutional environments. Spitz [1946; 1950] recorded his early observations of institutionalized infants. In one group, infants were raised primarily by their incarcerated mothers. In the second group, infants were raised in a clean and safe environment where they received good medical care, but daily caregiving was provided by a series of nurses, a system that allowed infants little opportunity for attachment to a caregiver. Spitz noted that despite the adequate physical care received by the second group of infants, these children later demonstrated deficits in intellectual and emotional functioning and physical health, whereas the infants raised by their mothers developed relatively normally. Spitz's conclusion was that the absence of maternal caregiving was the determining factor in differentiating these two groups of institutionalized infants. Bowlby's earliest research with delinquent adolescents [1944] also highlighted the significance of loss of attachment figures in the earliest years.

Tizard's [1977] findings regarding the effects of privation during infancy on children over the age of two "softened" this early pessimistic position. She found that, although many late adopted children had emotional and behavioral problems, more than half of them did not. These findings suggested that at least apparent recovery was possible under some conditions. More recently, children who have experienced severe privation in Romanian orphanages have been studied as they have been adopted in the United States [Cermak & Groza 1998; Groza & Ileana 1996; Groza et al. 1998], England [Rutter 1999] and Canada [Ames et al. 1992; Chisholm & Ames 1995; Chisholm et al. 1995; Goldberg 1998]. Groza and colleagues [Groza et al. 1998; Groza & Ileana 1996] provide an excellent review of the developmental processes potentially affected by experiences of institutionalization. Similar to Tizard's resilient group, the authors describe cases in which Eastern European adoptees have exhibited healthy later development (termed "Resilient Rascals"), and address factors associated with later developmental difficulties. Among the most problematic conditions associated with poor long-term functioning are periods of institutionalization of seven months and longer. Work by Cermak and Groza [1998] has pointed to difficulties with self-regulation among previously institutionalized children, including oversensitivity and undersensitivity to environmental stimuli.

Work by Rutter and his colleagues [1999] has suggested that subsequent social development is affected even when children are adopted at quite early ages. Effects of longer periods of privation are found related to more serious cognitive and social deficits. Ames and associates [1992] have found that children who experienced eight or more months in Romanian orphanages often showed anomalous behaviors with strangers, most notably indiscriminate friendliness, long after adoption. Further, greater physiological reactivity is seen years after adoption [Gunnar 1999]. These findings suggest that these children remain more emotionally and physiologically vulnerable to stress than other children long after the privation experience. Taken together, these results suggest that extreme privation can have long-term effects on physiological, psychological, and interpersonal functioning.

Abuse and neglect. Abuse and neglect usually represent less noxious experiences than extreme privation. The abused or neglected child usually has the opportunity to interact with others, even if the caregiving is nonoptimal. The gross insensitivity to infants' emotional and psychological needs that characterizes abusive and neglectful parenting, nonetheless, can have serious consequences for children's subsequent development. Difficulties for maltreated infants have been noted across a range of outcomes. Preschool children who have been abused are less likely than other children to respond empathetically to the distress of their peers and are more likely to respond aggressively [Main & George 1985]. Not surprisingly, such children are at increased risk for later difficulties with peers, including aggression and acting-out behavior [See Cicchetti et al. 1992; Dodge et al. 1994; George & Main 1979]. Problems have also been noted in affect-regulation, self-esteem, competence and motivation [See Aber & Allen 1987; Schneider-Rosen & Cicchetti 1984; Shields et al. 1994]. Infants who have been maltreated are much more likely than other children to show disorganized/disoriented attachments to maltreating caregivers [van IJzendoorn 1995]. The percentage of abused children showing disorganized attachments has hovered around 50% in most studies. As mentioned previously, these children are in the untenable position of needing to seek protection from caregivers who are the source of their fear. They appear to show a collapse in their attachment strategy when they are in need of their caregivers, being unable to respond in an organized fashion. These infants are at increased risk for becoming controlling of their caregivers over time [Main & Cassidy 1988]. For example, as toddlers, they may exhibit behaviors usually seen in parents rather than children, either "punishing" the parent (e.g., making embarrassing comments about parental behavior) or engaging in caregiving behavior (e.g., demonstrating parent-like concern for the caregiver's wellbeing).

Disruption in caregiving. The effects of disruption in caregiving have been examined somewhat less than abuse and neglect but appear no less important. These disruptions appear particularly significant for older infants as opposed to infants placed in care early in life. Indeed, infants placed early in adoptive homes do not appear to evidence attachment-related difficulties. Singer and colleagues [1985] found no relationship between timing of placement and infant-caregiver attachment in a sample of infants placed between 3 days and 10 months of age (mean placement age approximately 2 months).

In contrast to infants placed early, Yarrow and Goodwin [1973] found that infants placed into foster care at older than seven months of age showed problematic behavioral reactions. In our work, we have extended the time frame upward somewhat. We find that children placed into foster care prior to 12 months of age often form secure attachments readily to foster mothers who have autonomous states of mind [Stovall & Dozier in press]. Children placed later than about 12 months do not usually form secure attachments over an extended period of time, even when their foster mothers have autonomous states of mind. We also found that autonomous foster mothers believe that they have less influence on babies' development when babies are placed in their care after about 12 months of age than when babies are placed at earlier ages [Bates & Dozier 1998]. Thus, our own work suggests that infants' regulatory systems become somewhat less forgiving after the first year of life.

Attachment and Fetal Drug Exposure

Prenatal exposure to cocaine may result in infant withdrawal symptoms such as irritability, unpredictable and irregular sleep patterns, decreased alertness and sociability, and increased crying compared to control infants [See Allessandri et al. 1995; Soby 1994]. For some infants, prenatal drug exposure may be associated with hypersensitivity and difficult temperament in infancy. The long-term effects of prenatal exposure to many narcotics, however, do not seem to be as severe as had once been imagined [Mayes & Bornstein 1995; Peterson et al. 1995]. Studies indicate that when important confounding variables are controlled, infants who were exposed to drugs prenatally do not show developmental delays [Mayes & Bornstein 1995]. Nonetheless, a heightened risk for insecure attachment is found among infants prenatally exposed to drugs [Rodning et al. 1991], at least partly because the infants may not frequently engage in interactions that are rewarding to caregivers in early infancy.

Early problems in interactions, combined with biases regarding the long-term effects of prenatal substance exposure, may combine to create long-term problems between parent and child. Consider, for example, the case of a child known to have been exposed prenatally to cocaine. He exhibited early signs of irritability and became readily overstimulated. The parents, finding it difficult to interact with him, were convinced that he would benefit from less contact with them and decreased their interactions. Over time, however, the baby's hypersensitive neurological system had become better regulated, making increased stimulation not only possible, but also important for optimal development. The ongoing lack of stimulation of this child led him to withdraw socially, and he subsequently experienced delays in cognitive development. The parents' expectations that the child would show long-term effects of the prenatal substance exposure, combined with their early experiences in attempting to interact with him, led to a pattern of behavior that confirmed their expectations.

A more optimal scenario is the case of the parent who, provided with adequate knowledge of the development of drug-exposed infants, learns to gear interactions to the capacities of the child, gradually promoting social interaction. For example, early in the child's life, when the child is experiencing the greatest difficulty with self-regulation, the parent may minimize stimulation, interacting primarily when the infant appears alert and mimicking any of the child's social bids in an effort to reinforce those interactions. With such highly attuned caregiving, substance-exposed infants may gradually develop increased capacity for social interaction and stimulation.

The Special Case of Adopted Children

Consider the following vignette: David's adoptive parents have been distressed by his apparent indifference toward them. When he falls down, he often does not look to them. Similarly, in other situations where their biological children have shown distress, they notice that David does not. He simply acts as if nothing is wrong and turns away if they attempt to comfort him. David is 24 months old and was adopted four months earlier. Prior to his adoption, between the ages of 12 and 20 months, he was cared for by two different foster families. He was originally placed in foster care because of his biological mother's severe substance-abuse problem.

For a variety of reasons, infants and young children who become eligible for adoption have often experienced more than their share of problematic caregiving. Infants removed from the custody of their birth parents and ultimately raised by adoptive parents commonly have experienced abuse, neglect and parental unavailability. Further, a significant number of these infants have experienced prenatal exposure to drugs. As noted above, these children sometimes develop behaviors that serve to alienate their caregivers, thus perpetuating expectations that others will not be emotionally available. To this point, we have focused primarily on the effects of problematic early caregiving and fetal drug exposure from the perspective of the infant. Also important are the effects that infants' subsequent difficulties may have on the adoptive caregiver. Foster and adoptive parents often express bewilderment and distress over the behavior of their new children. Like the mother in the vignette regarding David, some wonder why their newly adopted children seem indifferent to nurturance. Others are upset by their adopted children's inability to settle effectively when distressed despite parental reassurance. Still others find it disconcerting that their children seem to treat strangers as warmly as they treat their parents.

The concerns of these parents are understandable. As we noted at the outset of this chapter, parents have certain expectations regarding interactions with their children, particularly with their infants. Stern [1977] has suggested that the interactions of the parent and child can be thought of as a dance, with the dance steps worked out between the two partners. In intact dyads, reciprocity usually develops smoothly, with the partners accommodating their own dance steps to those of their partners. For example, the child expresses a need in a way that he or she has learned can be responded to by the parent; the parent responds in a way that he or she has learned is comforting to the infant; and both partners are rewarded by the predictability and the reciprocity. Children who are placed in foster or adoptive care, however, may have learned dance steps that are ill-suited to their new caregivers. Rather than acclimate to the new caregivers, they may rigidly repeat the old dance steps. One might expect foster or adoptive parents to quickly modify the child's dance steps. However, we have found that even the most sensitive mothers tend to respond reciprocally to children's interactive behaviors [Stovall & Dozier in press]. Thus, a mother will tend to respond to a child who acts avoidant as if he does not need her. She will tend to respond to resistant behavior as if the child is being petulant. As a result, the child "drives" the interaction, or to return to the dance metaphor, seems to take the lead in the dance.

In cases like these, responding in kind to children's insecure attachment behaviors will likely only perpetuate such coping strategies on the part of the child. The challenge to new adoptive parents is, therefore, to begin to reinterpret their children's attachment cues, recognize the underlying distress, and respond accordingly. It is this skill that our intervention attempts to teach and reinforce.

An Attachment-Based Intervention for Foster and Adoptive Parents

A number of clinicians have begun to apply the tenets of attachment theory to interventions with foster and adoptive children [Fahlberg 1991; Hughes 1997; Johnson & Fine 1991; Keck & Kupecky 1995]. These clinicians stress the impediments involved in the development of a warm, trusting relationship between parent and child and emphasize the need for supportive interventions. For example, Fahlberg [1991] suggests providing the older child with preparation for a transition in care—a step increasingly taken by state agencies.

We have developed a brief intervention targeted to help new foster and adoptive parents understand, reinterpret, and respond differently to their infant's alienating attachment behaviors [Dozier & Albus 1998]. This intervention is expected to be particularly relevant to infants who have experienced such risk factors as late placement in foster care with adoptive families, exposure to trauma, and prenatal exposure to drugs. Through the use of videotaped vignettes and individualized discussion of their particular infant, parents are encouraged to see that all children need reassurance and nurturance when frightened, hurt, or otherwise distressed—whether they show their need directly or not. The intervention consists of two sessions conducted individually in parents' homes, homework assignments, and booster sessions every six months. The effectiveness of our intervention is currently being assessed in a randomized clinical trial. We present here an overview of the intervention, delineating its purpose and expected outcomes.

Session One

The first session begins with a brief overview of the significance of attachment. The trainer introduces the session by stressing that all babies need love and nurturance, but many adopted children and children in foster care have found that they cannot trust in the availability of others. Parents are asked to think about the experience of infants whose parents do not respond to their needs and subsequently to consider what these children learn about the world—namely, that their needs will not be met. The trainer then links children's expectations of unresponsive caregiving to types of insecure attachment behaviors and introduces the behavior seen in avoidant or resistant children. Parents are then asked about their own experiences with babies who seem to push them away or who seem difficult to settle. This technique begins to help parents recognize their own children's attachment behaviors.

The process of attachment is then described in more detail. Trainer and parents discuss the variety of ways that babies may let parents know they are needed, such as by reaching, smiling, crying, or moving toward them. At this point, a videotape of a child who has been separated from his mother for several minutes is presented. The child in this video exhibits clear signals upon reunion—reaching for mother, sinking into her shoulder when picked up, and demonstrating obvious relief of distress due to contact with the mother. These secure attachment behaviors are discussed as "clear" signals as to the baby's needs. The trainer then asks parents to describe what their reactions would be to such behaviors, attempting to make the connection between children demonstrating their needs clearly and parents having little difficulty interpreting such signals and responding appropriately. The trainer then links such responsiveness to what the baby learns from parent-child interactions—namely, that his or her needs will be met.

The trainer moves on to again discuss babies who have experienced problematic parenting and disruptions in their caregiving relationships, suggesting that a child's alienating behaviors might make sense if considered as strategies for dealing with a problematic caregiving history. Avoidance and resistance are introduced more explicitly through the use of additional videotaped vignettes of children who are being reunited with parents after a separation. The Strange Situation vignette shows a baby who exhibits obvious distress when the caregiver is gone from the room, but clearly ignores her upon her return. The trainer asks the parents how they would feel if their child were to respond in this way, attempting to elicit the parents' natural and normal responses—feelings of rejection or ineffectiveness and a response in kind to the baby of leaving him or her alone. The trainer then discusses with parents that, in fact, the child does need his parents, but the child has developed ways of appearing tough, to cope with past experiences of unavailable caregiving.

A similar procedure is followed in discussing resistant behavior. In the videotape presented, the child exhibits extreme difficulty settling when his mother returns, angrily pushing her away, yet continuing to cry. The parents are again asked how they would feel in such a situation, attempting to elicit parents' natural responses to children's irritability—in this case, feelings of helplessness, ineffectiveness, and annoyance at this "difficult" child. The trainer again stresses that the child's angry, fussy behavior comes neither from a difficult temperament nor ineffectiveness on the part of the caregivers, but rather from the child's insecurity with regard to parents' availability.

These principles are then applied to the parents' individual circumstances. For example, parents whose children exhibit avoidant, resistant, or secure behaviors have the opportunity to talk about their particular experiences. The trainer focuses first on how the children's behaviors make the parents feel, then how the parents respond, and then on potential reinterpretations of the infants' behaviors. Thus, for avoidant or resistant children, the parents are asked to reinterpret the children's coldness or anger as a strategy for dealing with histories of problematic caregiving. From here, parents and trainer consider new ways in which the parents may respond to children, thereby attempting to change the insecure patterns of behavior. In a sense, parents are being asked to respond therapeutically instead of reacting to their children's apparent cues. Parents, for example, may be encouraged to gently respond to avoidant children who have been hurt, despite their apparent lack of interest in the parents' attention. The session closes with additional video vignettes of secure, avoidant, and resistant infants. For further practice, parents are asked to interpret these infants' behaviors and to determine "new" appropriate responses with less guidance from the trainer.

Homework

Between Sessions One and Two, parents are asked to complete a brief homework assignment, noting instances in which their children are hurt. They are asked to pay particular attention to what the children do, as well as their own interpretation of and response to the behavior. In addition, they are asked to attempt to reinterpret the behavior of avoidant and resistant infants and to practice the new responses learned in Session One. Finally, they are asked to note any difficulties they experience in responding differently as well as any changes in their children's reactions.

Homework is expected to be useful in helping parents to recognize avoidant and resistant behaviors in their own children. For example, in the first session, one mother in our sample denied ever witnessing avoidance or resistance in her child. However, upon going over her homework during the next session, she reported, with some surprise, that she had been able to recognize avoidance behavior in her child once she had become sensitized to it. She was then better able to participate in the training by bringing up specific examples of her own child's behavior when distressed.

Session Two

The second session is primarily a review of Session One, with greater attention to parents' particular situations and to ways of maintaining new behaviors and noticing changes. Thus, the majority of the session focuses on the homework assignments and on the specific incidents recounted there. In addition, parents view a videotape of their own Strange Situation procedures, conducted prior to the first training session. This aspect of the training is a means of further personalizing the training experience for parents.

After a brief summary of the basic points covered in Session One, the trainer asks parents to refer to their homework and discuss how their children behaved when hurt, how parents interpreted the behavior, and how parents responded. Attention is directed to the parents' own experiences, although attachment behaviors other than those mentioned by the parents are reviewed as well. Once again, parents are asked to discuss their feelings when faced with secure, avoidant, and resistant behaviors. In this way, parents are allowed the opportunity to acknowledge the natural frustrations, insecurities, and doubts they feel about their children's behavior.

At this point in the session, the trainer reviews the personal Strange Situation procedure videotape and helps parents describe and interpret their children's behaviors and recount the thoughts and feelings they have as they view their children's reactions to their return. For example, the mother who initially could not recognize avoidant behavior in her child expressed some surprise when, in her own Strange Situation videotape, her child did not approach her upon reunion but instead turned away. Seeing her child's response on video enabled this mother to note and reinterpret her child's avoidance and to discuss potential ways of responding to it.

Special attention is given, at this point, to the barriers the parents feel in responding differently to their children. Some parents may state that they are frustrated by the lack of change seen in their children despite the parents' efforts. Others may express anger at their children's behavior or difficulty recognizing the times when children are upset. Still others may express fears that by responding to their children, they will "spoil" them. The trainer deals with the parents' frustrations and fears in an individualized manner, empathizing with their concerns but focusing on the ultimate goal of reinterpreting children's behavior and responding differently. The trainer also discusses ways that parents may begin to notice changes in their children. For example, parents may be helped to note and reinforce small changes, such as the child's looking at the parent more frequently or tolerating more parental nurturance. The trainer also acknowledges that changes in a child's avoidant or resistant behavior will likely happen slowly.

Session Two ends with the presentation of additional video-taped vignettes presenting avoidant and resistant dyads, to allow parents an additional opportunity to recognize, interpret, and respond to insecure attachment behaviors. In closing, the trainer helps the parents identify behavioral techniques they might use to remember and "stick with" their emerging skills. Parents are encouraged to keep journals, offer themselves rewards for practicing their new behaviors, and take time to reflect on their children's new behaviors.

Expectations Regarding Effectiveness

We expect this training program to be differentially effective depending upon characteristics of each participant. Of particular interest to us are parents' own states of mind with regard to attachment, and we not only expect differential treatment outcomes, but differential processes as well. Korfmacher and colleagues [1997] found that parents with autonomous states of mind were able to engage in more proactive problem solving in their intervention than other parents. Similarly, in research with adults with serious psychopathological disorders, Dozier [1990] found that persons with autonomous states of mind were more collaborative in treatment. In both of these studies [Dozier 1990; Korfmacher et al. 1997], those parents with dismissing states of mind were more rejecting of interventions. In our intervention, we expect that foster and adoptive parents with autonomous states of mind will be more collaborative with the trainer and will work harder to understand the concepts presented. Foster and adoptive parents with dismissing states of mind are expected to be less accepting of the concepts and less apt to work diligently to apply the principles in their work with their children.

With regard to outcomes, we expect that autonomous parents will need very little to achieve satisfactory relationships with their children. Because such parents have the internal resources that allow them to be generally sensitive to their babies' distress, they are likely to need help only in modifying the nature of the transactions with their children. Their needs are not at the more rudimentary level, requiring a reworking of the way they approach attachment or an enhanced sensitivity, but are related to reinterpreting and responding differently to their children's alienating behaviors. On the other hand, parents with nonautonomous states of mind—who find it difficult to respond to babies' distress even when babies show their needs directly—are most likely to require a more extensive and intensive intervention. Rather than focusing primarily on the child's behaviors and assuming that parents can modify their reactions accordingly, interventions with nonautonomous parents require a focus on parents' own attachment-related experiences and attitudes toward attachment. Parental state of mind with regard to attachment is assumed to be the limiting factor in these parents' ability to respond sensitively to their child's needs, and the intervention targets this parental dynamic. For example, a mother classified as dismissing might be helped to look at how her own attachment experiences may have led her to deal with attachment issues by minimizing them, and therapy may focus on how her interactions with her children could be affected by her own state of mind. This type of more intensive, therapeutic intervention is beyond the scope of the intervention described here and is not being tested in the current population.

Our experience with parents thus far is consistent with these expectations for differential use of treatment and differential effectiveness. For example, one foster mother with an autonomous state of mind in our sample responded to the treatment enthusiastically. Her child, placed with her when he was 14 months old, had been exposed to cocaine and alcohol prenatally and had experienced shifts in care between a foster home and the home of his birth mother during his first year of life. During the first session, this foster mother excitedly began to reinterpret the behaviors of her child that she had previously found puzzling. She later reported that she found it easy to respond in more nurturing ways to her child, and that the child had become cuddly and affectionate as a result. In contrast, another foster mother in our sample, who demonstrated a dismissing state of mind, remained convinced throughout the intervention that responding to her baby's cries would result in the child crying more and more. Observation of the mother and child suggested that the intervention had done little to alter the mother's behavior toward the child.

Research from our laboratory has also suggested that a child's age at placement in foster care has a significant effect on the transactions that occur between child and parent. Children placed after about a year of age have more difficulty trusting in the availability of their new caregivers [Stovall & Dozier in press]. Their parents are likely to behave in ways that serve to confirm these children's negative worldviews [Stovall & Dozier in press]. Parents with autonomous states of mind appear to develop a diminished sense of their importance when their children are older than one year of age when placed with them [Bates & Dozier 1998], perhaps leading to a sense of helplessness and frustration. Therefore, we think that we see a self-perpetuating cycle, whereby late-placed babies act in ways that serve to alienate caregivers, and parents develop a sense that what they do does not matter.

Directions for the Future

Given the significance of the difficulties associated with problematic early caregiving, we are quick to acknowledge that the intervention we have described is a sort of "Band-Aid" for a severe wound. Ultimately, improved outcomes for at-risk infants will likely stem from policy changes that minimize disruptions in caregiving and focus on early placement with permanent caregivers. All too often, a child is placed in a succession of nonpermanent homes until parental rights are eventually terminated, so that when the child reaches his or her adoptive parents, it is after a long series of traumatic disruptions.

Permanency planning, which focuses on minimizing caregiving disruptions and placing children in permanent care as early as possible, has increasingly become the accepted practice in social services. The Adoption and Safe Families Act of 1997 [PL 105-89] requires that whatever the child's ultimate placement (return home, adoption, or kinship care), permanency be achieved as early as possible. The Act pushes social service agencies to expedite reunification efforts and, when such efforts are unsuccessful, to work toward immediate placement with adoptive families. The ultimate goal of the permanency planning movement is to limit the disruptions in caregiving described in this chapter.

Conclusions

When infants are first placed in adoptive homes, the situations are often not as had been imagined by the adoptive parents. The children to whom the parents have made enduring commitments may seem indifferent or even angry with them. These babies have had to find ways to cope with loss and perhaps with inadequate caregiving—a situation further complicated for children exposed prenatally to substances. The strategies that these children develop allow them to cope with prenatal and postnatal insults, but are likely problematic in the context of their new relationships with their adoptive parents. For, although leaving them "safer" from subsequent harm, the strategies often interfere with their discovery that others can indeed be there for them. Adoptive parents may find that the children's behaviors alienate them, leaving them feeling angry or detached rather than loving. We have proposed an intervention aimed at helping adoptive parents reinterpret children's alienating behaviors. We suggest that, with support, adoptive parents can help their children modify their expectations of the world. In addition, we suggest that permanency-planning efforts are crucial, with a focus upon achieving stability as early and quickly as possible.

Notes

1.   Preparation of this chapter was supported by National Institute of Mental Health grant MH52135 to the first author. We thank Wanda Spotts, Chase Stovall, and Brady Bates for their help on the project. Also, our appreciation to Doris Loftin, Beverly Williams, Gerri Robinson, and Yvonne Gilchrist of Baltimore City Department of

Social Services; and to Kathy Goldsmith, Laura Miles, and Darlene Lantz of Delaware Department of Services for Children, Youth, and Their Families; and to case workers, foster families, birth families, and children at both agencies.

References

Aber, J. L. & Allen, J. P. (1987). Effects of maltreatment on young children's socioemotional development: An attachment theory perspective. *Developmental Psychology, 23*(3), 406–414.

Ainsworth, M. D. S., Blehar, M. C., Waters, E., & Wall, S. (1978). *Patterns of attachment: A psychological study of the Strange Situation.* Hillsdale, NJ: Erlbaum.

Allessandri, S. M., Sullivan, M. W., Bendersky, M., & Lewis, M. (1995). Temperament in cocaine-exposed infants. In M. Lewis & M. Bendersky (Eds.). *Mothers, babies, and cocaine: The role of toxins in development* (pp. 273–286). Hillsdale, NJ: Erlbaum.

Ames, E. W., Carter, M. C., Chisholm, K., Fisher, L., Gilman, L. C., Mainemer, H., McMullan, S. J., & Savoie, L. A. (1992). *Development of Romanian orphanage children adopted to Canada.* Symposium presented at the Annual Convention of the Canadian Psychology Association, Quebec City.

Bates, B. C. & Dozier, M. (1998). *Foster parents' working models of their infants.* Unpublished manuscript.

Bowlby, J. (1944). Forty-four juvenile thieves: Their characters and home-life. *International Journal of Psycho-Analysis, 25,* 19–53 and 107–128.

Bowlby, J. (1969). *Attachment and loss: Attachment.* New York: Basic Books.

Bowlby, J. (1973). *Attachment and loss: Separation.* New York: Basic Books.

Carlson, E. A. (1998). A prospective longitudinal study of disorganized/disoriented attachment. *Child Development, 69,* 1107–1128

Cassidy, J. (1994). Emotion regulation: Influences of attachment relationships. In N. A. Fox (Ed.), *The development of emotion regulation: Biological and behavioral considerations. Monographs of the Society for Research in Child Development, 59,* (2–3, Serial No. 240).

Cermak, S. & Groza, V. (1998). Sensory processing problems in post-institutionalized children: Implications for social work. *Child and Adolescent Social Work Journal, 15*(1), 5–37.

Chasnoff, I.J., Burns, W.J., Schnoll, S.H., & Burns, K.A. (1985). Cocaine use in pregnancy. *The New England Journal of Medicine, 313*(11), 666–669.

Chisholm, K., Carter, M. C., Ames, E. W., & Morison, S. J. (1995). Attachment, security and indiscriminantly friendly behavior in children adopted from Romanian orphanages. *Development & Psychopathology, 7*, 283-294.

Cicchetti, D., Lynch, M., Shonk, S., & Manly, J. T. (1992). An organizational perspective on peer relations in maltreated children. In R. D. Parke & G. W. Ladd (Eds.). *Family-peer relationships: Modes of linkage.* Hillsdale, NJ: Erlbaum.

Dodge, K. A., Pettit, G. S., & Bates, J. E. (1994). Effects of physical maltreatment on the development of peer relations. *Development and Psychopathology, 6*, 43–55.

Dozier, M. (1990). Attachment organization and treatment use for adults with serious psychopathological disorders. *Development and Psychopathology, 2*, 47–60.

Dozier, M. & Albus, K. E. (1998). *Training parents to understand the attachment strategies of infants who have experienced relationship disruption: A manual for training foster, biological, and adoptive parents.* Unpublished manuscript, University of Delaware, Newark, DE.

Elicker, J., Englund, M., & Sroufe, L. A. (1992). Predicting peer competence and peer relationships in childhood from early parent-child relationships. In R. D. Parke & G. W. Ladd (Eds.), *Family-peer relationships* (pp. 77–106). Hillsdale, NJ: Erlbaum.

Emde, R. N. (1980). Emotional availability: A reciprocal reward system for infants and parents with implications for prevention of psychosocial disorders. In P. M. Taylor (Ed.), *Parent-infant relationships* (pp. 87–115). Orlando, Florida: Grune and Stratton.

Erickson, M. F., Sroufe, L. A., & Egeland, B. (1985). The relationship between quality of attachment and behavior problems in preschool in a high-risk sample. In I. Bretherton & E. Waters (Eds.), *Growing points of attachment theory and research. Monographs of the Society for Research in Child Development, 50*, (1–2, Serial no. 209), 147–166.

Fahlberg, V. (1991). A developmental approach to separation/loss. In E. D. Hibbs (Ed.), *Adoption: International perspectives* (pp.27–34). Madison, WI: International Universities Press.

Fonagy, P., Steele, H., & Steele, M. (1991). Maternal representations of attachment during pregnancy predict the organization of infant-mother attachment at one year of age. *Child Development, 62,* 891–905.

Fox, N. A., Kimmerly, N. L., & Schafer, W. D. (1991). Attachment to mother/attachment to father: A meta-analysis. *Child Development, 62,* 210–225.

Fullard, W. & Reiling, A. M. (1976). An investigation of Lorenz's "babyness." *Child Development, 47,* 1191–1193.

George, C., Kaplan, N., & Main, M. (1985). *Attachment interview for adults.* Unpublished manuscript, University of California, Berkeley.

George, C. & Main, M. (1979). Social interactions of young abused children: Approach, avoidance, and aggression. *Child Development, 50,* 306–318.

Goldberg, S. (1998). The assessment of sensitivity. Unpublished manuscript.

Groza, V. & Ileana, D. (1996). A follow-up study of adopted children from Romania. *Child and Adolescent Social Work Journal, 13*(6), 541–565.

Groza, V., Proctor, C., & Guo, S. (1998). The relationship of institutionalization to the development of Romanian children adopted internationally. *International Journal of Child and Family Welfare, 98*(3), 198–217.

Gunnar, M. (1999). Long-term physiological effects of early privation. In M. Dozier, *The continuum of caregiving deprivation: Effects on psychophysiological, emotional, and cognitive functioning.* Symposium presented at biennial meetings of Society for Research in Child Development, Albuquerque, NM.

Hughes, D. A. (1997). *Facilitation developmental attachment: The road to emotional recovery and behavioral change in foster and adoptive children.* Northvale, NJ: Jason Aronson.

Johnson, D. & Fein, E. (1991). The concept of attachment: Applications to adoption. *Children and Youth Services Review, 13,* 397–412.

Keck, G. & Kupecky, R. M. (1995). *Adopting the hurt child.* Colorado Springs, CO: Pinon Press.

Korfmacher, J., Adam, E., Ogawa, J., & Egeland, B. (1997). Adult attachment: Implications for the therapeutic process in a home visitation intervention. *Applied Developmental Science, 1*, 43–52.

Lamb, M. E. (1987). Predictive implications of individual differences in attachment. *Journal of Consulting and Clinical Psychology, 55*(6), 817–824.

Lyons-Ruth, K. (1996). Attachment relationships among children with aggressive behavior problems: The role of disorganized early attachment patterns. *Journal of Consulting and Clinical Psychology, 64*(1), 64–73.

Main, M. & Cassidy, J. (1988). Categories of response to reunion with the parent at age 6: Predictable from infant attachment classification and stable over a 1-month period. *Developmental Psychology, 24*(3), 415–426.

Main, M. & George, C. (1985). Responses of abused and disadvantaged toddlers to distress in agemates: A study in the day care setting. *Developmental Psychology, 21*(3), 407–412.

Main, M. & Goldwyn, R. (In press). Adult attachment rating and classification system. In M. Main (Ed.), *A topology of human attachment organization assessed in discourse, drawings, and interviews.* New York: Cambridge University Press.

Main, M., & Hesse, E. (1990). Parents' unresolved traumatic experiences are related to infant disorganized attachment status: Is frightened and/or frightening parental behavior the linking mechanism? In M. T. Greenberg, D. Cicchetti, & E. M. Cummings (Eds.), *Attachment in the preschool years* (pp. 161–182). Chicago: University of Chicago Press.

Main, M., & Solomon, J. (1990). Procedures for identifying infants as disorganized/disoriented during the Ainsworth Strange Situation. In M. T. Greenberg, D. Cicchetti, & E. M. Cummings (Eds.), *Attachment in the preschool years* (pp. 121–160). Chicago: University of Chicago Press.

Mangelsdorf, S., Gunnar, M., Kestenbaum, R., Lang, S., & Andreas, D. (1990). Infant proneness-to-distress temperament, maternal personality, and mother-infant attachment: Associations and goodness of fit. *Child Development, 61*, 820–831.

Marvin, R. S., & Pianta, R. C. (1996). Mothers' reactions to their child's diagnosis: Relations with security of attachment. *Journal of Clinical Child Psychology, 25*, 436–445.

Mayes, L. C., & Bornstein, M. H. (1995). Developmental dilemmas for cocaine-abusing parents and their children. In M. Lewis & M. Bendersky (Eds.). *Mothers, babies, and cocaine: The role of toxins in development* (pp. 251–272). Hillsdale, NJ: Erlbaum.

Peterson, L., Burns, W. J., & Widmayer, S. M. (1995). Developmental risk for infants of maternal cocaine abusers: Evaluation and critique. *Clinical Psychology Review, 15* (8), 739–776.

Rodning, C., Beckwith, L., & Howard, J. (1991). Quality of attachment and home environments in children prenatally exposed to PCP and cocaine. *Development and Psychopathology, 3,* 351–366.

Rutter, M. (1999). Social and cognitive deficits following early privation. In M. Dozier, *The continuum of caregiving deprivation: Effects on psychophysiological, emotional, and cognitive functioning.* Symposium presented at biennial meetings of Society for Research in Child Development, Albuquerque, NM.

Schneider-Rosen, K. & Cicchetti, D. (1984). The relationship between affect and cognition in maltreated infants: Quality of attachment and the development of visual self-recognition. *Child Development, 55,* 648–58.

Shields, A. M., Cicchetti, D., & Ryan, R. M. (1994). The development of emotional and behavioral self-regulation and social competence among maltreated school-age children. *Development and psychopathology, 6,* 57–75.

Singer, L. M., Brodzinsky, D. M., Ramsey, D., Steir, M., & Waters, E. (1985). Mother-infant attachment in adoptive families. *Child Development, 56,* 1543–1551.

Soby, J. M. (1994). *Prenatal exposure to drugs/alcohol: Characteristics and educational implications of fetal alcohol syndrome and cocaine/polydrug effects.* Springfield, IL: Charles C. Thomas.

Spitz, R. A. (1946). Hospitalism: A follow-up report. *The Psychoanalytic Study of the Child, 2,* 113–117.

Spitz, R. A. (1950). Anxiety in infancy: A study of its manifestations in the first year of life. *International Journal of Psycho-Analysis, 31,* 138–143.

Sroufe, L. A. (1983). Infant-caregiver attachment and patterns of adaptation in preschool: The roots of maladaptation and competence. In M. Perlmutter (Ed.), *Minnesota Symposia in Child Psychology, Volume 16* (pp. 41–83). Hillsdale, NJ: Erlbaum.

Sroufe, L. A. (1988). The role of infant-caregiver attachment in development. In J. Belsky & T. Nezworski (Eds.), *Clinical implications of attachment* (pp. 18–38). Hillsdale, NJ: Erlbaum.

Stern, D. (1977). *The first relationship*. Cambridge, MA: Harvard University Press.

Stovall, K. C. & Dozier, M. (in press). The evolution of attachment in new relationships: Single subject analyses for ten foster infants. *Development and Psychopathology*.

Thompson, R., Cicchetti, D., Lamb, M., & Malkin, C. (1985). The emotional responses of Down syndrome and normal infants in the Strange Situation: the organization of affective behavior in infants. *Developmental Psychology, 21,* 828–841.

Tizard, B. (1977). *Adoption: A second chance*. New York: Free Press.

van IJzendoorn, M. H. (1995). Adult attachment representations, parental responsiveness, and infant attachment: A meta-analysis on the predictive validity of the Adult Attachment Interview. *Psychological Bulletin, 117(3),* 387–403.

Ward, M. J. & Carlson, E. A. (1995). Associations among adult attachment representations, maternal sensitivity, and infant-mother attachment in a sample of adolescent mothers. *Child Development, 66,* 69–79.

Yarrow, L. J. & Goodwin, M. S. (1973). The immediate impact of separation: Reactions of infants to a change in mother figure. In L. J. Stone, H. T. Smith, & L. B. Murphy (Eds.), *The competent infant: Research and commentary* (pp. 1032–1040). New York: Basic.

8

Societal Attitudes Toward Drug-Using Women and Their Children: Past and Present

Stephen R. Kandall

Introduction

Although the recent national "drug scare" may suggest that drug abuse is a recent phenomenon in this country, the use and abuse of addicting substances has been part of the American culture for over 200 years [Kandall 1996]. Warnings about the dangers of drug use are also not new. Beginning in the mid-19th century, when drug use in America first began to be called a "problem," warnings regarding the dangers of addicting drugs, taken either medicinally or recreationally, were sounded by many physicians [Day 1868; Chase 1873; Howard 1879; Kane 1881; Grover 1894]. Admonitions regarding the growing number of addicts created by the injudicious prescribing of opiates by physicians and pharmacists were echoed by the Hearst-dominated lay press in articles such as the 1893 story entitled "Doctors Largely Responsible for Drunkenness and the Opium Habit" [Silver 1979]. This campaign, waged in the popular press, continued into the early years of the 20th century, most notably with Samuel Hopkins Adams' blistering series in Collier's Weekly on the dangers of commonly-used opiate-laden patent medicines [Adams 1907]. During the next 90 years, sensationalistic media reporting buttressed society's attempts to control cocaine use in the 1900s-1920s, marijuana in the 1930s, and heroin and psychedelic drugs in the 1960s.

Understanding this tradition, it is not surprising that another media blitz began in the mid-1980s, concomitant with the "crack"

199

epidemic, and extending to the present day. In this most recent antidrug campaign, television, radio, and print media have focused prismatically on the relationship between drug use and social and economic conditions such as poverty, homelessness, crime, prison overcrowding, job-related accidents and absenteeism, and spread of infectious diseases, most notably AIDS—all of which were portrayed as sapping America's moral and financial strength. The magnitude and extent of the drug problem, reinforced by media coverage, produced a feeling of panic among American citizens, many of whom were ready enlistees in the "war on drugs."

Although judicial efforts to stem drug use in America actually began in San Francisco in 1875 with the passage of limited municipal antiopium legislation, our national "war on drugs" is often historically dated from the passage of the Harrison Anti-Narcotic Act of 1914. It should be noted, however, that this legislation was only a tax act, and that America's "zero tolerance" approach to drug control really began in 1919 with two Supreme Court decisions, *U.S. v. Doremus* (1919), which confirmed the constitutionality of the Harrison Act, and *Webb et al. v. U.S.* (1919), which ruled that physicians could not prescribe narcotics to addicts simply for the purpose of maintaining that addiction. In more recent memory, the "war on drugs" was formalized in the early 1970s by President Nixon, who called drug use "Public Enemy No. 1." In accordance with this national initiative, the federal antidrug budget grew from $86 million in 1969 to $418 million in 1972, and subsequently grew to over $16 billion in 1997.

Despite this exponential increase in spending to control drug abuse, vocal critics have belittled these national efforts. Listed among the many criticisms are that (1) the entire philosophical underpinning of the "war on drugs"—namely that drug use can be eliminated (in 1988, Congress passed a resolution stating that America would be "drug-free" by 1995)—is merely hubris and hyperbole; (2) repressive tactics have failed to differentiate between "hard" and "soft" drugs, resulting in alienation of a large segment of the American public, mass imprisonments, and unnecessary loss of life through preventable violence and disease; (3) the bellicose terminology attached to the "drug war" diverts attention from the fact that drug use should be treated primarily as a medical and public health issue; (4) antidrug money is being misspent, in that two-thirds to three-quarters of the antidrug budget is allocated to policing and interdiction rather than to prevention, education, and treatment; and (5) the total budget, regardless of its distribution, is inadequate since estimates of the total societal cost of the drug scourge now run to almost $98 billion annually [Swan 1998]. Although the ideological struggle is still being fought between the "drug warriors" and those trying to stimulate a national dialogue which includes decriminalization and legalization, by far the prevailing attitude in American society today is for continuance of the repressive "zero tolerance" approach to drug control, which has characterized U.S. drug policy for the past 80 years.

Embedded in this matrix of anger and frustration over national and international failures to control drug use was an issue which had historically been given little attention—drug use by women [Kandall 1996]. Beginning in the mid-to-late 1980s, an attitude of anger, blame, and demonization toward drug-using women, especially those who were pregnant and "crack" users, became integrated into a tough national stand against drugs. Once again, the media weighed in with sensationalism. The term "crack babies" was coined, and with little or no medical evidence, the press characterized these infants as undergrown, brain damaged, and congenitally stigmatized [Brody 1988]. These "crack babies" soon grew into "cocaine toddlers" and "crack children," who were reportedly doomed to be unlovable, unteachable, and unadoptable [Balmaseda 1989; Blakeslee1989; Kantrowitz 1990]. These children were portrayed as the "innocent victims" of selfish and uncaring women who had lost their maternal instincts under the influence of drugs [Hinds 1990; Fackelmann 1991]. Ignoring much of the issue's subtlety, pregnant addicts were portrayed as using drugs "voluntarily" and quick to abandon their babies in neonatal intensive care units, cocaine-littered hallways, or on America's street corners in exchange for their next drug high [Mayer 1989].

Other news stories branded these "crack babies" as "poisoned" [Rosenthal 1996] or as "genetic inferiors" [Krauthammer 1989] who were "troubled' and "tormented" [Goodman 1992]. These irresponsibly premature and dire predictions reflected society's anger and helped to sculpt the groundswell of blame heaped upon these women. With articles such as "Crack babies: The worst threat is Mom herself," [Besharov 1989], it was not surprising to find letters to the editor such as the one published by the New York Times in December, 1989, entitled "Imprison addicts, for the children's sake."

This chapter will explore the historical roots of societal attacks on drug-using women and the basis of the current anger and resentment toward these women, and will offer strategies that might provide some answers to this persistent problem in American society.

Historical Roots of the Attacks on Drug-Using Women

The relatively recent display of anger toward drug-using women may be viewed as surprising in light of the fact that from the middle to the end of the 19th century, at a time during which drug addiction was becoming increasingly common, approximately two-thirds to three-quarters of the opium addicts in the United States, as well as significant numbers of users of cocaine, chloroform, and cannabis, were women [Earle 1880; Nolan 1881; Hull 1885; Kandall 1996].

Despite the fact that drug use was frowned upon by many, the relatively benign approach that society took to drug use by women was predicated on the prevailing stereotype. Although, in reality, the spectrum of female addiction was quite broad, generally these women tended to be portrayed as genteel, southern, white, upper-middle class women, whose "problem" tended to be family-centered rather than society-centered. Such prototypes made their loosely-fictionalized appearances in characters such as Helen Mathews in Maria Weed's 1895 novel, A Voice in the Wilderness, and better known figures such as the chloral addict Lily Bart in Edith Wharton's 1905 novel The House of Mirth, and opium-addicts such as Mrs. Henry Lafayette Dubose in Harper Lee's To Kill a Mockingbird and Mary Tyrone in Eugene O'Neill's Long Day's Journey Into Night.

Although nonmedicinal use was certainly common, the most important reason for the increase in opiate consumption during the mid-to-late 19th century was the prescribing and dispensing of legal opiates by physicians and pharmacists. An almost limitless list of real and imaginary complaints was treated with opiates by medical professionals who possessed a very limited therapeutic armamentarium. Victorian women were not only treated with opiates for the same illnesses as men, but in addition, they were considered less capable of managing painful conditions and thus, more in need of medication. Indeed, as R.V. Pierce, who built a huge business based on opiate-laden medications, advised, "[When woman, the] last and crowning handiwork of God....is disturbed by disease, when the nicely-adjusted balance of her complex nature deviates from its true and intended poise...its importance should elicit...the most scientific administration of the choicest, rarest, and purest medicinal elements in the whole range of nature" [Pierce 1895, p. 684].

The most common conditions for which women were medicated with opiates were "female problems." Marshalls's 1878 survey revealed that the most frequent cause of the opium habit in females was the taking of opiates to relieve painful menstruation and diseases of the female reproductive organs. Another physician noted that, in women, "a large part of the deviations from health which induce the use of some form of opiate, are dependent on disorders peculiar to their sex" [Mattison 1879, p. 332]. Dr. T. Gaillard Thomas, President of the American Gynecological Society, wrote: "For the relief of pain, the treatment is all summed up in one word, and that is opium. This divine drug overshadows all other anodynes....you can easily educate her to become an opium-eater" [Thomas 1879, p. 316]. R. V. Pierce offered pages of testimonial from satisfied women who used his patent medications for conditions such as "falling of the womb," "paralysis and uterine disease," "indigestion, constipation, and uterine disease," "female weakness," "severe flowing," vaginitis," and "suppressed menstruation and nervous debility" [Pierce 1895, pp. 727-771]. As late as 1913, women who suffered from painful menstruation passed on the word that "paregoric, laudanum, etc. is a specific" [Wholey 1913, p. 724].

Women were also widely treated for neurasthenia, or "nervous weakness," a vague disorder which encompassed an enormous range of symptoms, including tenderness of the scalp, spine, and body;

vague pains and flying neuralgias; flushing and fidgitiness; variability of pulse and palpitations; strength giving out or legs giving way; sensitivity to hot or cold water; sensitivity to weather changes; ticklishness; insomnia; nervous dyspepsia; partial memory failure; sexual exhaustion; depression and morbid fears; headache; pain and heaviness; floating specks before the eyes; noises in the ears; and chills and heat flashes [Mortimer 1901]. As an 1886 medical textbook explained: "To women of the higher classes, ennuyeed (sic) and tormented with neuralgias or the vague pains of hysteria and hypochondriasis, opium brings tranquility and self-forgetfulness" [Wilson 1886, p. 649].

Since these women, both written about in fiction and discussed in the medical literature, had become addicted through the misuse and overuse of addicting but legal drugs prescribed by their physicians or pharmacists, they posed no immediate threat to society. Viewed more with sympathy and pity than with scorn, drug-addicted women did not incite sentiment for antidrug legislation.

The fact that antidrug legislation experienced an upsurge in the latter part of the 19th century and first two decades of this century was explained to a large extent by dramatic changes in the sociodemographics of drug use in America. When dominant drug-use patterns changed from female to male, from white to minority, from southern rural to northern urban, and from wealthy to poor—in other words from "mainstream" to "deviant"—it became easier to mobilize the American people in a campaign to eradicate drug use in this country. The use of antidrug laws to control minority populations considered to be "socially deviant" extends back over a century in U.S. history. Following passage of the first antiopium legislation in San Francisco, which was intended to keep whites from frequenting Chinese opium dens, similar laws were passed in Virginia City, Nevada, in 1876, and in New York State in 1882. Despite their general lack of efficacy in controlling drug trafficking or drug usage, every state except Delaware, and many cities as well, had passed ordinances against either cocaine, opiate, or both by 1912 [Kolb 1962]. National antidrug legislation was introduced unsuccessfully in 1880 and 1884, but those efforts eventually came to fruition in the Harrison Anti-Narcotic Act in 1914 and the two 1919 Supreme

Court decisions, *U.S. v. Doremus*, and *Webb et al. v. U.S.*, which ushered in the repressive approach to drug control that has characterized the country's approach for over eighty years.

As suggested, much of the early antidrug legislation in the U.S. was intended to counter the social and economic threats posed by emerging minorities, such as Asian immigrants and African Americans. To advance this initiative, women began to be portrayed as helpless targets of drug-crazed, sexually predatory minority men. The sensationalistic Hearst-dominated lay press ran frequent stories of women lured into Chinese opium dens or the white slave trade. San Francisco authorities feared that "many women and young girls . . . were being induced to visit the dens, where they were being ruined, morally and otherwise" [Kane 1882, p. 1]. Hamilton Wright, one of the architects of early drug policy, was extremely concerned about opium and "the large number of women who have become involved and were living as common-law wives or co-habitating with Chinese in the Chinatowns of our various cities" [Wright 1910, p.44]. In response to the escalating use of cocaine in Southern African Americans after the turn of the twentieth century, testimony was offered before the U.S. House of Representatives that its use was involved in "a great many of the southern rape cases" [Morgan 1981, p.93]. One year later, Wright [Marshall 1911, p.12] stated that cocaine "is used by those concerned in the white slave traffic to corrupt young girls, and....it is but a short time before such girls fall to the ranks of prostitution."

Once drug use was *de facto* criminalized, addicted women slunk into the shadowy margins of society. Many women were forced into lives of prostitution and crime to support their drug habits. When it was realized that the events of 1919 had thrown a large number of addicts onto the streets with no organized treatment, a primitive network of 44 clinics hurriedly sprung up around the country to bolster the few scattered clinics that had been started as early as 1912 [Kandall 1996]. During the last six months of 1919, the New York City clinic treated 1,532 women, approximately one-fourth of the registered addicts. In many other clinics, women made up between 25% and 35% of the patients [Kandall 1996]. Drug treatment clinics reduced crime in the cities in which they were located and, despite wide variability in their quality, offered women the opportunity to cope with their addiction in a legal and medically supervised way. Because they ran counter to the repressive approach being developed by the federal government, however, these clinics were never popular with the Narcotics Unit of the Treasury Department, and the last clinic in Shreveport, Louisiana, was closed in March 1925 [Kandall 1996].

Not all drug-using women were poor. Society women, movie stars, and the "idle rich" dabbled with cocaine, marijuana, and even opium smoking during the 1920s and 1930s. On the screen as well, drugs were big business in Hollywood. Beginning in 1894 with a 30-second kinetograph entitled "Chinese Opium Den," which was made for Thomas Edison, Hollywood produced over 200 known films dealing with drug themes, many portraying women as vulnerable targets of drug-involved men [Starks 1982]. The extent to which drug use, often associated with female sexuality, permeated the Jazz Age music scene is reflected in songs such as Duke Ellington's "Hophead," Louis Armstrong's song about marijuana, "Muggles," and Cab Calloway's "Minnie the Moocher," "Kicking the Gong Around," and "Reefer Man," among many others.

Somewhat later, through the 1940s, 1950s and 1960s, treatment options for drug-addicted women remained extremely limited, as these women were largely ignored. Between 1941 and 1965, almost 15,000 female patients, constituting 18% of all admissions, were treated at the Lexington Federal Farm, the only organized treatment system in the country. Living conditions were primitive and depressing [Hughes 1961], and were compared to conditions described in Mary Jane Ward's 1946 expose of conditions in asylums treating mental disease, *The Snake Pit*. Not surprisingly, relapse rates were high among women discharged from Lexington, and many became "winders," patients who spent much of their lives in and out of treatment seeking the elusive cure for their addictions.

Treatment opportunities did begin to expand in the 1960s. Detoxification, which had the longest history, remained a therapeutic option showing limited success. Women were among early enrollees in therapeutic communities, first with the opening of Synanon in 1958 in Ocean Park, California, followed by other programs such as Daytop, Odyssey House, and Phoenix House. Religion-based alternatives, outpatient nonmaintenance treatment, inpatient chemical dependency treatment, and correctional treatment programs, all offered drug treatment to women in limited ways, usually based on models more suited to the treatment of male addicts. In all of these "therapeutic" settings, women often had to contend with insensitivity, hostility, voyeurism, and even outright sexual abuse.

The most important therapeutic option for women was the development of methadone maintenance. During the early 1960s, Drs. Vincent Dole and Marie Nyswander pioneered the use of methadone, a synthetic opiate that they found could block both the euphoriant effects of heroin and the addict's craving for the drug. [Dole & Nyswander 1965; Dole et al. 1966]. Although the original Dole-Nyswander methadone trials excluded women, a small group of women did soon enter treatment and appeared to derive significant benefit from methadone maintenance. Between 1969 and 1973, women made up almost 10,000 of the 40,000 patients treated in federally funded drug treatment programs. Today, women still comprise between 25% and 33% of methadone-maintained patients [Center for Substance Abuse Treatment 1994].

A major development in the approach to female addicts occurred in the early 1970s. During those years, the Women's Movement, bolstered by other self-help groups, created a setting in which a discussion of women and drugs could flourish. The National Institute on Drug Abuse (NIDA) opened in 1974 with an early focus on women and drugs, and by 1975 had launched an innovative series of comprehensive drug treatment demonstration grants located in six cities, using pregnancy as the entry point. Thus, programs such as the Family Center program in Philadelphia, the Pregnant Addicts and Addicted Mothers Program (PAAM) in New York, and the Hutzel Hospital program in Detroit pioneered efforts to provide drug-using women with a network of comprehensive services to meet their varied needs. Whereas in the past, treatment for addicted women had been clumsily grafted onto a model more suitable for men, in the early 1970s the idea of "comprehensive care" for pregnant drug-women was taking shape. For the first time, although in a very limited number of settings, pregnant women could receive their medical, obstetric, and drug treatment care in a single facility. This concept has been subsequently expanded, and it is now recognized that features of comprehensive care considered essential for success include: a continuum of addiction services (e.g., residential, outpatient, home-based); multiple counseling modalities (e.g., individual, group, family); counseling on other issues such as sexual abuse and domestic violence; services for children (e.g., day care, play therapy, child developmental monitoring, parenting training); concrete services such as housing, food, and transportation; comprehensive health care (e.g., family planning, prenatal care, HIV prevention); educational training such as job training and high school equivalency; appropropriate staffing (female, supportive, non-confrontational, and culturally and racially sensitive); legal and advocacy support; and aftercare (e.g., twelve-step, transitional housing, individual counseling) [Kandall & Chavkin 1992].

By the end of the 1970s, the "treatment glass" for women could be viewed as half-full or half-empty. On the positive side, an enlightened attitude had taken hold and more women were finding their way into drug treatment. On the negative side, however, the need for services overwhelmed the available treatment slots; too many programs did not accept women; many programs were still providing inadequate gender-based services; and women were having difficulty reaching levels of administrative responsibility within programs. A 1979 nationwide survey found only 25 programs that described themselves as specifically geared to female addicts [Beschner & Thompson 1981]. Even in these programs, more than half of the women reported that they did not receive gynecological care, three-fourths did not receive contraceptive counseling, and nonminority women received the majority of available treatment.

The Current Environment of Anger and Resentment Toward Drug-Using Women

If, in fact, slow but perceptible progress in treating drug-addicted women was being made through the 1970s and extending into the

1980s, why did a venomous national anger against these women take root in the mid-1980s? Broadly, an attack on drug-using women, stereotypically defined as poor, urban minority women, fit well with the Reagan administration's initiatives to limit women's reproductive options, reduce social welfare spending, and socially marginalize the "welfare queens" who were bankrupting the country. In addition, the attack resonated with the concept that enforcement and expansion of antidrug laws could control or even eliminate drug use in America. This tough "zero tolerance," supply-side approach found expression in the Comprehensive Crime Control Act of 1984, the Anti-Drug Abuse Act of 1986, and the Anti-Drug Abuse Amendment Act of 1988. Although funding for interdiction and policing increased, funding for drug prevention, education, and treatment declined by about $65 million between 1981 and 1985 as the federal prevention campaign devolved to the First Lady's slogan, "Just Say No." National frustration increased in 1986, when top administration officials admitted that these policies by themselves were not slowing the use of drugs. Just at that time, the concomitant emergence of two drug-related phenomena—"crack" cocaine and the onslaught of AIDS, both of which were threatening, indeed terrifying, to Middle America—fueled this national anger.

One of the avenues into which this national anger and resentment was channeled was the prosecution of pregnant, drug-using women. Although isolated prosecutions had taken place—such as in California in 1977 [*Reyes v. Superior Court 1977*], the majority of such prosecutions occurred after 1987. By 1997, over 240 women in 35 states had been charged with similar crimes under statutes which had clearly never been intended to be applied in this context [Rhodes & Marshall 1997]. The case which received the most notoriety was the 1989 Florida prosecution of Jennifer Johnson, who was convicted of delivery of drugs to a minor, the narrow interpretation being that she had transferred cocaine to her newborn infant in the few seconds between delivery and cutting of the umbilical cord. Following imposition of a rather harsh sentence, the lower court conviction was upheld by the Florida Appellate Court, by a vote of two male judges to one female judge. In 1992, however, the Florida

Supreme Court unanimously overturned Ms. Johnson's conviction and condemned the creative misuse of existing statutes to criminalize behavior not specifically addressed by law [*Johnson v. State* 1992].

Until recently, despite continuing prosecutorial activity directed against women who had used drugs during pregnancy, appellate or State Supreme Courts had overturned every lower court conviction against these women. In 1997, however, in a stunning verdict, a cocaine-using woman was found guilty of involuntary manslaughter under a South Carolina Supreme Court ruling that a woman could be held criminally liable for actions that endanger the health of a viable fetus [*Whitner v. State* 1997]. Following that decision, which the United States Supreme Court let stand, both Wisconsin and South Dakota in 1998 passed bills which allowed the involuntary detention of pregnant women who abuse drugs or alcohol [Nelson 1997].

The current environment of anger and resentment toward drug-using women can be explained by a number of factors: the growing number of drug-exposed babies; the increased risk of child abuse and neglect to which drug-exposed infants have been subjected; the increase in the number of babies being born with medically-related conditions such as low birthweight and sexually transmitted diseases such as congenital syphilis and HIV positivity, all of which have led to increased societal costs and higher infant mortality; and the increasing visibility of drug-using women in the criminal justice system.

Growing number of drug-exposed babies

During the 1980s, the United States experienced a sharp increase in the number of births of drug-exposed babies. The use of opiates such as heroin during pregnancy had remained at a persistently stable level, but the use of cocaine had grown, and almost all of the media attention focused on the exponential increase in cocaine-exposed babies. Studies of individual cities, primarily in the Northeast, confirmed the increase in drug-exposed newborns. In the late 1980s, one Boston hospital found that 17% of women who had delivered infants had used an illicit drug during their pregnancy [Frank at al.1988]; a later study from the same hospital found that 31% of the women had used marijuana and 18% had used cocaine [Zuckerman et al. 1989]. In New York City during the 1980s, babies born to cocaine-using mothers rose twentyfold [Health Systems Agency of New York City 1994]. Similar statistics were reported from around the country, including Philadelphia, Rhode Island [U.S. Department of Health and Human Services 1992], and California [Vega 1993].

Nationally, studies estimated the number of drug-exposed babies at between 37,000 and 100,000 [Dicker & Leighton 1991] and the most comprehensive study by NIDA estimated the number to be 220,000 [U.S. Department of Health and Human Services 1996]. The only figure quoted by the press, however, was the highest estimate, that of 375,000 babies annually, or 11% of infants, published by Chasnoff [1989]. Exploitation of the highest number fit the agendas of activists on both sides of the political spectrum, those who wished to demonize drug-using minority women and those who wished to procure additional funding for drug treatment programs.

Child abuse and neglect

With the heightened attention to the sharp increase in the number of infants born drug-exposed, women have also been chastised, prosecuted, and incarcerated for their deficiencies as "child rearers." The failure of many drug-using mothers to meet their socially-designated responsibility as child caregivers has been judged to be a moral failing. With little understanding of the fact that many such women avoid the healthcare system—fearing anger, resentment, discrimination, and even prosecution—the public has been quick to condemn these women as unfit mothers who care little about their children. Directly blaming mothers, but not fathers, for an inability to care for their children, the media ended their contest to find the youngest "crack" dealer when a 10-year-old was identified [Schmitt 1989]. Others blamed mothers for accidental ingestion of cocaine and methadone by toddlers, or still worse, for deaths in homemade drug cookshops [Cooper 1995; Lii 1997]. The media coverage reinforced the notion that drug-using women were worthy of society's enmity.

Statistics bore out this concern. In the late 1980s, the number of reports of child abuse and neglect tripled when both parents were drug users [Falco 1989]. This trend led to a rapid increase in foster care placements. The New York Times ["No parent" 1989] editorialized on the growing foster care crisis, noting an increase in foster care placements of children in New York City from about 23,700 in 1977 to almost 40,000 in 1989. Nationally, the number of children in foster care rose from 280,000 to 360,000 between 1986 and 1989, and increased again to 500,000 by 1997 [Kilborn 1997]. The national geographic distribution of this foster care load was extremely uneven, with California, Illinois, New York, Pennsylvania, and Ohio making up 50% of the cases. In 1994, the New York State Council on Children reported that parents of 75% of the children in foster care were substance abusers [Health Systems Agency 1994].

With the growth in the number of reports of child abuse and neglect and the number of children entering foster care as a result of parental substance abuse, the number of children needing adoption planning and services also began to increase. It is currently estimated that as many as 110,000 children in foster care will need adoptive families [U.S. Department of Health and Human Services 1999]. Although there is no definitive data, some portion of children in foster care who will not be reunited with their families and who will need adoption services will have histories of prenatal substance exposure [Edelstein 1995]. Child welfare experts point to the particular difficulties encountered in attempting to reunify substance-involved mothers with their children [Child Welfare League of America 1991], though there are examples of success. For some children, however, adoption services will be necessary as a result of the challenges faced by mothers in overcoming addiction in an environment that is not supportive of women's treatment needs and the children's own medical and developmental problems that result from prenatal drug exposure.

Medically-related conditions

A third factor that has contributed to the environment of anger and resentment toward substance abusing women are medical conditions associated with prenatal substance exposure: sexually transmitted diseases and HIV, low birthweight, and increased neonatal and infant mortality rates.

Sexually transmitted diseases and HIV. The increase in drug use seen during the 1970s was clearly linked to increased rates of acquisition of sexually transmitted diseases. One notable example was congenital syphilis, a disease which had been practically eradicated by the early 1980s, but which reappeared and increased in numbers during the mid-to-late 1980s [Ricci at al. 1989; Lewin 1992].

Even more devastating was the increase in HIV acquisition by women, especially drug-using women. Already by 1984, 50% to 60% of street addicts were HIV-positive [Novick et al. 1986]. By September 1993, 40,000 (12%) cases of AIDS in women could be counted among the 330,000 known cases of AIDS in the United States, and more than 28,000 of the cases were felt to be drug-related. By mid-1994, AIDS had become the fourth leading cause of death among women of child-bearing age. It was widely accepted that, in addition to direct injection by sterile needles, promiscuous high-risk sexual behavior, either trading sex directly for drugs or selling sex for money to buy drugs, were important factors in the spread of HIV.

Despite this horrendous toll, it was not until 1993 that the Office of Research on Women's Health (ORWH) realized that women were being systematically excluded from trials of useful, even potentially life-saving drugs. Shortly thereafter, ORWH, the prestigious Institute of Medicine, and NIDA addressed the issue of inclusion of women in clinical trials of new medications and therapies. This issue took on critical significance in 1994, following the release of data from the NIH-sponsored clinical trial of the antiviral agent zidovudine (AZT), which showed that treatment of HIV-positive women during pregnancy and continued treatment of their infants for six weeks after birth could reduce the rate of perinatal HIV transmission by two-thirds [Connor et al. 1994]. This development was especially important because, by 1994, almost all pediatric HIV was acquired through transmission of the virus from mother to her newborn infant, either transplacentally or through breastfeeding.

Issues related to pediatric HIV became intertwined in the heated debate as to whether pregnant women should be forced to undergo mandatory HIV testing. Emotions ran high on both sides, and a woman's refusal to accept mandatory testing was often interpreted as unwillingness to cooperate for her own health and the health of her baby, rather than as a legitimate civil rights issue or fear of stigmatization and discrimination. Recently, in an effort to diffuse the emotional debate surrounding the issue and focus on treatment for the 8,000 pregnant women who are HIV-infected, a 13-member committee of the Institute of Medicine recommended that the determination of the HIV status of all pregnant women should be established as a standard of care in obstetric practice [Leary 1998].

Emotions have also run high regarding needle exchange programs, which have been shown to offer a significant health benefit to injecting drug users. In one cross-sectional analysis of 5 needle exchange programs, 30% of the 2,525 intravenous drug users were women [Paone et al. 1995]. Following enrollment in these programs, borrowing used needles—often referred to as "works"—fell from 25% to 10%, passing on syringes fell by 50%, using bleach to disinfect needles increased by 26%, and using alcohol pads to clean the skin increased by 116% [Paone et al. 1995]. After finding that needle exchange programs reduced HIV transmission in 75 programs in 55 cities, a prestigious panel of the National Academy of Sciences in April 1998 recommended federal financing of such programs. Despite their own expert panel's recommendations regarding the benefits of needle exchange, the Clinton Administration declined to approve federal financing of such programs [Stolberg 1998].

Low birthweight babies and the associated costs. Although the media has overdramatized the impact of maternal drug use on infant birthweight and has inaccurately portrayed the typical cocaine-exposed baby as tiny and sick, it is clear that some infants have suffered direct effects of maternal drug abuse. Whether attributable to maternal lifestyle associated with street drug use or to the direct harmful effects of drugs on the pregnancy, drug-complicated pregnancies in New York City, for example, were associated with a quadrupling of low birthweight (under 5 lbs., 8 oz.) rates during the years 1985 to 1987 [City Health Information 1989].

The increase in the number of births of low birthweight babies suggested by this data coincided with pressure brought by the government and managed care organizations to reduce health costs. In 1989, the San Francisco Chronicle reported that caring for 250 cocaine-exposed infants the previous year had cost the state of California $3.5 million in excess of Medical-Cal reimbursement. A New York study found that intrauterine exposure to cocaine increased infant hospital costs by over $5,000 per baby [Phibbs et al. 1991]. Nationally, the Inspector General's Office of the Health and Human Services Department estimated that the birth of 100,000 cocaine-exposed babies would cost the country $20 billion annually [Wagner 1990]. It would hardly be unreasonable for the American people to conclude that valuable healthcare dollars were being siphoned from "legitimate" medical needs to fund the care of "innocent" babies being born to "unfeeling" and "uncaring" drug-using mothers [Blakeslee 1989; Goodman 1992].

Increased neonatal and infant mortality rates. Factors associated with maternal drug use, including low birthweight and risks of HIV transmission, have been connected to increased neonatal and infant mortality rates. Early data from Philadelphia showed that drug-exposed infants had higher mortality rates than a control group [Finnegan et al 1977]. A later study in New York City revealed that the mortality rate among drug-exposed infants during the first year of life was 34.1 per 1,000 live births, almost 3 times that of non-exposed infants [City Health Information 1989]. By contrast, a recent study from Detroit found that mortality rates in the first 2 years of life were no higher among opiate-exposed infants than among matched controls [Ostrea 1997]. The increased mortality noted in earlier studies may be attributed to an increased risk of Sudden Infant Death Syndrome among drug-exposed infants [Kandall et al. 1993], with recent strategies, such as smoking reduction or cessation and placing infants to sleep in the supine position on firm bedding, playing a role in reducing that risk significantly.

Women in the criminal justice system

As previously noted, drug-using women as criminals became more visible following passage of the Harrison Act in 1914. Prior to the 1960s, female addicts who entered the judicial system had been primarily arrested for nonviolent crimes such as drug sales, prostitution, theft and shoplifting. Arrest rates for women rose rapidly during the 1960s and 1970s, with the addition of such offenses as burglary, auto theft, fraud, and embezzlement [Silverman 1982]. Between 1965 and 1977, narcotics violations among women rose significantly, rising from just over 1% of total arrests to more than 6% [Silverman 1982]. Even more striking was the increase in narcotic-related female juvenile arrests from less than 7 per 100,000 population to more than 150 per 100,000 population [Silverman 1982].

During the 1980s and 1990s, women continued to enter the criminal justice system at an alarming rate. Between 1980 and 1992, the number of women in prison in the United States tripled to about 75,000. Between 1984 and 1989 the average daily population of women in local jails rose by 95%. At the end of the 1980s, women comprised 12% of the more than 4 million adults in the care or custody of correction agencies. Most of the arrests and confinements were not due to violent crimes, but were byproducts of the "war on drugs": between 1982 and 1991, the number of women arrested for drug offenses increased by 89% [Federal Bureau of Investigation 1992]. A national survey found that nearly 1 in 3 female inmates was serving a drug-related sentence in 1991 compared to 1 in 8 in 1986 [Snell 1994]. By the late 1990s, the rate of incarceration had followed a steeper trajectory for women than for men among the nearly 300,000 drug offenders in our nation's prisons.

Incarceration appeared to be punitive much more than rehabilitative for drug-using women. Ironically, despite the recognition that treatment services were of great benefit to female addicts, services provided to incarcerated female drug users have always been grossly inadequate. Although exact figures are difficult to obtain, a national survey in 1990 found only about 11% of incarcerated female drug users were receiving drug treatment [Wellisch et al. 1993]. The survey further found that only one-third of the prisons had separate reception and diagnostic facilities for women; most of the facilities were built and were being administered by men; gynecological-obstetric care was available in only half of the jails, but in about four-fifths of the prisons; most of the facilities did not offer either extended visits with families or on-site child care during visits; and only one-quarter of the jails, but more than four-fifths of the prisons offered any vocational programs for women [Wellisch et al. 1993].

Intervention Strategies

Society's view of women who use drugs has varied according to the cultural values of the period and how mainstream America has chosen to define the "drug problem." From the mid-19th century through the beginning of the 20th century, women made up the majority of opiate addicts and a significant fraction of those who used other addicting drugs. During the Classic Era (1920s-1950s), following the institution of a repressive, zero tolerance approach to drug control, the percentage of addicts who were female declined to about 20%, but the rate rose again to about 30% beginning in the 1980s. It should be remembered that if addictions to legal drugs such as psychopharmaceutical agents were included, these percentages would be considerably higher since women have made up the great majority of users of those preparations, which have often been targeted specifically for use by women.

Throughout the past 150 years, drug-using and addicted women have been subjected to a range of indignities, from benign neglect during the last century to repression, victimization, persecution, and prosecution during the current century. As a group, these women have been pushed to the shadowy margins of society and socially ostracized, if not overtly hated. This marginalization, aided by propagation of the myth that drug users are "them" and not "us," and that female addicts are minority "crack mothers" who are ripping off the system at the expense of their children and society, has done little to foster a dialogue as to how best to help them. Sensationalistic press treatment, dating back to the Hearst portrayals early in the century, sells newspapers and TV advertising spots, but does little to illuminate the tangled roots of addiction.

The need to help women who are struggling with addiction has taken on added urgency. In the previous century, many women trapped in the prison of addiction lived in secure, intact families and had no need to resort to crime to support their habit. The "sea change" that resulted in passage of the Harrison Act and its sequelae set the stage for the current web of drug-associated poverty and disintegrating family structure. Addicted women face increased risk from "hard drugs," as well as health impairment or even death from serious illnesses acquired in "crack houses" or "shooting galleries." To make matters worse, these dangers are being faced in a society becoming both more socially conservative and fiscally conservative, and thus less willing to allocate needed dollars for comprehensive treatment programs which might benefit marginal members of society.

While the debate rages over whether or not drugs can be eradicated from U.S. society, whether policy should become more repressive or less repressive towards drug addiction, and whether decriminalization or legalization represents a legitimate talking point, the ravages of drug abuse continue to take their toll. As opposing factions on the right and left of the drug-use spectrum continue to verbally spar, the center appears to be expanding [Wren 1997], offering hope that the gulf can be bridged.

Although answers remain elusive, it is clear that whereas providing services may not always work, certainly not providing services will never work. Unfortunately, history provides few answers as to what really works. Past attempts at treatment, whether by private physicians, in sanitaria, in short-lived drug clinics in the early 1920s, or later in the Lexington-Forth Worth facilities, were limited in scope, lacked firm scientific foundation, and were never properly assessed.

Even today, effective therapeutic interventions such as methadone maintenance are misunderstood and maligned. Overwhelming evidence exists that methadone maintenance offers significant and often essential benefits to opiate-addicted women seeking to positively restructure their lives. As one San Francisco addict commented, "with methadone, you don't have to go out and use any other drugs. You have a choice" [Wenger & Rosenbaum 1994, p. 4]. Women who give up heroin and enter methadone treatment engage in less illegal behavior, decrease their rates of needle use and HIV acquisition, experience an improvement in general health and nutrition, show better obstetrical outcomes, receive more consistent prenatal care, and are better prepared for parenting. Despite these facts, methadone has been politicized as "just another addiction," akin to substituting whisky for gin.

Another strategy to be considered—family unification—must be approached with caution. Sensationalistic press reports detailing failures notwithstanding, successful programs of well-supervised family unification should be expanded. Operation PAR (Parental Awareness and Responsibility) in St. Petersburg, Florida, began providing residential care for substance-abusing women in 1971, and by 1990 was serving a hundred women. Programs such as The Coalition on Addiction, Pregnancy, and Parenting in Cambridge, Massachusetts, Shields for Families in Compton, California, and Families First in Lansing, Michigan, are examples of other programs that were developed to emphasize family unification in the context of maternal substance abuse. Cities such as San Francisco, Los Angeles, and New York developed programs under social supervision which allowed mothers to take their newborn infants home from the hospital. The Federal Government even included a provision in a crime bill in 1994 to allow nonviolent offenders to serve their sentences in supervised settings where their children could live with them, but funding was not included in the 1996 Department of Justice appropriations.

Conclusion

The history of women and addiction extends back over 150 years in America. Although the true extent of "addiction" would obviously depend on which drugs are included under the term "addiction," the spectrum of female addiction extends well beyond those women who make the headlines by abandoning or battering their children. For other less visible women, such as those addicted to prescription medications, their addiction may be the result of media manipulation, inappropriate overmedication by physicians not unlike in the mid-19th century, or their own attempts to cope with social or occupational barriers preventing equality and self-fulfillment. However tragic their individual circumstances, substances-abusing women are bound in a sisterhood which has generated societal enmity and whose human costs are inestimable.

References

Adams, S. H. (1907). *The great American fraud* (4th ed.). Chicago: American Medical Association Press.

Balmaseda, L. (1989, January 29). Cocaine toddlers. *The Miami Herald,* p. G1.

Beschner, G. M. & Thompson P. (1981). *Women and drug abuse treatment: needs and services.* (DHHS Publication No. (ADM) 81-1057). Washington, DC: U.S. Department of Health and Human Services, National Institute on Drug Abuse.

Besharov, D. (1989, August 6). Crack babies: The worst threat is Mom herself. *The Washington Post,* p. B1.

Blakeslee, S. (1989, September 17). Crack's toll among babies: A joyless view, even of toys. *New York Times,* p. A1.

Brody, J. (1988, September 6). Cocaine: Litany of fetal risks grows. *New York Times,* p. C1.

Center for Substance Abuse Treatment. (1994). *Practical approaches in the treatment of women who use alcohol and other drugs.* (DHHS Publication No. (SMA) 94-3006). Rockville, MD: U.S. Department of Health and Human Services.

Chase, A. W. (1873). *Dr. Chase's family physician, farrier, bee-keeper and second receipt book.* Toledo, OH: Chase Publishing.

Chasnoff, I. J. (1989). Drug use and women: Establishing a standard of care. *Annals of the New York Academy of Sciences, 562,* 208–210.

Child Welfare League of America. (1991). *Children at the front.* Washington, DC: Author.

New York City Department of Health. (1989). Maternal drug abuse—New York City. *City Health Information, 8*(8).

Connor, E. M., Sperling, R. S., Gelber, R., Kiselev, P., Scott, G., O'Sullivan, M. J., VanDyke, R., Bey, M., Shearer, W., Jacobson, R. L., Jimenez, E., O'Neill, E., Bazin, B., Delfraissy, J-F., Culnane, M., Coombs, R., Elkins, M., Moye, J., Stratton, P., & Balsey, J.(1994). Reduction of maternal infant transmission of human immunodeficiency virus type 1 with zidovudine treatment. *New England Journal of Medicine, 331,* 1173–1180.

Cooper, M. (1995, December 25). Boy's mother charged with abuse. *New York Times,* p. A43.

Day, H. (1868). *The opium habit*. New York: Harper and Brothers.

Dicker, M. & Leighton, E. A. (1991). Trends in diagnosed drug problems among newborns: United States, 1979–1987. *Drug and Alcohol Dependence, 28*, 151–165.

Dole, V. P. & Nyswander, M. E. (1965). A medical treatment for diacetylmorphine (heroin) addiction. *Journal of the American Medical Association, 193*, 646.

Dole, V. P., Nyswander, M. E., & Kreek, M. J. (1966). Narcotic blockade. *Archives of Internal Medicine, 118*, 304–309.

Earle, C. W. (1880). The opium habit: A statistical and clinical lecture. *Chicago Medical Review, 2*, 442–446.

Edelstein, S. (1995). *Children with prenatal alcohol and/or other drug exposure: Weighing the risks of adoption*. Washington, DC: Child Welfare League of America.

Fackelmann, K. A. (1991). The maternal cocaine connection. *Science News, 140*(10), 152–153.

Falco, M. (1989). *Winning the drug war*. New York: Priority Press.

Federal Bureau of Investigation. (1992). *Crime in the United States, 1991*. Washington, DC: U.S. Department of Justice.

Finnegan, L. P., Reeser, D. S., & Connaughton, J. F. (1977). The effects of maternal drug dependence on neonatal mortality. *Drug and Alcohol Dependence, 2*, 131–140.

Frank, D. A., Zuckerman, B. S., Amaro, H., Aboagye, K., Bauchner, H., Cabral, H., Fried, L., Hingson, R., Kayne, H., Levenson, S. M., Parker, S., Reece, H., & Vinci, R. (1988). Cocaine use during pregnancy: Prevalence and correlates. *Pediatrics, 82*, 888–895.

Goodman, E. (1992, January 16). Beyond the "crack" baby horror lies the pain of troubled kids. *Miami Herald*, p. A23.

Grover, G. W. (1894). *Shadows lifted*. Chicago: Stromberg, Allen.

Health Systems Agency of New York City. (1994). *Charting new directions: Planning substance abuse treatment services in New York City*. New York: Health Systems Agency of New York City, Inc.

Hinds, M. (1990, March 17). The instincts of parenthood become part of crack's toll. *New York Times*, p. A8

Howard, H. (1879). *Domestic medicine*. Philadelphia: Hubbard Brothers.

Hughes, H. M. (1961). *The fantastic lodge.* Boston: Houghton Mifflin

Hull, J. M. (1885). The opium habit. *Iowa State Board of Health Biennial Report, 3,* 535–545.

Johnson v. State, 602 So.2d 1288 (Fla. 1992).

Kandall, S. R. (1996). *Substance and shadow.* Cambridge, MA: Harvard University Press.

Kandall, S. R. & Chavkin W. (1992). Illicit drugs in America: history, impact on women and infants, and treatment strategies for women. *The Hastings Law Journal, 43,* 615–643.

Kandall, S. R., Gaines, J., Habel, L., Davidson, G., & Jessop, D. (1993). Relationship of maternal substance abuse to subsequent sudden infant death in offspring. *Journal of Pediatrics, 123,* 120– 126.

Kane, H. H. (1881). *Drugs that enslave.* Philadelphia: Presley, Blakiston.

Kane, H. H. (1882). *Opium smoking in America and China.* New York: G. P. Putnam's Sons.

Kantrowitz, B. (1990, February 12). The crack children. *Newsweek, 115,* 62–63.

Kilborn, P. T. (1997, April 20). Priority on safety is keeping more children in foster care. *New York Times,* p. A1

Kolb, L. (1962). *Drug addiction.* Springfield, IL: Charles C. Thomas.

Krauthammer, C. (1989, July 31). Crack babies: Genetic inferiors. *New York Daily News,* p. 24.

Leary, W. E. (1998, October 15). Panel urges HIV tests for all pregnant women. *New York Times,* p. A22.

Lewin, T. (1992, November 23). Syphilis cases among newborns climb with the rise in crack use. *New York Times,* p. A13.

Marshall, E. (1911, March 12). "Uncle Sam is the worst drug fiend in the world." *New York Times,* Part 5, p. 12.

Mattison, J. B. (1879). Opium habituation. *Medical Record, 16,* 332–333.

Mayer, J. (1989, October 10). Addiction's child: How a Florida mother needing cash for crack handed over her baby. *The Wall Street Journal,* p. A1.

Morgan, H. W. (1981). *Drugs in America: A social history 1800–1980.* Syracuse, NY: Syracuse University Press.

Mortimer, W. G. (1974) *History of Cocoa.* San Francisco: And/Or Press.

Nolan, D. W. (1881). The opium habit. *Catholic World, 33,* 827–835.

Novick, D. M., Khan, I., & Kreek, M. J. (1986). Acquired immunodeficiency syndrome and infection with hepatitis viruses in individuals abusing drugs by injecting. *Bulletin on Narcotics, 38,* 15–25.

Ostrea, E. M., Ostrea, A. R., & Simpson, P. M. (1997). Mortality within the first 2 years in infants exposed to cocaine, opiates, or cannabinoid during gestation. *Pediatrics, 100,* 79–83.

Paone D., Caloir, S., Shi, Q., & Des Jarlais, D. C. (1995). Sex, drugs, and syringe exchange in New York City: Women's experiences. *Journal of the American Medical Women's Association, 50,* 109–114.

Phibbs, C. S., Bateman, D. A., & Schwartz, R. M. (1991). The neonatal costs of maternal cocaine use. *Journal of the American Medical Association, 266,* 1521–1526.

Pierce, R. V. (1895). *The people's common sense medical adviser in plain English.* Buffalo, NY: World's Dispensary.

Reyes v. Superior Court, 75 Cal. App. 3d 214 (1977).

Ricci, J. M., Fojaco, R. M., & O'Sullivan, M. J. (1989). Congenital syphilis: The University of Miami/Jackson Memorial Medical Center experience, 1986–1988. *Obstetrics and Gynecology, 74,* 687–693.

Rosenthal, A. M. (1996, January 16). The poisoned babies. *New York Times,* p. A17.

Schmitt, E. (1989, February 2). Family court judge finds 10-year-old did sell crack. *New York Times,* p. B2.

Silver, G. (1979). *The dope chronicles (1850–1950).* San Francisco: Harper and Row.

Silverman, I. J. (1982). Women, crime and drugs. *Journal of Drug Issues, 12,* 167–183.

Snell, T. J. (1994). Women in prison: Survey of state prison inmates. *Bureau of Justice Statistics Special Report* (Document NCJ-145321). Washington, DC: U.S. Department of Justice.

Starks, M. (1982). *Cocaine fiends and reefer madness: An illustrated history of drugs in the movies.* New York: Cornwall Books.

Stolberg, S. G. (1998, April 21). Clinton decides not to finance needle program. *New York Times,* p. A1.

Swan, N. (1998). Drug abuse cost to society set at $97.7 billion, continuing steady increase since 1975. *NIDA Notes.* (NIH Publication No. 98-3478). Rockville, MD: National Institute of Health.

The no parent child. (1989, December 24). *New York Times*, p. E10.

Thomas, T. G. (1879). Clinical lecture on diseases of women. *Medical Record, 16*, 316.

U.S. vs. Doremus, 249 U.S. 86 (1919).

U.S. Department of Health and Human Services. (1992). *Maternal drug abuse and drug exposed children: Understanding the problem* (DHHS Publication No. (ADM) 92-1949). Washington, DC: U.S. Department of Health and Human Services.

U.S. Department of Health and Human Services, National Institute on Drug Abuse (1996). *National Pregnancy & Health Survey—Drug Use Among Women Delivery Livebirths: 1992* (NCADI Pub. No. BKD 192). Rockville, MD: National Clearinghouse for Alcohol and Drug Information.

U.S. Department of Health and Human Services. (1999) AFCARS Report 1999. [Online]. Available: http://www.acf.dhhs.gov/programs/cb.

Vega, W. A., Kolody, B., Hwang, J., & Noble, A. (1993). Prevalence and magnitude of perinatal substance exposures in California. *New England Journal of Medicine, 329*, 850–854.

Wagner, L. (1990, March 26). Cost of maternal drug abuse drawing notice. *Modern Healthcare, 21.*

Webb et al. v. U.S., 249 U.S. 96 (1919).

Wellisch, J. M., Anglin, M. D., & Prendergast, M. L. (1993). Numbers and characteristics of drug-using women in the criminal justice system: implications for treatment. *Journal of Drug Issues, 23*, 7–30.

Wenger, L. D. & Rosenbaum, M. (1994). Drug treatment on demand—not. *Journal of Psychoactive Drugs, 26*, 1–11.

Whitner v. State, 492 S.W.2d 777 (S.C. 1997).

Wholey, C. C. (1913). Psychopathologic phases observable in individuals using narcotic drugs in excess. *Pennsylvania Medical Journal, 16*, 721–725.

Wilson, J. C. (1886). The opium habit and kindred afflictions. In W. Pepper (Ed.), *System of practical medicine* (pp. 647–660). Philadelphia: Lea Brothers.

Wren, C. S. (1997, September 1). New voice in drug debate seeks to lower the volume. *New York Times*, p. A10.

Wright, H. (1910, February 21). *Report on international opium: The opium problem.* Senate Document 377 (61st congress, 2nd Session).

Zuckerman, B., Frank, D. A., Hingson, R., Amaro, H., Levenson, S. M., Kayne, H., Parker, S., Vinci, R., Aboagye, K., Fried, L. E., Cabral, H., Timperi, R., & Bauchner, H. (1989). Effects of maternal marijuana and cocaine use on fetal growth. *The New England Journal of Medicine, 320,* 762–768.

9

Emerging Legal Issues in the Adoption of Drug-Exposed Infants

Judith Larsen & Harvey J. Schweitzer

Legal problems, while not unique to drug-exposed infants, can be significant. A large proportion of drug-exposed infants are not symptomatic at birth and present as healthy babies [Lester & Tronick 1994], and as a result, they may have no more legal difficulty on the road to adoption than any infant. Adoption may be fraught with difficulty, however, when newborns are medically fragile, spending early weeks in the neonatal intensive care units, or obviously symptomatic, as with Fetal Alcohol Syndrome, Fetal Alcohol Effects, or heroin withdrawal. These infants, often characterized as being "special needs" children who are eligible for assistance from the state [Government Accounting Office (GAO) 1998], may have attachment and bonding problems that cause more than ordinary concern about shifts in caregivers and hiatuses in nurturing [Mayes et al. 1995; Lester & Tronick 1994; Miller 1996]. Finding a permanent, safe, and healthy home—important for all infants—becomes essential to the future development of neonates who are medically compromised.

Fetal exposure to drugs or alcohol can cause physical effects or behaviors in later childhood that are not apparent when an infant is adopted. Although some research tells us that as they mature, many cocaine-exposed children achieve the performance levels of their non-exposed peers [Barth & Needell 1996], other research suggests that cocaine-exposed children may fall behind their peers in "executive functioning"—language skills and the ability to make judgments and organize information—which may become more apparent as a child matures [Carta et al. 1997; Lester et al. 1998]. There is also a

227

recognized potential for certain late-emerging problems for children prenatally exposed to alcohol, including cerebal palsy [Streissguth et al. 1989]. Many problems associated with prenatal substance exposure are unpredictable, as research data are just beginning to accumulate in many areas. Because of this uncertainty, it is important that adoptive families receive advice and support. Knowledgeable preadoptive negotiation with a state agency, when one is involved, is essential to ensure adequate future health coverage for children with special needs.

Intercountry adoptions also have turned a strong light on problems related to prenatal substance exposure. Infants may be adopted from countries where maternal alcohol and drug use is prevalent, but medical records and social histories are sketchy or nonexistent. A challenge for adoption agencies is how to explain these risks to prospective adoptive parents, protect against wrongful adoption suits, and provide quality services. A challenge for adoptive parents is how to forecast the risks and avoid unconscionable contracts with adoption agencies.

In this chapter, we look at three areas in which emerging legal issues impact the adoption of drug-exposed infants. In the first section, we examine the policies of The Adoption and Safe Families Act of 1997 (ASFA). In the second section, we consider adoption from three viewpoints: that of drug-involved birth parents, the adopting foster parents, and that of the child. In the third section, we explore adoptions in which adopting parents have sought to hold agencies legally liable for negligence or fraud.

Fast-Tracking Drug-Affected Infants Toward Adoption

The Agency's Role in Speeding Children Toward Adoption

The Adoption and Safe Families Act (ASFA) has the plain purpose to put children who are in state foster care on a fast track toward adoption. Targeted for this effort are "special needs" infants. ASFA accomplishes its goal primarily by instructing state child welfare agencies regarding the policies they must develop to qualify for generous federal subsidies. The means through which ASFA speaks to state agencies is The Social Security Act, which ASFA amends. State courts also are directed to take certain actions, many of which are designed to enforce the fast-tracking adoption policies promoted by ASFA.

The frequently-stated standard of ASFA is "safety and health of the child," a radical change from the theme of "family reunification" which dominated the prior Adoption Assistance and Child Welfare Act of 1980. Under the new law, each case of child abuse or neglect entering the child welfare agency-court continuum will be analyzed for safety and health and sped on its way through use of certain operating principles. Court decisions about the best permanent home for a child must be made within approximately one year of the child's entry into foster care.

While services may be offered to reunify and stabilize the family during that year (an excellent package of appropriate services is specified), the agency is encouraged to plan concurrently for out-of-home alternatives. In fact, ASFA describes instances in which reunification services do not even have to be offered, including the murder or assault of a child and a prior involuntary termination of parental rights [42 U.S.C. § 671(a)(15)]. The required "reasonable efforts" to reunify are redefined to apply to services that promote the child's safety and health, and state agencies are required to use "reasonable efforts" to develop adoptive placements when the court approves that objective [42 U.S.C. § 671 (a)(15)]. There is a detailed description of the circumstances under which parental rights can be terminated, including provisions to ensure that children waiting for permanent families are adopted. Judges are urged to terminate parental rights whenever it is in the child's "best interests" [ASFA transition rules and rule of construction, sec. 103(c)-(d)].

Fast tracking of adoptions is also promoted through monetary incentives to states to quickly place children with special needs in adoptive homes. The placement of a special needs child in an adoptive home may qualify a state for up to $6000 as an incentive payment—$4000 for each child placed beyond the number placed the year before, and an additional $2000 for each child with "special needs" placed beyond the number of such children placed the year before [42 U.S.C. § 673b (d) (1)]. Many drug-exposed infants are likely to be included in the "special needs" category, as the term refers to physical, mental, or emotional disabilities, as well as other factors that make it reasonable to conclude that a suitable adoptive family cannot be found unless adoption or medical assistance is provided [42 U.S.C. § 673 (c)].

When one looks behind the specific requirements described by ASFA to strategies for technical assistance offered to states by the U.S. Department of Health and Human Services, the purpose of ASFA is unmistakable. Technical assistance focuses on fast-tracking adoptions for children in foster care [42 U.S.C. § 673b (i)] and primarily addresses:

- models to encourage fast tracking of adoptions for children who have not attained one year of age,
- development of programs that place children with preadoptive families prior to termination of parental rights,
- development of special child welfare agency units to move children toward adoption,
- risk assessment tools to identify children who will be at risk if returned home,
- best practices for expediting termination of parental rights, and
- models to encourage concurrent planning.

While the movement toward swifter decisions about permanency may be cheered by proponents of adoption, ASFA merely expresses the will of Congress. The outcomes may be different than those the legislators envisioned. For example, although Congress may have intended to encourage voluntary consents to adoption by permitting state agencies to move immediately to terminate the rights of parents whose rights to another child have been involuntarily terminated [42 U.S.C. § 671(a)(15)], the actual effect may be quite different. Parents' attorneys may urge their clients to contest efforts to terminate parental rights and pursue appeals more vigorously. Expanded numbers of appeals could slow the adoption process, although some states are considering expedited appeals procedures for termination of parental rights cases.

Adoptive Parents' Role in Negotiating Health Care for Infants with Special Needs

Although agencies do not guarantee the future security of adopted children, they tacitly share responsibility with adoptive parents for providing for the children's future needs. The following ASFA language addresses this mutual responsibility:

In determining cost-sharing requirements, the State shall take into consideration the circumstances of the adopting parent or parents and the needs of the child being adopted consistent to the extent coverage is provided through a State medical assistance program, with the rules under such program [42 U.S.C. § 671(a)(21)(D)].

The adoptive parents have a significant role, as only they can explain how their economic "circumstances" relate to their ability to meet the health needs of the child they are adopting. Can they meet the present and future needs of a drug-exposed infant, given that problems not evident in infancy may emerge long after the adoption is final?

The traditional way of creating an opportunity for individuals at every economic level to adopt children with special needs has been through an adoption assistance agreement that encompasses health care and includes other kinds of aid such as maintenance payments [42 U.S.C. § 673]. The general parameters of adoption assistance agreements are set out in The Adoption Assistance and Child Welfare Act of 1980, which provides states with latitude to develop more specific criteria for assistance. Drug-exposed children may qualify for adoption assistance if three criteria are met: they have symptoms of physical, mental, or behavioral problems; "reasonable efforts" have been made to reunite the family; and the judge indicates in a court order that the child should be removed from the custody of the birth family. Adoption assistance is obtained through a contract between the placement agency and the preadoptive family on the basis of the child's eligibility under Title IV, Part E of The Social Security Act or under the Supplementary Security Income (SSI) program.

While the potential for awarding this assistance continues under ASFA in the sense that ASFA does not preclude nor amend the rules for awarding adoption assistance, there now is a particular emphasis on health care for children with special needs who are adopted. ASFA states that health insurance coverage is to be provided for:

> any child who has been determined to be a child with special needs, for whom there is an adoption assistance agreement…between the State and an adoptive parent or parents and who the State has determined cannot be placed with an adoptive parent or parents without medical assistance because such child has special needs for medical, mental health or rehabilitative care…. [42 U.S.C. § 671(a)(21)]

Health care coverage can be provided through one or more state programs, but it must provide at minimum the services that the state Medicaid program offers.

Whether Medicaid services can meet the lifetime health needs of drug-exposed children is not clear. There is a question as to whether Medicaid provides sufficient support for adoptive families, particularly as primary pediatric services have been placed within managed care systems and little incentive may exist to make referrals to expensive specialists. Complicating the picture further are changes in the eligibility criteria for the Supplemental Security Income (SSI) program, which has served as a basis for Medicaid coverage for children with disabilities [42 U.S.C. § 1382 c(a)(3)(C) (i)]. Drug-exposed children must manifest very distinct physical disabilities in order to qualify for the financial benefits of the SSI program. The scientific literature teaches, however, that many of the disabilities of drug-exposed children are difficult to quantify and may be subtle cognitive or behavioral effects—problems that the new SSI rules do not recognize as a basis for benefits [Lester et al. 1998].

There is, however, a new program offering health care benefits to children, the Children's Health Insurance Program (CHIP) created by the Balanced Budget Act of 1997 [P.L.105-33, 111 Stat.251 (1997)]. CHIP constitutes a new Title XXI to The Social Security Act, amending the Medicaid program in Title XIX. In order to increase the number of low income children receiving health care,

CHIP allows states to extend Medicaid coverage to additional children, develop a separate state child health insurance program, or combine the two strategies. Irrespective of the approach used in implementing CHIP, the services offered to children must include those available through the standard Medicaid program, including the Early and Periodic Screening, Diagnosis, and Treatment (EPSDT) benefit [42 U.S.C. § 1396 d(r)].

Although adoption subsidies are not specifically mentioned in CHIP, all indications are that they will be administered just as they were prior to the inception of CHIP. If a child's preadoptive status permits access to CHIP coverage, these benefits will "travel" with the child through the adoption subsidy. If adoptive parents are fully employed and receive health insurance through a job, it is likely that they will select that insurance to cover the child's health needs, at least to the extent that the coverage is equivalent to services provided by Medicaid. At present, as a result of the 1993 Omnibus Budget and Reconciliation Act [P.L. 102-66], children placed with adoptive families who are insured under group health plans through the parent's employer receive plan benefits when they are in preadoptive status.

As adoptive parents work with child welfare agencies regarding health care coverage for their child, they should be aware of the programs that exist within the state and the benefits associated with each program in relation to their child's individual needs. For children for whom Medicaid is likely to be the selected health care coverage, adoptive parents should understand that children with special needs who are in foster care or who are receiving adoption assistance are not required to enroll in a managed care plan unless the state has received a waiver permitting such enrollment [42 U.S.C. § 1396v (a)(2), as authorized by the 1998 Balanced Budget Act, sec. 4701(a)]. Critical to effective negotiation of benefits for a child who is prenatally substance exposed is the adoptive parents' understanding of their child's current health status. A pediatrician specializing in the field of pediatric drug effects should review the child's medical records and examine the child. Adoptive parents also should have an understanding of the potential developmental and behavioral problems associated with prenatal drug and alcohol exposure that could arise in the future. Finally, in negotiating an adoption assistance agreement that includes health care coverage, adoptive parents should consider representation by knowledgeable counsel.

Defining a Child's Legally-Protected Interest in an Adoptive Family

Does a child have a legally-protected interest in a permanent, safe, and healthy home? There seems to be an instinctive sense that there should be such a right. Congress expressed its sentiment by enacting ASFA, encouraging swift placement of children in safe, permanent homes. There has been public anger, as reflected by the news media, when a child is removed from long-term membership in an adoptive or preadoptive family and returned to an uncertain future with birth parents who are strangers to her ["Baby Jessica," *In re Clausen* (1983); "Baby Richard," *In re Kirchner* (1995)]. Bills have been introduced in Congress and state legislatures to force different results in such cases.

Despite these developments, courts in the past have held that children do not have a legally-protected interest in a safe and healthy home. Courts and legislatures, however, may be moving closer to a different view of children's interests. Most recently, a federal district court in New York State defined "family" in a way that gives a preadoptive foster family, in certain circumstances, a right to speak on behalf of the child with an authority equal to that of birth parents. In determining whether this case is a significant advancement of a child's interests in the integrity of a permanent safe and healthy home, one must first examine some principles that the case seeks to modify.

Constitutional Protection for the Birth Parents' Right to Raise a Child

In the 1920s, the U.S. Supreme Court, in two cases, accorded parents the power to bring up their children letting their conscience be their guide, *Meyer v. Nebraska* (1923) and *Pierce v. Society of Sisters* (1925). The Court held that this parental right, an individual right to exercise judgment free from unreasonable government interference, falls within the protection of the Fourteenth Amendment of the U.S.

Constitution. Parents are constitutionally assured "due process" of the law to protest and rectify any violation of their right to raise their children.

This constitutional provision provides the foundation for the strong position that birth parents hold in any preadoptive relationship, including foster care, and sometimes even after an adoption has been declared by a court to be final. No other stakeholder in the adoption constellation has been recognized by the U.S. Supreme Court to have such secure constitutional protection—not the child, the foster parent, the preadoptive family, nor, in some circumstances, the adoptive family. In 1982, the U.S. Supreme Court held that "clear and convincing evidence" of parental unfitness is required to terminate parental rights [*Santosky v. Kramer* 1982], emphasizing the gravity of undoing the birth family relationship.

The protected position of the birth family has been attacked in court many times, and while the constitutional defense in the main has held, courts are beginning to define the rights of birth parents more narrowly. Courts have viewed the closest relationship as that of mother and child, a recognition that has implications in the area of substance abuse by pregnant and parenting women. In recent years, the public has become familiar with the issues involved in substance abuse during pregnancy. The debate has focused on whether the fetus is a "person" who, when threatened by toxic substances ingested by the mother, should be protected by the government. Alternatively, is the fetus solely part of the mother's birth system, and therefore, subject to her health decisions? While *Roe v. Wade* [1973] and subsequent cases leave the mother free to make judgments until the fetus is viable, the cases recognize that the government's authority to intervene increases in the third trimester. In South Carolina, criminal incarceration of substance-abusing pregnant women for the offense of endangering the fetus has been held to be a permissible legal sanction [*Whitner v. State* 1977], and in a number of other states, civil commitment of a pregnant woman who abuses drugs or alcohol is permitted.

Once a substance-exposed infant becomes a "person" through birth, the government can intervene aggressively to protect the child, but termination of parental rights remains a challenging legal task. In most states, before a newborn can be separated involuntarily from the mother, she must harm the child or have such a history of neglect or abuse of other children that danger to the newborn is imminent. Traditionally, termination of parental rights follows only after attempts to keep the family together have failed, and there is a showing of clear and convincing evidence of parental unfitness [*Santosky v. Kramer* 1982].

ASFA may speed the journey to adoption through fast-tracking provisions that include the latitude to seek termination of parental rights without offering family reunification services when there are "aggravated circumstances"; concurrent planning policies that encourage identification of adoptive homes at the same time that reunification is attempted; and authorization to file termination of parental rights petitions directly after permanency decisions. Nevertheless, permanency plans of adoption inevitably will bump against constitutionally-protected rights of parents, which have not been tested as yet in the post-ASFA era by courts of highest jurisdiction.

Because the history of parental rights for unmarried fathers follows a path that differs from that of mothers, the implications of ASFA may be different. When parental substance abuse is involved, identification of a child's father may be difficult. Life on the street for drug-using parents often includes shifting addresses, periods of incarceration, and anonymous sexual encounters. When mothers do not name their partners, identifying a child's father may seem to be a hopeless pursuit. To what extent can an agency's failure to identify and properly notify a father of his right to contest the adoption of his child be a barrier to swift adoption?

For most of our domestic relations history, it was unnecessary to obtain the consent of unmarried fathers who were not financially and physically active in caring for their children. In 1972, however, the U.S. Supreme Court recognized a general right of unmarried fathers to parent their children in a case in which the unmarried father had lived with the children and their mother for 18 years and actively cared for them [*Stanley v. Illinois* 1972]. Since that time, courts have considered the rights of fathers whose relationships were less committed than the father in that case and have defined those rights more narrowly. Courts have required that once an unmarried father becomes aware of parenthood, he must "grasp that opportunity" by "coming forward" to raise the child [*Lehr v. Robertson* 1983], such as by paying child support, visiting, or showing other signs of an unmistakable intention to be involved in the child's life.

Courts, in continuing to define the parental rights of birth fathers in relation to adoption, have focused on two points: whether the agency made a credibly energetic attempt to identify and locate the father and notify him of the pending adoption; and whether the father's assumption of responsibilities for the child were vigorous enough to merit constitutional protection equal to those of the mother. The better reasoned cases hold that if the father knows he is a parent and has failed to aggressively assert the rights and responsibilities of fatherhood, the court may grant an adoption without his consent and is not required to accord him a termination of parental rights hearing [*Adoption of Kelsey S.* 1992]. Other decisions, however, have held that adoption agencies must attempt to obtain the father's consent even when the father is unable to assume parental responsibilities because he is in prison or patently unfit [*Adoption of R.W.S.* 1997; *Michels v. Hodges* 1998].

An unidentified birth father, or a birth father who has been identified but has not been located or given proper notice of the pending legal action, can be a barrier to adoption. When an adoption agency is involved, it must make every effort to ensure that the birth father is identified, located, and given notice of the adoption, and that he provides consent. The painful lesson of a few recent cases is that an adoption may be quickly undone by the appearance of a birth father whose attempts to exercise his parental rights have been thwarted [*In re Clausen* 1993; *In re Kirchner* 1995; *Brumfeld v. Yard* 1996].

Redefining "Family"

Who is the child's "parent"? Who is the adult with legal authority to speak for the child as she moves through various family constellations in her journey from the birth family to the adoptive family? Specifically, can foster parents who wish to adopt the child assume aspects of that role?

While a child is with her birth family, her birth parents represent her legal interests. When the home poses severe environmental risks for the child, such as those associated with parental substance abuse, does the child have a constitutional right to government intervention to ensure her safety and health even if her birth parents, who speak for her, oppose such an effort? The U.S. Supreme Court in *DeShaney v. Winnebago County Department of Social Services* [1989] held that children do not have a constitutionally-based entitlement through the Fourteenth Amendment to adequate care and protection by the government. Moreover, as the Michigan Supreme Court made plain in "Baby Jessica," children's interests are inextricably intertwined with parents' interests and cannot be independently promoted. Parental rights, however, are affected once a court has jurisdiction over a child, as in a case in which neglect or abuse has been determined and the child removed from the parent's custody. In such cases, the court can make decisions for the child, and the authoritative voice for the child usually is the child welfare agency to which custody is transferred. Until parental rights have been terminated, however, the parent retains residual parental rights that impact important aspects of the child's life.

In the search for a permanent, safe, and healthy home for a child, it is crucial to find a responsible adult who can protect the child's interests. Foster parents have in the past attempted to fill that role. Their interests in relation to the children in their care were rebuffed, however, by the U.S. Supreme Court. While continuing to respect constitutional protections for birth parents, the Court declined to extend such rights to foster parents [*Smith v. O.F.F.E.R.* 1977]. A recent case in federal district court in New York challenges that position. In *Rodriguez v. McLoughlin* [1999], the foster mother had cared for a four-year-old child since infancy. His birth parents' rights had been terminated; his foster mother had filed an adoption petition; and the adoption was almost final. An agency caseworker arrived at the home for a scheduled visit and found the little boy in the care of his 12-year-old foster brother. When the foster mother, Ms. Rodriguez, did not return after two hours, the caseworker removed the child to another foster home. Ms. Rodriguez tried over several months to arrange a visit with the boy to reassure him, but the agency refused to let her contact him. Meanwhile, she appealed through administrative procedures the agency's decisions to remove the child from her home and deny her contact with him. After it was determined that her absence from home was excusable and there was no neglect, the child was returned to Ms. Rodriguez and the adoption process resumed.

Ms. Rodriguez decided to pursue the matter further through litigation, as she believed that she should have been accorded the constitutionally-guaranteed due process of law of a parent rather than the lesser administrative process available to a foster parent. She contended that if she had been a birth parent, a refusal to grant her request to visit with her child would have triggered the right to an immediate review of that decision. She argued that she was entitled to a higher standard of legal process because the child had no other parents; she was the only parent he knew, as he had lived with her since infancy; and she was close to becoming his parent through adoption.

The federal district court agreed with Ms. Rodriguez. The judge recognized "a constitutionally-protected liberty interest in the stability and integrity of the relationship between…a foster mother and foster child." The court was careful to define this right very narrowly to situations in which parental rights had been terminated; the foster parent has cared for the foster child continuously for more than twelve months since infancy; and the foster parent has entered into an adoptive placement agreement for the child. It is interesting to note that the position taken by the judge is similar to that found in ASFA, in which foster and preadoptive parents are given notice and an opportunity to be heard in neglect and abuse cases. Ms. Rodriguez prevailed on the merits of her case at trial. If Ms. Rodriguez prevails on the merits of her case and the case is upheld on appeal, it would be a step away from the exclusive right of birth parents to due process through the Constitution's Fourteenth Amendment and a step toward a new definition of "family."

Considering a Child's "Best Interests"

Perhaps it is not surprising that legislatures have been quicker than courts to require that a child's "best interests" be weighed in the removal of a child's custody from the parent. While courts repeatedly have focused on the liberty interest in parenthood in the decades since Meyer and Pierce, legislatures have attempted to enact laws which promote the best interests of children even at the expense of parents' rights. Congress made clear in ASFA that it is in a child's best interests to have a safe and healthy home. It further specified that termination of parental rights actions may be taken early within ASFA's time frames if a court determines that it is in a child's best interest. Similarly, in the wake of the "Baby Jessica" case, legislation was introduced in the U.S. House of Representatives that would have required courts hearing a birth parent's objection to an adoption to consider a child's best interests before changing custody from the preadoptive parents to the birth parents [H.R.4164]. At the state legislative level, "best interest" of the child has not been utilized as the exclusive basis for termination of parental rights, as statutes uniformly require that the parents initially be found unfit. These statutes, however, define what is not in the child's interests. Maryland's statute is typical in permitting termination if the child was "born addicted" or with the presence of a significant amount of illegal substances in the blood, and the parent refuses drug treatment [Md. Family Law Stat. § 5-313(d)(iv)].

Recently a number of carefully considered state courts of appeal opinions have raised "best interests" as a barrier to returning a child from a preadoptive family to the birth parents, even if the parents demonstrate stability and fitness to parent. Two such cases are from New Jersey. In *Adoption by R.* [1998], a father learned of his paternity six months after his child's birth and immediately began paying child support and visiting. Although the appeals court agreed that the father's challenge to the adoption sufficed to dismiss the adoption petition, it decreed that custody should not change from the long-term preadoptive home unless the impact on the child was weighed in a "best interests" hearing and change in custody was recommended by the trial court judge. The court noted that removal of the child from his psychological parents would be tantamount to termination of their "parental rights." Noting that both New Jersey courts and the New Jersey legislature recognize the harm caused a child when separated from a long-term caregiver, the court held that ignoring a child's "best interests" in the course of the child's journey from termination of parental rights through adoption is "plain error."

In a second New Jersey case, *Adoption by P.S.* [1998], a mother who had recovered from substance abuse sought the return of her substance-exposed, severely impaired nine-year-old child, whom she had voluntarily placed with a relative-foster family. The trial court held that, because the mother was fit, her right to raise her own child could not be denied and the adoption could not go forward. The court of appeals disagreed, directing the trial court to explore whether the child's interest in remaining with her bonded family outweighed the mother's interest in the limited relationship she had with the child. The court of appeals noted that although the parent-child relationship was part of a "precious package" of constitutionally protected individual rights and liberties, those rights are not absolute.

Wrongful Adoptions

Once the barriers to adoption have been surmounted and the child becomes a part of her new family, there may be additional legal issues. Some families have returned to court with their child, claiming "wrongful adoption." These parents claim that the children they adopted developed severe physical, mental, or behavioral problems for which the agency either intentionally or negligently failed to prepare the adoptive parents. Usually the claimants seek monetary compensation for unforeseen medical costs, although in some cases they seek to return the child to the adoption agency and annul or rescind the adoption [*Adoption of Kay C.* 1991; *Adoption of Lisa Diane G.* 1988].

Proof of Wrongful Adoption

In a wrongful adoption case, the adopters claim that the agency did not accurately portray the child they adopted. Usually the inaccuracies involve the child's physical, mental, or emotional condition at the time of adoption or the child's behavioral and developmental history. In some cases, the inaccuracies pertain to the background of the birth parents, including alcohol and drug abuse or the presence of other diseases or conditions in the birth family.

The agency may give an inaccurate picture of the child or family by withholding, failing to uncover, or negligently or intentionally misrepresenting information about the child. In the first successful wrongful adoption case, *Burr v. Board of County Commissioners of Stark County* [1986], the adopters were told that the 17-month-old child was a "healthy baby boy," whose 18-year-old unwed mother had cared for him since birth. Long after the adoption was final, it was discovered that the agency knew that the mother was a 31-year-old patient in a mental hospital, and that the child had been in foster care since birth. Similarly, in 1995, another court held that an agency could be liable for failing to disclose the birth mother's known history of mental illness [Juman v. Lousie Wise Services (1995)]. In Meracle v. Children's Service Society of Wisconsin (1998), the adopters were told that the child's father had tested negative for Huntington's disease, when in fact no such test existed.

The reported wrongful adoption cases contain a bewildering variety of agency misinformation, omitted details, honest error, and willful bad behavior. The law provides guidance as to when and under what circumstances agencies will be liable when accused of wrongful adoption, using the principles of negligence, negligent misrepresentation, intentional misrepresentation, and fraud. By way of example, negligence may be found if an agency fails to collect and review the records of a 3-year-old girl who had been in foster care her whole life. Negligent misrepresentation may start with the same facts—a 3-year-old in foster care since birth—but the agency tells the adopters that the child is healthy and normal, without reviewing any of the child's records. Intentional misrepresentation may be found if the agency reviews the child's records, discovers that the child's mother drank heavily during her pregnancy, but when asked about the mother's alcohol use by the adopters, replies that the mother had no such problem. Fraud may be found if the agency discovers evidence of prenatal alcohol abuse, destroys the records, and tells the adopters that the mother had no relevant medical concerns.

Wrongful adoption law continues to develop, and it is not possible to discern any clear trends. There are very few cases—only about 20 reported appellate cases since 1986, of which 7 were reported in the last 2 years. All wrongful adoption cases are fact-sensitive, that is, the unique circumstances yield a particular result. As an example, a caseworker in an agency might be expected to recognize obvious features of Fetal Alcohol Syndrome, but may not be expected to identify or report more obscure symptoms. Moreover, state laws and regulations control these cases and, as a result, a set of facts leading to successful recovery in one state may not lead to the same result in another state.

What is the future of wrongful adoptions and what impact will such suits have, if any at all, on adoption and especially on the adoption of drug-exposed children? Because agencies are concerned about being sued for wrongful adoption, the mere existence of such potential liability will affect agency practices, including those re-lated to the adoption of drug-exposed infants. Whether current trends will help or hinder the adoption of such children is impossible to predict.

Agencies should use care when placing drug-exposed infants for adoption, including situations in which the child's history is un-known or when maternal drug abuse is suspected. The better prac-tice, and one which will protect agencies in court, is full disclosure and frank appraisal of all known information. Adopters should be told when information is unreliable (for example, a notation in a foreign orphanage record that the parents did not drink) or unavail-able (for example, the behavior and environment of birth parents of an abandoned infant). When information about a particular child is not available, adopters should be told the reasons. Agencies should provide pictures and videotapes of children whenever possible and encourage adopters to obtain a review of all available information by a medical or child development specialist. Agencies should not overlook the potential problems adoptive families may face when adopting a child who is at risk for developmental problems as a result of prenatal substance exposure. Although full disclosure may dis-courage adopters who would be hesitant to adopt a high-risk child, prospective adoptive families may be more prone to adopt if they are confident that they have been provided all relevant information and warned of possible problems.

Wrongful adoption cases also have revealed the need for better postadoption services and a heightened responsiveness to adoptive families. In cases in which adopters subsequently complain that the agency failed to give them accurate information about their child's background, agencies should respond in a caring and helpful manner. Failure to respond appropriately could lead adopters to conclude that the agency is attempting to conceal a failure to provide information and, perhaps more importantly, could delay or even prevent proper attention to the child's needs. Agencies that place drug-exposed children should develop postadoption services that address the problems that are likely to arise after the adoption is finalized. As with full disclosure, the existence of such services could reduce risk of suit and encourage the adoption of at-risk children.

Agency Limitation of Liability

It is standard practice that agencies ask adopters to sign agreements that set out the terms and conditions of the agency's role and efforts and other important aspects of the adoption process. Engaged in responsibly, this practice can benefit agencies, adopters, and children needing permanent families. These agreements may include "exculpatory clauses" that state that the agency is not responsible for events that negatively affect the adoption process. Such clauses may contain such wording as the following:

> I/we hereby waive any and all claims which I/we may have now or in the future against the Agency and its directors, officers, employees, and agents, including doctors. We agree to hold the Agency and its above described directors, officers, and employees harmless against any claims known or unknown now existing or in the future, which may arise out of this application, receipt of services from, or adoption through the Agency.

Although many may argue that agencies should not, as a matter of public policy, be allowed to escape liability for their own actions through the use of exculpatory clauses, it is a practice that recent court decisions have allowed on the theory that an adoption agreement is a contract like any other into which two parties enter with their eyes open [*Regensberger v. China Adoption Consultant, Ltd.* 1998; *Ferenc v. World Child, Inc.* 1997].

It remains to be seen whether the use of exculpatory clauses will promote or hinder the adoption of drug-exposed children. It is possible that agency use of exculpatory clauses that reduce or eliminate the risk of suit for negligence, but allow suit for fraud or intentional misrepresentation will actually promote the adoption of at-risk children, including children prenatally exposed to drugs or alcohol. If agencies are freed from the cost of negligence suits, they may be encouraged to place drug-exposed children for adoption, knowing that only an intentional or fraudulent act will subject them to liability. Even though adopters would have no recourse if the agency were merely negligent, they would be able to sue if the agency acted fraudulently or intentionally misinformed them.

If agencies could totally insulate themselves from all suits, would adoptions of drug-exposed children be promoted or reduced? At first glance, it would seem that precluding all agency liability would promote adoptions, but the answer is not so clear. In fact, an end to agency liability might severely reduce the number of drug-exposed children who would be adopted. Without liability, agencies may have less incentive to adopt full disclosure practices that would provide an accurate, comprehensive presentation of a child. The number of people willing to offer homes to at-risk children may be reduced, because adopters would know that the adoption of a child who could be drug-exposed is enormously risky, and that if the agency has been negligent, it could not be held accountable in a law suit.

The Duty to Disclose and the Duty to Investigate

The most difficult area for agencies to navigate, and one of great importance to the adoption of drug-exposed children, involves the duty to investigate. There is a difference between a duty to disclose information, which has been established by the wrongful adoption cases, and a duty to investigate, which has not been imposed.

Currently, agencies need only to report information that would normally be generated in an adoption placement. If there were a duty to investigate, an agency could be held liable if it could have discovered relevant information about a child through investigation, but made no effort to do so. Agencies maintain that if they were held liable for information that could have been discovered, they would become the guarantor of the child's health and development.

A legal duty to investigate would pose severe problems for agencies and most likely have a direct impact on the extent to which drug-exposed children would be adopted. Under a duty to investigate, an agency could be found liable for failure to undertake an investigation, even in those cases when the need for such investigation did not become clear until after the adoption was finalized. The scope of an investigation would be difficult to determine, as there may always be one more document to collect or one more expert to consult. The agency's cost of undertaking mandated investigations is another factor, one which might well discourage it from attempting to place drug-exposed children for adoption. It is exactly these kinds of children who may call for intensive investigations and who may engender future wrongful adoption cases for a failure to competently investigate.

Can the two duties of disclosure and investigation best be sorted out by statute? A Washington State adoption statute, which attempts to allocate duties and risks between agency and adopter, approaches the issue by requiring agencies (and others) to make "reasonable efforts to locate records and information" concerning the child, family background, and social history, but expressly states that aside from an obligation to provide the information, the agency has "no duty…to explain or interpret the records or information…." [Wash. Rev. Code 1994]. It is too soon to determine whether such a statutory scheme is the right approach.

Wrongful Adoption in the Future

Wrongful adoption lawsuits still are quite rare, and there is no indication that agencies will face an onslaught of litigation. Courts seem unwilling to enlarge the exposure of agencies to liability;

legislators are finding ways to encourage responsible agency conduct and protect adopters; and agencies seem ready to adopt practices that will enable them to continue to place children, while minimizing their risks of being sued.

Are domestic adoptions more likely to produce wrongful adoption suits than intercountry adoptions in the future? Although both types of adoptions present similar issues, a reading of the reported cases suggests some differences. As a starting point, there is no reported example of a successful international wrongful adoption case. Agencies engaged in international adoptions recognize that accurate information regarding children is scarce, and available information may well be highly unreliable. They tend to take elaborate steps to ensure that prospective adopters are aware that they may adopt a child whose medical and developmental history and condition are unknown. When an adopter later sues the agency, courts have been willing to conclude that the adopter entered into the adoption process knowing that they may unintentionally and unknowingly adopt a child with serious medical conditions. Agencies engaged in international placements have not hesitated to use exculpatory clauses that insulate them from liability [*Regensberger v. China Adoption Consultants, Ltd.* 1998; *Ferenc v. World Child, Inc.* 1997].

Conclusion

A drug-exposed infant may encounter several challenges on the journey toward adoption. First are the legal complexities involved in terminating the rights of birth parents. Clear and convincing evidence of unfitness to parent must be produced to overcome parents' constitutionally-protected right to raise their child. Second are the challenges related to placing substance-exposed children with adoptive families. Agencies may have a difficult time finding a preadoptive home for drug-exposed infants who demonstrate special needs, including physical, mental, or emotional disabilities. The process, however, may be aided by the current fast-track approach to adoption under The Adoption and Safe Families Act. States now are offered financial incentives to make an extra effort to place children with special needs quickly, and adoption assistance agreements can help families meet children's current and future health needs. Adoptive parents, however, need expert advice on pediatric drug effects and well-drafted contracts to protect access to health care for later-emerging health problems.

When preadoptive parents are part of a state's foster care system, there are indications that the law gradually may be according them certain constitutional protections extended to birth parents. ASFA provides foster parents with notice of hearings and opportunity to be heard, and the recent federal court ruling in *Rodriguez v. McLoughlin* [1999] accorded foster parents a constitutionally-protected liberty interest under certain circumstances. These judicial and legislative developments may signal a greater level of legal protection for children's interim family relationships as they await adoption.

The third challenge relates to wrongful adoption suits, which have caused great unease among adoption agencies. When drug-exposed infants manifest serious disabilities that were not apparent at the time of adoption, adoptive parents may decide that they were intentionally or negligently misled by the agency. Some agencies have protected themselves by inserting exculpatory clauses into their contracts with prospective adoptive parents to foreclose wrongful adoption suits. In two intercountry adoption cases, these clauses were enforced by courts of appeals. The best legal protection for agencies rests in disclosing the information that is reasonably available, clarifying situations when information cannot be obtained, and offering resources and guidance to adoptive parents who are seeking a full understanding of the child's history.

The three emerging legal issues in the adoption of drug-exposed infants—fast tracking toward adoption, defining a child's legally protected interest in an adoptive family, and wrongful adoption—have important implications for current and future practice. While much is currently understood, ongoing developments in each of these areas will affect policy and practice bearing on the adoption of children with special needs in the future.

Appendix I. Referenced Cases Annotated

Adoption of Child by R., 705 A.2d 1233 (N.J. 1998). Where incarcerated father did not learn of baby until six months after birth and immediately began paying child support and expressing interest, court was right to dismiss adoption petition, but wrong to deny prospective adoptive custodial parents a "best interests" hearing so that impact on child of move to father could be weighed.

Adoption of Child by P.S., 716 A.2d 1171 (N.J. 1998). Despite constitutional protections, mother's interest in limited relationship with child to date should be weighed against child's best interests, before child is returned from adoptive family to mother

Brumfeld v. Yard, 673 N.E. 2d 461 (Ill.1996). Father, who made vigorous attempts to obtain custody of child, prevailed over long-term custodial family.

Burr v. Board of County Commissioners of Stark County, 491 N.E. 2d 1101 (Ohio 1986). Adoptive parents successfully sued county agency that made deceitful and material misrepresentations about child.

Clausen, In re, 502 N.W.2d 649 (Mich.1993). "Baby Jessica." Where custodial, preadoptive parents knew nine days after baby came into their care that mother had revoked adoption consent, and where they constantly defied court orders to return child to birth parents, state's highest court finds that they have no claims to child based solely on their custody of her.

DeShaney v. Winnebago County Dept. of Social Services, 489 U.S. 189 (1989). The Constitution does not create a general duty to protect children from neglect and abuse; the government is not obliged to guarantee its citizens a minimum level of safety and security.

Ferenc v. World Child, Inc., 977 F. Supp.56 (D.D.C. 1997). Adoptive family sued because important information about their adopted Russian child was inaccurate or not provided. Trial court dismissed suit, ruling that contract between adopters and agency minimized agency's obligations, warned adopters of risks of adoption, and waived their right to sue.

Juman v. Louise Wise Services, 211 A 2d 446 (N.Y. 1995). Adoptive parents' suit against agency will be permitted if agency fraudulently concealed information.

Kay C., Adoption of, 228 Cal.App.3d 741; 281 Cal. Rptr. 907 (1991). California law allows an adoption to be set aside if adoptive parents had no notice or knowledge of mental illness or developmental disability of adopted child.

Kelsey S., Adoption of, 823 P.2d 1216 (Cal.1992). California Supreme Court, interpreting the 1973 Uniform Parentage Act, said unwed father's parenting rights are equal to mother's if he demonstrates full commitment to responsibilities.

Kirchner, In re, 649 N.E.2d 324 (Ill.) cert. Denied, 515 U.S. 1152 (1995). "Baby Richard." After mother told father child had died, father located baby and vigorously attempted to gain custody; adoption was vacated and child given to father.

Lehr v. Robertson, 462 U.S. 248 (1983). Mere existence of a biological link does not merit equivalent constitutional protection; father must manifest specific interest by "coming forward to participate in the rearing of his child."

Lisa Diane G., In re, 537 A 2d 131 (R.I.1988). An adoption may be nullified if important information about child – in this case, an emotionally disturbed eight year old who should not have been placed for adoption – intentionally is withheld from adopters.

Meracle v. Children's Service Society of Wisconsin, 437 N.W.2d 532 (Wisc.1998). Agency made negligent misrepresentation about medical tests performed on biological parent.

Meyer v. Nebraska, 262 U.S. 390 (1923). Parents have a liberty interest in bringing up their children according to dictates of their own consciences.

Michels v. Hodges, 956 P.2d 184 (Ore.1998). Lacking father's consent to adoption, prospective adoptive parents cannot plead and prove father's unfitness on TPR grounds.

Pierce v. Society of Sisters, 268 U.S. 510 (1925). Parents, not the government, have the right and duty to direct the upbringing of a child.

Regensberger v. China Adoption Consultants, Ltd., 138 F.3d 1201 (7th Cir.1998). Adoptive parents sued a company providing travel and support services to those adopting from the People's Republic of China. Court dismissed parents' claims and enforced contract in which adopters acknowledged risks of international adoption and waived right to sue.

Rodriguez v. McLoughlin, 1999 W.L. 9834 (S.D.N.Y.). Federal district court extends certain constitutional protections to foster parent-adoptive child relationships, if parental rights have been terminated.

R.W.S,.Adoption of, 951 P.2d 83 (1997). Even though incarcerated father had not paid child support, as long as support obligation was stayed by court, consent to adoption required.

Roe v. Wade, 410 U.S. 113 (1973). A fetus is not a "person" in the Constitutional sense of the word; termination of pregnancy is a private decision protected by the 14th Amendment, except that other rights must be balanced against it when the fetus is viable in the third trimester.

Santosky v. Kramer, 455 U.S. 745 (1982).Government must provide clear and convincing evidence of parental unfitness before terminating parental rights.

Smith v. Organization of Foster Families for Equality and Reform (O.F.F.E.R.), 431 U.S. 816 (1977). Supreme Court considers, but does not decide, whether foster parents have a constitutionally-protected interest in their relationship with child.

Stanley v. Illinois, 405 U.S. 645 (1972). State may not terminate parental rights absent showing that father is unfit parent.

Whitner v. State, 492 S.E.2d 777 (S.C.1997). State's highest court finds that a fetus is a person for purposes of criminal law, and that woman who ingested drugs during pregnancy can be criminally prosecuted for harm to child.

Appendix II. Referenced Statutes And Administrative Rules Annotated

Adoption Assistance and Welfare Act of 1980, P.L.96-272; 42 U.S.C. 670 et seq. Version of the child welfare portion of the Social Security Act that governed adoptions until amended by the Adoption and Safe Families Act of 1997.

Adoption and Safe Families Act of 1997, P.L.105-89; 42 U.S.C. 620 et seq. Recent amendment of the Social Security Act that changes parts of the Adoption Assistance and Welfare Act of 1980.

The Balanced Budget Act of 1997, P.L. 1005-33 (August 5, 1997). Established Children's Health Insurance Program.

Maryland Family Law Statute, Md. Family Law Code Ann. §5-313(d)(iv) (1999). Best interests of child in parental termination proceeding.

Omnibus Budget and Reconciliation Act of 1993, P.L.103-66 (Aug. 10, 1993). Permits prospective adoptive children, as well as adopted children with pre-existing conditions, to be included in adoptive parent's group health insurance.

Proposed Act to amend Title 28, United States Code, with respect to the enforcement of child custody and visitation orders, H.R. 4164, 105th Cong., 2nd Sess., July 15, 1998. Would have required best interests of child to be considered prior to removal from an adoptive home and return to biological parents.

Washington Rev. Code Ann., §26.33.350(4); §26.33.380(2) (1994).Describes agency responsibilities for duty to disclose information, and duty to investigate.

References

Adoption Assistance and Welfare Act of 1980, P.L.96-272; 42 U.S.C. §§ 670 et seq. (1980).

Adoption and Safe Families Act of 1997, P.S. 105-89; 42 U.S.C. §§ 620 et seq. (1997).

Adoption of Child by P.S., 716 A.2d 1171 (N.J. 1998).

Adoption of Child by R., 705 A.2d 1233 (N.J. 1998).

Balanced Budget Act of 1997, P.L. 1005-33 (1997).

Barth, R. P. & Needell, B. (1996). Outcomes for drug-exposed children four years postadoption. *Children and Youth Services Review, 18*(1–2), 37–56.

Brumfeld v. Yard, 673 N.E.2d 461 (Ill. 1996).

Burr v. Board of County Commissioners of Stark County, 491 N.E.2d 1101 (Ohio 1986).

Carta, J. J., McConnel, S. R., McEvoy, M. A., Greenwood, C. R., Atwater, J. B., Baggett, K., & Williams, R. (1997). Developmental outcomes associated with in utero exposure to alcohol and other drugs. In M. Haack (Ed.), *Drug Dependent Mothers and their Children* (pp. 64–90). New York: Springer.

Clausen, In re, 502 N.W.2d 649 (Mich. 1993).

DeShaney v. Winnebago County Dept. of Social Services, 489 U.S. 189 (1989).

Ferenc v. World Child, Inc., 977 F.Supp. 56 (D.D.C. 1997).

Government Accounting Office (1998). *Foster care: Agencies face challenges securing stable homes for children of substance abusers.* Report to the Chairman, Committee on Finance, U.S. Senate. Washington, DC: U.S. General Accounting Office.

Juman v. Louise Wise Services, 211 A.2d 446 (N.Y. 1995).

Kay C., Adoption of, 228 Cal.App.3d 741; 281 Cal.Rptr.907 (1991).

Kelsey S., Adoption of, 823 P.2d 1216 (Cal. 1992).

Kirchner, In re, 649 N.E.2d 324 (Ill. 1995), *cert. denied*, 515 U.S. 1152 (1995).

Lehr v. Robertson, 462 U.S. 248 (1983).

Lisa Diane G., In re, 537 A.2d 131 (R.I. 1988)

Lester, B. M., LaGasse, L. L., & Seifer, R. (1998). Cocaine exposure and children: The meaning of subtle effects. *Science, 282,* 633–634.

Lester, B. M. & Tronick, E. Z. (1994). The effects of prenatal cocaine exposure and child outcome. *Infant Mental Health Journal, 15*(2), 1007–1120.

Md. Family Law Code Ann. § 5-313(d)(iv) (1999).

Mayes, L. C., Bornstein, M. H., Chawarska, K., & Granger, R. H. (1995). Information processing and developmental assessments in 3-month-old infants exposed prenatally to cocaine. *Pediatrics, 95*(4), 539–545.

Meracle v. Children's Service Society of Wisconsin, 437 N.W.2d 53 (Wisc. 1998).

Meyer v. Nebraska, 262 U.S. 390 (1923).

Michels v. Hodges, 956 P.2d 184 (Ore. 1998).

Miller, H. (1996). Prenatal cocaine exposure and mother-infant interaction: Implications for occupational therapy intervention. *The American Journal of Occupational Therapy, 51*(2), 119–131.

Omnibus Budget and Reconciliation Act of 1993, P.L. 103-66 (1993).

Pierce v. Society of Sisters, 268 U.S. 510 (1925).

Regensberger v. China Adoption Consultants, Ltd., 138 F.3d 1201 (7th Cir. 1998).

Rodriguez v. McLoughlin, 1999 WL 9834 (S.D.N.Y.).

Roe v. Wade, 410 U.S. 113 (1973).

R.W.S., Adoption of, 951 P.2d 83 (1997).

Santosky v. Kramer, 455 U.S. 745 (1982).

Smith v. Organization of Foster Families for Equality and Reform (O.F.F.E.R.), 431 U.S. 816 (1977).

Social Security Rules, 20 C.F.R. § 404, Subpart P, App. 1, sec.112.00C.2 & 112.02B.2.c.(2).

Stanley v. Illinois, 405 U.S. 645 (1972).

Streissguth, A. (1989). Neurobehavioral dose-response effects of prenatal alcohol exposure in humans from infancy to adulthood. *Annals N.Y. Academy of Sciences, 562*(145), 145–158.

Wash. Rev. Code § 26.33.350(4); 26.33.380(2) (1994).

Whitner v. State, 492 S.E.2d 777 (S.C. 1977).

10

The Adoption of Children Prenatally Exposed to Alcohol and Drugs: A Look to the Future

Madelyn Freundlich

Despite all that is known about prenatal alcohol and drug exposure through research, practice, and policy, much is not fully understood, particularly in the context of the adoption of children affected by prenatal substance exposure. As adoption professionals look to the future, there is a need to expand upon the vital information currently available through research, build further on the existing practice base, and address many of the policy issues in this area. Research is needed to provide a fuller understanding of the postnatal factors associated with developmental outcomes for substance-exposed children. Practice needs to give greater attention to the recruitment and preparation of prospective adoptive parents, staff training, and ongoing support for families following adoption. Policy needs to be evaluated carefully to determine its impact on essential service delivery issues for prenatally substance-exposed children and their adoptive families, particularly with regard to maternal substance abuse during pregnancy, the current emphasis on adoption as a permanency alternative for substance-exposed children, and the need for postadoption services. This chapter considers the directions that research, practice, and policy should take in the future to strengthen services for children affected by prenatal alcohol and drug exposure and their adoptive families.

Research and Directions for the Future

The Existing Research

Research on the scope, nature, and effects of prenatal alcohol and drug exposure in relation to adoption is limited. The research, however, provides a significant knowledge base on the effects of prenatal substance exposure, which can inform adoption practice and policy. The key learnings from the current research can be summarized as follows:

Although imprecise, estimates regarding the extent of prenatal alcohol and drug exposure suggest that prenatal exposure continues to have a significant impact on large numbers of children, including children who are adopted from other countries.

Estimates of prenatal drug exposure vary and have been framed from a variety of perspectives. With regard to prenatal drug use and exposure:

- Chasnoff [1989] has estimated that 11% of the infants born each year are exposed to illicit drugs.
- Gomby and Shiono [1991] have projected that 739,000 women each year use one or more illegal drugs during pregnancy.
- Schipper [1991] has calculated that a substance exposed infant is born more frequently than every 90 seconds.
  With regard to prenatal alcohol exposure and its effects:
- Some 2.6 million infants are believed to be prenatally exposed to alcohol each year [Gomby and Shiono 1991].
- Fetal Alcohol Syndrome (FAS) has been determined to affect between 1.3 and 2.2 children per 1,000 live births yearly in North America [US Department of Health and Human Services 1990; Streissguth & Giunta 1988]
- Cases of Alcohol Related Birth Defects (ARBD) are believed to exceed cases of FAS by a ratio of 2:1 to 3:1, with between 16,500 and 22,000 children born annually exhibiting the effects of prenatal exposure to alcohol [Streissguth & Giunta 1988; Abel & Kintcheff 1984]

Internationally, there is very little data on rates of prenatal substance exposure, although Aronson, as her chapter indicates, has found that children adopted from Russia disproportionately meet the strictest requirements for FAS—eight times greater than the world FAS incidence.

These data suggest that prenatal substance exposure affects significant numbers of children each year, and given recent data regarding parental drug and alcohol use [Feig 1998; U.S. Department of Health and Human Services 1996], it can be anticipated that large numbers of children will continue to be exposed prenatally to alcohol and drugs.

Many potential effects of prenatal alcohol and drug exposure on development have been identified; the extent to which an individual child will experience these effects, however, cannot be readily determined.

A range of possible effects of prenatal alcohol and drug exposure on newborns has been well documented. Researchers have confirmed potential effects of prenatal exposure to cocaine, opiates, amphetamines and methamphetamines, PCP, marijuana, and alcohol [Brady et al. 1994]. The impact of prenatal substance exposure on an individual child, however, cannot be predicted. A wide range of effects, from severe conditions such as neurological damage and growth retardation to normal developmental outcomes, have been observed [Sameroff 1986]. Prenatal factors affecting outcomes for children—which help to explain the variations observed in individual infants—include the type of drug to which the child was exposed; exposure history, including timing, amount, and duration of exposure; maternal comorbidity [the presence of associated mental health and social problems]; maternal health and medical history; and access to medical care [Myers et al. 1992; Weston et al. 1989].

The impact of prenatal alcohol and drug exposure on a child's long-term development varies, depending not only on prenatal factors, but also on the child's own biological vulnerability and the nature of the postnatal environment.

Understanding of the longer-term developmental impact of prenatal substance exposure has evolved significantly with ongoing research. The early research, conducted in the 1970s through the early 1990s, associated prenatal substance exposure with significant health and

developmental problems and extremely poor prospects for intellectual and social functioning. As research yielded information on
broader samples of children and studied the development of substance-exposed children over time, it became apparent that a range
of outcomes was associated with prenatal substance exposure, including the absence of significant problems. The research also
demonstrated that, in addition to the nature and degree of prenatal
substance exposure and maternal health status during pregnancy,
postnatal factors play an important role in a child's long-term
development, an influence not taken into account in the early
research.

In general, postnatal factors such as the quality of caregiving the
child receives [Daghestani 1988; Lester & Tronick 1994], the stability of the family environment [Free et al. 1990; Rodning et al. 1991],
and socioeconomic factors [Powell 1991; Storkamp et al. 1993] have
been found to play important roles in children's developmental
outcomes. Some studies have suggested that the nature of the
interaction between mother and child and other social factors have
a greater effect on certain outcomes than does prenatal substance
exposure [Myers et al. 1992; Barth 1991]. Research further indicates
that biologically vulnerable infants are affected to a greater degree by
stresses in the postnatal environment than infants whose biological
status is within normal limits [Escalona 1982].

Specifically, poorer developmental outcomes for children have
been associated with environmental factors such as poverty [Storkamp
et al. 1993]; inadequate caregiving, inappropriate parent-child interactions, and lack of adult supervision [Howard & Kropenske 1991;
Free et al. 1990]; ongoing parental abuse of alcohol and other drugs,
often accompanied by mental disorder [Chavkin et al. 1993]; family
disorganization and instability [Tarter et al. 1993]; and child abuse
and neglect [Murphy et al. 1991]. Conversely, the research indicates
that child development is optimized by favorable caregiving environments [Zuckerman 1993]. Research consistently has found that
positive factors in the social environment can promote the social,
cognitive, and emotional development of prenatally substance-
exposed children [Beckwith 1990; Tronick & Beeghly 1992].

The small body of existing research regarding prenatally substance-exposed children who are adopted suggests that they generally fare well developmentally, although caution must be taken not to overinterpret these findings.

As Barth and Brooks report in their chapter, research indicates that children who were prenatally exposed to drugs and then adopted have comparable developmental outcomes to adopted children who were not prenatally substance-exposed. Their research found that, like the adoptive parents of nonexposed children, adoptive parents of prenatally substance-exposed children express high levels of satisfaction with adoption. Their research points to the impact of the child's preadoption history on developmental outcomes, with findings that suggest that placements of children at older ages and multiple placements prior to adoption have a more negative effect on development than does prenatal drug exposure.

The findings of Barth and Brooks are consistent with those of Ornoy, Michailevskaya, and Lukashov [1996], which revealed differences based on prenatal exposure and postnatal environment. Ornoy and associates found that at age five, children who were prenatally exposed to heroin functioned as well as children who were not prenatally exposed; children who were prenatally exposed to heroin and then reared by their birth parents functioned more poorly than heroin-exposed children who were adopted; and children who had not been exposed in utero to heroin, but who had been reared in "neglecting" or "abusing" environments functioned even less well than children born to heroin-dependent mothers. These findings led the researchers to conclude that developmental outcomes for children of heroin-dependent mothers were primarily influenced by the environment.

Several cautions, however, must be noted regarding the interpretation of these findings. There is evidence that adopted children exposed to drugs and alcohol in utero may be more vulnerable to learning difficulties and language delays [Barth & Needell 1996]. Although these vulnerabilities have not been associated with significant impairments in children's early years [Barth & Needell 1996], these findings suggest that more attention needs to be given to the development of services to assist adoptive parents and children with what may be difficult transitions in adolescence and adulthood. Barth and Brooks, in their research reported in this volume, also raise several cautionary notes about the future for children who are adopted following prenatal substance exposure, especially children adopted at older ages. Although they find that the satisfaction level of parents who adopt drug-exposed children is not different from that of parents who adopt nonexposed children, the level of parental satisfaction decreases significantly over time. Despite the fact that the children in their study are in their preteens, an age at which parents may find them most enjoyable as they become more competent and independent but have not yet developed a "rebellious" side, they found a notable decline in parental satisfaction. That finding, coupled with the high level of these children's participation in special education, may presage stresses as the youngsters enter their adolescent years.

Research also cautions against an overemphasis on the benefits of a nurturing postnatal environment in remediating problems associated with prenatal substance exposure, particularly in the case of prenatal alcohol exposure. As Cadoret and Riggins-Caspers report in their chapter, prenatal alcohol exposure is likely to have detrimental and enduring effects on future behavior, irrespective of environmental factors. A continuum of negative effects is associated with Fetal Alcohol Syndrome even when an optimal caregiving environment is provided, as the research of Cadoret and Riggins-Caspers indicates that exposure to alcohol in utero contributes to the development of adult psychiatric problems even after exposure to postnatal risk factors has been taken into account. These researchers also find, however, that when prenatal exposure combines with an adverse postnatal environment, the number of psychiatric symptoms in adult adoptees substantially increases. The adoptees in their study who were exposed to alcohol prenatally and to adverse adoptive home factors reported two to three times the number of psychiatric symptoms as adoptees who were exposed only to adverse adoptive home factors.

Research on attachment suggests that caregivers with certain characteristics can promote positive outcomes for children who are prenatally exposed to alcohol or drugs.

Attachment theory is based on the premise that infants' earliest relationships with their primary caregivers serve as a blueprint for subsequent relationships [Bowlby 1969/1982]. This early parent-child relationship provides the child with an opportunity to develop a sense of security, a conception of self, and expectations that establish a basis for later social relationships [Johnson & Fein 1991; Fahlberg 1996]. There is some evidence that children's opportunities to attach are limited by early privation, relationship disruption, and abuse and neglect [Cermak & Groza 1998; van IJzendoom 1995; Yarrow & Goodwin 1973]. Prenatal drug exposure may also be associated with attachment problems, although the extent of the impact on individual children varies significantly [Rodning et al. 1991]. For children whose attachment opportunities may have been limited by early experiences, adoption may present an opportunity for attachment by providing the child with "new relationships with those who nurture them and enhance their security and protection" [Johnson & Fein 1991, p. 406; see also Hughes 1997; Keck & Kupecky 1995]. As Dozier and Albus report in their chapter, the sensitivity of a child's caregiver and the way in which a caregiver responds to a child's avoidant behavior may play an important role in facilitating a child's attachment. Their research suggests that adoptive parents can learn effective ways of interpreting and responding to potentially alienating behaviors on the part of children whose early experiences with caregivers have limited their opportunities to learn how to attach. As other researchers have noted, however, the impact of nurturing parenting may be limited when a child has sustained central nervous system dysfunction as a result of prenatal alcohol or drug exposure [see Brown et al. 1991; Kelley 1992].

Implications for Future Research

Research has provided information on the range of effects of prenatal alcohol and drug exposure on newborns; the longer-term effects that are observed in some, although by no means all, children with histories of prenatal substance exposure; and the extent to which the postnatal environment may exacerbate or remediate the effects of prenatal substance exposure. Because, however, of the multiple variables that bear on the longer-term effects of prenatal alcohol and drug exposure—involving the prenatal drug or alcohol use itself, the biological vulnerability of the individual fetus, and an array of medical, social, and psychological factors that impact maternal functioning during pregnancy—it has not been possible to definitively determine the effects of prenatal exposure on an individual child. Further, because of the complexity of child development and the multiplicity of postnatal factors that may affect children's developmental outcomes, research has not been able to provide sufficient information to allow projections of future outcomes for individual children. It appears unlikely that future research could provide definitive information on developmental outcomes on an individualized basis.

Future research, however, could contribute to a fuller understanding of the impact of adoption through additional and more comprehensive studies that consider postnatal environmental factors on long-term developmental outcomes. As the work of Orny and colleagues [1996] suggests, much can be learned by comparing outcomes for children prenatally exposed to substances and reared by their birth families to outcomes for substance-exposed children who are adopted. Similarly, the work of Barth and Brooks, which compares outcomes for adopted children who are drug-exposed and adopted children who are not drug-exposed, demonstrates that research can provide significant information about longer-term outcomes for children who are adopted. A more complete research-based understanding of the benefits and limits of positive postnatal environments would enhance agency practice in preparation and support services for the adoptive parents of children with histories of prenatal substance exposure. Such an understanding will require more extensive longitudinal research that follows substance-exposed children into adolescence and adulthood; utilizes a full range of comparison groups, including substance-exposed children reared by birth families and by adoptive families, and non-exposed children reared by birth families and by adoptive families; and a broader range of outcome measures across a spectrum of psychological, social, and intellectual functioning.

Similarly, further research is needed into the specific aspects of the postnatal environment that promote positive developmental outcomes for children who display a range of effects related to prenatal drug and alcohol exposure. Building on the research of Dozier and Albus, more information is needed to understand such questions as: Are there caregiver characteristics that are associated with more effective parenting of children with prenatal histories of substance exposure? Are there aspects of the postnatal environment other than caregiver characteristics that are more or less supportive of positive developmental outcomes? Are there certain aspects of the environment that are more critical, depending on the nature of the effects of the child's prenatal exposure? Finally, what is the role of different types of support systems, both formal and informal, in supporting and enhancing efforts to maximize positive developmental outcomes for substance-exposed children?

Adoption Practice and Directions for the Future

Current Practice

As reflected by Aronson, Dozier, and Edelstein and colleagues in their chapters, a significant practice base of services for substance-exposed children and their adoptive families has developed. Practitioners who have specifically focused on this population of children and families have defined quality adoption planning and services. The practice base that has evolved from their work primarily has focused on five areas:

- Sound information gathering from birth families regarding health and other background factors, including high-risk factors that suggest the use of alcohol or drugs during pregnancy, or, in the case of international adoption, the gathering of information from medical records and other available sources;

- Assessment of children to determine the extent to which there are health or development problems associated with prenatal alcohol or drug exposure;
- Solid preparation of adoptive families—both kin and families who are unrelated to the child—regarding the uncertainties of adoption in general and, specifically, the adoption of children who have been prenatally exposed to alcohol or drugs;
- Ongoing support for adoptive families and children, including counseling, financial and/or medical assistance, services to meet the child's health and developmental needs, support and education for the adoptive family, and advocacy; and
- Training for professionals who work with prenatally substance-exposed children and their adoptive families to enhance their knowledge of the effects of prenatal alcohol and drug exposure; their ability to work effectively with birth parents, adopted children, adoptive parents, foster parents and extended family members; and their skills in working with other disciplines to respond effectively to the needs of children and families. [Edelstein 1995].

Despite this sound practice base, challenges in serving substance-exposed children and their adoptive families remain. A key practice area that is fraught with difficulties is permanency planning for children in foster care who are affected by prenatal alcohol and drug exposure. Reunification of substance-exposed children with their parents is complicated by the uncertainties related to parents' ability to achieve and maintain sobriety; the limited availability of substance abuse treatment services; and the often protracted course of drug/alcohol treatment [Kaplan-Sanoff & Rice 1992]. As a result, children removed from the custody of substance-involved parents are far less likely to return home than are children removed from the custody of parents who are not abusing drugs or alcohol [Walker 1994]. As it has become apparent that reunification in these cases generally will not be easily realized, there has been a shift from the stance in the early 1990s that adoption should rarely be considered for prenatally substance-exposed children [McCullough 1991] to greater interest in adoption as a permanency option for these children. This new focus has important implications for recruitment and preparation of prospective adoptive parents, postplacement and postadoption support for adoptive families, and education of adoption professionals.

Similar practice issues have arisen in private adoptions in which birth parents voluntarily place their children for adoption and in international adoptions. While there are no definitive statistics, private adoption agencies in the United States indicate that, increasingly, infants and young children whom they place for adoption have "special needs," many of which are related to prenatal alcohol and drug exposure [Goldwater 1997; Legg 1997]. Additionally, as Barth and Brooks point out in this volume, parents in this country knowingly adopt drug-exposed children through attorneys and physicians. From the international perspective, reports from the field indicate that children adopted from abroad, particularly from Russia and the Eastern Republics, are at particular risk of prenatal exposure to alcohol and that many manifest the effects of prenatal exposure to alcohol. As Aronson indicates in her chapter, trends in Russia reflect a significant increase in the rate of alcoholism among women and higher rates of adolescent pregnancy, factors which have been associated with higher levels of fetal alcohol exposure. These trends highlight the need for solid adoptive parent preparation programs, ongoing support and services following adoptive placements, and training of adoption professionals on drug and alcohol exposure issues.

Implications for Practice in the Future
It can be anticipated that there will continue to be a significant need for adoption planning and services for children affected by prenatal alcohol and drug exposure, both domestically and internationally. Domestically, the use of crack-cocaine may be declining, but the use of other drugs, including heroin and methamphetamines, is on the rise [General Accounting Office 1998], and use of drugs by pregnant

and parenting women remains at a significant level [US Department of Health and Human Services 1996]. Internationally, prenatal alcohol exposure will continue to be an issue for adoption practice in the future if, as anticipated, the number of adoptions continues at its rate of steady growth and a substantial percentage of adoptions continues to be of children from Russia and Eastern Europe [Adoptive Families of America 1998].

A key area of focus for adoption practice in the future will be the recruitment and preparation of adoptive families for children in the foster care system, for whom reunification is not feasible and for whom adoption is the permanency plan. Currently, many public child welfare agencies report that they have only a limited number of adoptive families available to them [General Accounting Office 1998]. These agencies may face particular challenges in recruiting sufficient numbers of families to adopt children affected by prenatal substance exposure because of misperceptions that these children are significantly "damaged" and fears that the challenges of parenting these children are too difficult to overcome. An essential component of recruitment efforts will be, as Edelstein and colleagues propose in their chapter, education and preparation services that provide prospective adoptive parents with the information and support they need to consider adoption in a fully informed manner and make the decision to adopt.

Although adoptive parent recruitment may be less of a challenge in private domestic and international adoption because of the high level of interest in adopting younger children, including those with special needs, preparation of prospective adoptive parents who may adopt a child with a history of prenatal substance exposure is equally critical. In private domestic adoptions, as with the adoptions of children in foster care, the full nature of a child's prenatal substance exposure and the longer-term impact of that exposure are not always clear. As a result, it is essential that adoptive parents be assisted to understand "what the challenges could look like," and that although a child may appear healthy at the time of adoption, problems may occur as the child enters later developmental stages [Klein 1998]. Components of this preparation include educational materials that outline the potential impact of prenatal substance exposure, casework services to assist the family to understand and integrate the information, encouraging the family to talk with other families who have adopted children with histories of prenatal sub-stance exposure, and, whenever possible, consultative services with pediatricians with expertise in prenatal alcohol and drug exposure [Klein 1998].

Families who choose to pursue international adoption require the same preparatory and support services. In the case of children adopted from other countries, information regarding a child's prena-tal history, including the extent to which a child may have been exposed to alcohol or drugs, may be even more limited than is the case in the United States. For many children adopted internation-ally, medical records provide only minimal information, and birth families are often not available to supplement the information in the records maintained by the orphanage or institution in which the child lives. In both domestic and international adoption practice, providing prospective adoptive parents with an opportunity to develop realistic expectations supports informed decision making and, as the research demonstrates, enhances the stability of adoptive placements [Brodzinsky et al. 1998].

A second critical area for practice in the future is postadoption services. Traditionally, services following adoption finalization have been neglected as a component of adoption programs: fewer than one-third of the states have formal programs to serve adoptive families of children in foster care after adoptions are legalized [Barth 1997], and postadoption services for families who adopt privately, either domestically or internationally, are not widely available [Sullivan 1998]. As an initial matter, this dearth of postadoption support is likely to bode poorly for enhanced recruitment of adoptive families for children in foster care who have been prenatally exposed to alcohol and drugs. The assurance of the availability of financial assistance and services following adoption, as Edelstein and col-leagues emphasize, plays a critical role in many prospective adoptive parents' decisions to go forward with adoption. Additionally, postadoption support is critical in assisting families to cope with health and developmental issues that may surface after adoption, often during a child's pre-school, school-age and adolescent years. Practitioners consistently have highlighted the importance of postadoption support and services in ensuring stability of adoptive families in general [Voice for Adoption 1997], and these services are likely to be even more important for families who have adopted children whose long-term development may be affected by prenatal substance exposure.

One approach to the development and implementation of a comprehensive and integrated program of preparation and postadoption services for families who adopt children affected by prenatal alcohol or drug exposure is set forth by Sullivan [1997]. She advances a multifaceted service system that includes social acceptance and support; education about adoption; counseling and mental health services; specialized health, development, legal, and financial services; and advocacy. The following table, based on her framework, outlines the services that should be provided to fully prepare families to adopt children with special needs, including children affected by prenatal substance exposure, and to provide support following adoption.

Finally, practice in the future will need to address the education of adoption professionals about the potential effects of prenatal substance exposure, the variations in outcomes for children exposed prenatally to drugs and alcohol, and the impact of the postnatal environment on developmental outcomes. When professionals lack an understanding of the research, their views of substance-exposed children may be shaped by media accounts portraying children and their prospects for the future in a highly negative light. Unfamiliarity with the research may cause them to question whether adoption should be pursued for these children, and they are likely to be uncertain as to how best to advise and prepare prospective adoptive parents considering adoption of a child affected by prenatal substance exposure. Because it is likely that prenatal substance exposure will continue to be an issue in private domestic, international, and special needs adoption, professionals in all areas of adoption need education that provides a sound understanding of the research, so that they can plan appropriately for children and provide adoptive parents with the education and support they need.

Table 10-1. A Comprehensive Adoption Support and Services Program (Adapted from Sullivan 1997)

Service Type	For Adopted Individuals	For Birth Families
Social Acceptance and Support Services	• Provide adopted individuals with opportunities to normalize the experience of becoming a family member through adoption	• Provide birth families with validation of their decision as a responsible choice and of adoption as a valued and acceptable plan for the child born to them
Education about Adoption	• Provide adoptive parents and children with knowledge and skills in resolving common problems that adoptive families experience; provide adoptive families with specific preparation and training on issues related to prenatal alcohol and drug exposure	• Provide birth families with an understanding of the postadoption stresses that birth parents commonly experience
Counseling and Mental Health Services	• Help adopted adults with issues such as search and reunion with their birth families	• Assist birth families experiencing significant post-adoption stress

Table 10-1. Continued

Specialized Health Care and Developmental Services		• Provide services that meet the special health needs of adopted children; for children affected by prenatal alcohol and drug exposure, provide developmental and special education services
Legal Services	• Provide adoptive families with help in finalizing adoptions	
Financial Assistance	• Provide adoption assistance to support adoptive families in meeting the child's ongoing special needs	• Provide adoption assistance to support adoptive families in meeting the child's ongoing special needs
Advocacy	• Integrate throughout the service framework to ensure that the needs of adoptive families and children, adopted adults and birth families are recognized and addressed, and that policy decisions that impact adoption are well grounded on an understanding and appreciation of the needs and interests of all parties to adoption	• Integrate throughout the service framework to ensure that the needs of adoptive families and children, adopted adults and birth families are recognized and addressed, and that policy decisions that impact adoption are well grounded on an understanding and appreciation of the needs and interests of all parties to adoption

Similarly, practice needs to recognize the importance of training mental health and other professionals who serve adopted children and their families on the effects of prenatal substance exposure, the range of health and developmental outcomes associated with prenatal exposure to drugs and alcohol, and the influence of postnatal environmental factors on developmental outcomes. Because a range of professionals from a variety of disciplines respond to issues that affect substance-exposed children and their adoptive families—including social work, medicine, psychology, the law, education, and occupational therapy—multidisciplinary training models need to be developed and implemented. Additionally, as Edelstein and colleagues point out, practice is enhanced when service systems develop opportunities to convene various disciplines for case conferences and consultations, as well as broader service planning.

Policy and Issues for the Future

Policy related to substance abuse and prenatal substance exposure generally has not focused on the treatment needs of women who are substance-involved, nor on the service needs of their children as a result of prenatal alcohol or drug exposure. Policies related to drug and alcohol use by pregnant and parenting women, according to Kandall in this volume and others [Carter & Larson 1997; Nelson & Marshall 1998], have concentrated on interventions designed to punish maternal substance abuse. Broad family and child welfare policy efforts rather than policies specific to the needs of substance-exposed children have shaped responses to prenatal substance exposure. These broader policies have included the reconstruction of "safety net" programs, often in ways that may erode rather than strengthen services needed by substance-exposed children, their birth parents, and their adoptive families; and efforts to free larger numbers of children for adoption, often without adequate consideration of the supports needed by children and their adoptive families.

Current Policies Regarding Parental Alcohol and Drug Abuse and Their Future Impact

In his chapter in this volume, Kandall argues that blame and punitiveness have characterized the policy environment surrounding maternal alcohol and drug use since the mid-to-late 1980s. He maintains that policy largely has developed in the context of intense media attention to "crack" babies, with characterizations of mothers as uncaring and irresponsible, and of infants as uniformly underdeveloped, brain-damaged, and incapable of attaching to any caregiver [Blakeslee 1990; McFadden 1990]—portrayals borne out neither by research [Zuckerman 1991] nor practice [Edelstein 1995]. Three policy approaches to maternal substance abuse have emerged: criminalization, resulting in the arrest of women for drug use during pregnancy; involuntary civil commitment of substance-abusing pregnant women for purposes of fetal protection; and child welfare interventions at the time of a newborn's birth on grounds of child abuse or neglect, often resulting in the child's placement in foster care [Nelson & Marshall 1998].

In contrast to the limited use of criminalization and involuntary civil commitment procedures to punish or control substance abuse during pregnancy [Carter & Larson 1997; Figdor & Kaeser 1998], there has been a broad use of child protective service interventions when newborns evidence the effects of prenatal alcohol or drug exposure [Nelson & Marshall 1998]. A number of states have developed policies under which a newborn's positive drug toxicology and other evidence of maternal alcohol or drug use provide a basis for initiating a child protective service investigation; substantiating a finding of child abuse or neglect; and supporting the involuntary removal of the child from the parent's custody [Nelson & Marshall 1998]. Research supports the benefits of early protective service interventions that comprehensively assess safety and well-being issues for infants born with positive drug toxicology results [Jaudes & Ekwo 1997]. It further suggests that more positive outcomes are associated with foster care services for children at significant risk of harm and ongoing home-based services for children who are discharged to their families [Jaudes & Ekwo 1997].

As maternal drug use has grown over the past decade and child protection policies have been implemented in response, parental substance abuse has become the foremost factor in the increase in the number of children entering foster care because of abuse or neglect

[Albert & Barth 1996; Feig 1990]. Although not all children who enter foster care because of parental substance abuse are physically affected by drugs or alcohol, a significant number of children in foster care have histories of prenatal substance exposure [Jaudes & Ekwo 1997]. The General Accounting Office [1994] found that the percentage of children in care who were considered at risk for significant health problems as a result of prenatal drug exposure grew from 29% in 1986 to 62% in 1991.

Given the difficulties in reuniting children in foster care with their substance-involved parents and the growing interest in adoption as a permanency alternative for substance-affected children, termination of parental rights has begun to receive greater attention as an outcome of foster care entry [National Center on Addiction and Substance Abuse 1999]. The federal Adoption and Safe Families Act (ASFA) [1997], enacted in 1997, provides a legal framework for broader and more timely efforts to terminate parental rights and free children for adoption. ASFA requires, as Larsen and Schweitzer point out in their chapter, that a permanency hearing be held for a child within 12 months of entry into care, and that a petition to terminate parental rights be filed, with some exceptions, when a child has been in foster care for 15 of the most recent 22 months. These provisions, designed to promote adoption "fast tracking" for children in care, may particularly impact cases in which maternal alcohol or drug use precipitated the child's entry into foster care and continues to be a factor that precludes reunification. These cases, in fact, may present the very type of situation for which the expedited termination of parental rights provisions of ASFA were intended: success rates for drug and alcohol treatment are variable; years of treatment may be required even in the more successful situations; and children of drug and alcohol-involved parents historically have remained in foster care for lengthy periods of time pending efforts to reunify them with their parents [Besharov 1996].

ASFA may prompt changes in state laws that set forth the substantive grounds for termination of parental rights. States are currently in the process of amending their statutes to conform to ASFA requirements and thereby ensure that they will continue to be eligible for federal child welfare funding [U.S. Department of Health and Human Services 1998; New York Public Welfare Association 1998]. Currently, only a few states statutorily permit termination of parental rights to be based on drug- or alcohol-related incapacity and a history of repeated, unsuccessful efforts at treatment [Hardin & Lancour 1996]. Other states may move to incorporate such grounds into their termination of parental rights statutes, a policy direction that would be consistent with the approach taken in the federal welfare reform act [Personal Responsibility and Work Opportunity Reconciliation Act of 1996] with regard to adult drug and alcohol addiction and drug-related crimes. If such changes in state laws on termination of parental rights were to occur in connection with the implementation of the federally-mandated time frames for pursuing termination of parental rights, there could be a significant increase in the number of substance-exposed children in foster care freed for adoption.

Although ASFA requires that states pursue termination of parental rights in a more expedited manner, it also creates certain exceptions to this mandate. Such actions, for example, need not be pursued if the state agency has failed to provide parents with the services necessary for the safe return of the child to them [42 USC § 675(e)(4)(E)]. In the case of mothers who need alcohol and drug treatment services, the limited availability of community-based services theoretically could result in the exemption of these cases from termination of parental rights requirements. The argument could be made that termination of parental rights is not justified when substance-involved parents cannot receive rehabilitative services because, as is the case in many communities, treatment services for women are not available or long waits for residential treatment beds or outpatient services are commonplace [Woolis 1998; American Humane Association 1994; Kumpfer 1991]. On the other hand, there appears to be a growing intolerance for drug-involved parents and more strident insistence that the rights of substance-involved parents be terminated in a timely fashion and their children provided with the permanency and security of adoption [Besharov 1996].

The tension that exists between ASFA's mandate to more expeditiously terminate parental rights and the broad exceptions that carve out many cases from this mandate mirrors the conflicts that have characterized permanency planning for alcohol- and drug-exposed children. Child welfare practice has recognized, on the one hand, that substance-involved parents should be provided with the treatment resources they need to stabilize their lives and demonstrate their ability to parent, and, on the other, that substance-affected children should be provided with stable and nurturing families as early as possible in order to maximize their health and development [Children's Aid Society 1996]. Current efforts in the areas of concurrent planning [Katz 1999] and therapeutic mediation [Heath 1998] may assist in resolving the tensions and complexities in permanency planning for this group of children and their parents. As states implement ASFA and more fully utilize these nontraditional approaches to permanency planning, it will become clearer whether the number of adoptions for children in foster care will increase substantially. If, as many anticipate, more children are freed for adoption, policies that address the ongoing needs of children affected by prenatal substance exposure and their adoptive families will become even more critical.

Current Policies Affecting Services to Children Who Are Prenatally Substance Exposed and the Policies' Impact

Current family and child welfare policy is likely to have an impact on services for children affected by prenatal substance exposure and their adoptive families in the future. Child welfare practice related to the provision of postadoption services will be affected by policy to the extent that federal legislation and state budgetary allocations place or fail to place emphasis on such services. Additionally, support for substance-exposed children and their adoptive families will be affected by federal and state adoption subsidy policy; the extent to which the Supplemental Security Income [SSI] program for children with disabilities provides supports for substance-exposed children; and the impact of managed care on the availability of health care services in the private sector and through Medicaid.

Policies Supporting Postadoption Services. There has been only limited policy attention to the development and provision of the wide array of postadoption services needed by substance-exposed children and their adoptive families. Some support for developing postadoption services has been available through the federal Adoption Opportunities Program, but the limited resources provided by this program generally have been used to develop and test new approaches rather than institutionalize proven ones. Most recently, the Adoption and Safe Families Act targeted funding under the federal family preservation program (now renamed the Promoting Safe and Stable Families Program) to postadoption services to preserve adoptive families, a step that may strengthen postadoption services in many communities. At the same time, some states have independently focused on postadoption services. Although not every pioneering effort to provide adoption preservation services has been successful, postadoption service programs in Oregon, Massachusetts, and Illinois have demonstrated the benefits of intensive postadoption services at times of crisis in adoptive families' lives [Barth et al. 1996]. The successes of these programs suggest the importance of policies that support the development of services that stabilize adoptive families faced with the challenges of parenting children in an increasingly taut socioeconomic environment.

A specific service area in which adoptive families need support is temporary out-of-home care services for their children. Out-of-home care, particularly residential treatment, is an important component in the array of postadoption services that may be needed, in particular, by youngsters affected by prenatal substance-exposure. These children, having experienced significant genetic, prenatal, and postnatal threats to their well-being, enter adolescence with a range of needs which remain misunderstood. The vulnerabilities they face as adolescents may not be effectively addressed by family efforts and community-based services, and a therapeutic setting may be indicated. The expenses associated with residential care, even on a temporary basis, however, have presented significant challenges for adoptive families [Vobeja 1998]. Residential placements are generally not covered by private or public health insurance or covered only for extremely short periods of time in certain types of facilities, and as a result, families may be faced with the choice of incurring insurmountable expenses associated with out-of-home treatment or returning their child to foster care [Vobeja 1998]. Policies that offer

financial coverage for time-limited residential treatment can provide a significant support to ensure that children and their adoptive
families sustain their legal and emotional connections at times of
greatest crisis. The fact, however, that only a few states such as
California provide such assistance and do so without federal cost-
sharing highlights the need for greater attention at the policy level
to this need.

Adoption Subsidy. The federal adoption subsidy program—
which provides children with "special needs" with financial benefits
and medical assistance in the form of Medicaid—is a key postadoption
service for children with health and developmental problems who
exit foster care through adoption [Avery 1998]. All states operate
federally-assisted adoption subsidy programs, but there is significant
variation among state programs regarding eligibility, scope of benefits, and policies governing subsidy programs [Avery 1998]. Further
variation results from the fact that some states also have state-funded
adoption subsidy programs with eligibility criteria, benefits, and
payment levels that differ from the state's federally-funded subsidy
program [Sullivan 1998]. Under some of these state-funded programs, children with "special needs" outside the foster care system
qualify for subsidy and health care benefits [Sullivan 1998].

When children are affected by prenatal exposure to drugs or
alcohol, subsidy may be a key consideration on the part of prospective adoptive parents. Two issues are often raised: the child's threshold eligibility for subsidy and the amount of the subsidy itself. With
regard to eligibility, states often qualify financially-eligible children
for subsidy if they have a physical, mental, or emotional disability or
condition [Avery 1998], but may not qualify children who have
histories of substance exposure but do not manifest any current
disability or condition. As a consequence, many children who have
been prenatally exposed to alcohol or drugs may not qualify for
subsidy. For those children who do qualify on the basis of an existing
condition or disability, some states engage in a form of means
testing—an assessment of adoptive parent income and resources—
to determine whether to offer a family an adoption subsidy for the
child whom they plan to adopt. Avery's research [1998, pp. 41-42]
revealed that as many as one-third of the states utilize such an

approach, failing to inform parents who are considered "wealthier" of subsidy availability, based on assumptions that subsidy is "not necessary." In such cases, subsidy is simply not discussed, irrespective of the fact that the child's needs or condition qualifies the child for subsidy.

A second issue is the amount of subsidy once the child is determined to be eligible for such support. Adoption subsidies do not, even in the case of children with needs that are less demanding than those of many substance-exposed children, cover the costs associated with rearing a child [Avery 1998]. Under the current program, the level of payment only partially subsidizes the costs of rearing a child with special needs [Avery 1998], a situation that may be compounded by the extensive needs of many substance-exposed children. Irrespective of this inadequacy, it seems unlikely that adoption subsidy levels will be increased in the future. Increasingly, states have grown concerned about the costs of their adoption subsidy programs and have begun to consider ways to contain subsidy costs [Sullivan 1998]. Cost containment considerations may result in a tightening of eligibility criteria and a reluctance to make any upward adjustments in subsidy levels. If states were to take such measures and subsidy support becomes less available as a result, there could be a negative impact on the recruitment of adoptive parents for substance-exposed children, as well as the availability of resources to meet these families' postadoption support needs.

The Supplemental Security Income (SSI) Program. The Personal Responsibility and Work Opportunity Reconciliation Act of 1996 [PL 104-193], in addition to making significant changes in the federal welfare program, made substantial changes in the SSI program as it relates to children with disabilities. The law narrowed the definition of "child disability" and eliminated individualized functional assessments of children—changes which principally affect children with mental and emotional disorders and those with multiple impairments [National Health Law Program, National Center for Youth Law & National Senior Citizens Law Center 1996]. It is conservatively estimated that some 135,000 children who previously qualified for SSI benefits lost their benefits as a result of these changes [Social Security Administration 1997], and it is anticipated that the number of children who will qualify for SSI in the future will be significantly reduced from early 1990 levels [Social Legislation Information Service 1997]. The changes in SSI brought about by welfare reform have already resulted in the denial of benefits to children with Fetal Alcohol Syndrome and other conditions associated with prenatal alcohol and drug exposure [Singleton 1998]. It seems likely that in the future SSI will play a diminished role as a resource for children with medical and developmental problems resulting from prenatal substance exposure, requiring adoptive families to seek financial support and health care coverage for their children through other avenues.

Health Care Coverage. One of the critical postadoption services for families who adopt children affected by prenatal alcohol and drug exposure is health insurance adequate to cover children's ongoing health care needs. As Edelstein and colleagues note in their chapter, the physical, mental health, and developmental needs associated with prenatal substance exposure can be extensive and the costs of the needed services significant. For substance-exposed children who move from foster care to adoption, Medicaid has been the primary health insurance program [DeWoody 1994]. For substance-exposed children adopted outside the public child welfare system, employment-based family health insurance generally has been the primary vehicle for health coverage.

In recent years, significant changes have occurred in the health insurance industry in general and in the Medicaid program in particular. Both private health insurance and publicly- funded Medicaid programs have shifted from traditional fee-for-service reimbursement models to managed care approaches that place emphasis on preventive and primary care, limit health care choices and services, and utilize other measures—such as preauthorization requirements and stringent "medical necessity" criteria—to contain health care costs [Battiselli 1996]. These features of managed care have given rise to serious concerns about the capacity of managed care plans to respond effectively to the complex health and developmental problems of children with "special needs," including children affected by prenatal alcohol and drug exposure [Simms, et al. 1999]. Recent data validate these concerns, demonstrating that managed care has reduced access to specialty care for all insured children with chronic or disabling conditions, whether they are covered by Medicaid or private insurance [Hughes & Luft 1998].

These effects of managed care may have particular impact on families who adopt children in foster care. Many of these families value Medicaid-based health care coverage that accompanies a subsidy or SSI to a greater degree than the direct financial benefits associated with these programs [Sullivan 1998]. With the advent of Medicaid managed care, however, the actual scope of health care coverage has become far less certain, as plans have restricted the types of health, mental health and developmental services that children can receive, the number of visits to mental health professionals that are permitted, and the extent to which specialized and expensive treatments may be utilized [Battiselli 1996].

Access to health care services for children with special needs is likely to continue to be a serious issue under managed care [Kilborn 1997], with implications for the long-term health and developmental status of children affected by prenatal alcohol and drug exposure. Absent changes within the health care industry itself, the issue ultimately may need to be addressed by federal legislation that sets standards for health care access and quality for all served, but particularly for highly vulnerable populations [Pear 1997].

Conclusion

As adoption professionals look to the future, they may draw on a rich research and practice base as they develop services to meet the needs of children prenatally exposed to drugs and alcohol and their adoptive families. There are, however, limits on the current research and practice-based knowledge, with a number of issues that need to be addressed. Research can contribute to stronger practice in the future by providing a firmer understanding of the postnatal environmental factors that may optimize positive developmental outcomes for children. Practice can be strengthened through a focus on recruitment of adoptive families for children in foster care, including children who have been prenatally exposed to drugs and alcohol; the development of strong preparation and education programs for prospective adoptive parents of substance-exposed children in the United States and from other countries; the implementation of comprehensive postadoption services; and the education of adoption professionals on issues related to prenatal alcohol and drug exposure.

Current policies may present particular challenges for the future. On the one hand, there is a policy emphasis on increasing the number of adoptions of children in foster care, many of whom are affected by prenatal alcohol and drug exposure. On the other hand, recent changes in policy have set significant limits on ongoing supports for children with disabilities and their families, and, as a result of managed care, have limited access to many health care services. As these policies are fully implemented, the effects on vulnerable children, including children affected by prenatal drug and alcohol exposure, will need to be carefully evaluated. Policy in the future can support these children and their adoptive families by extending its focus beyond increasing the number of adoptions to strengthening adoption as a service. Policies that promote the availability of a range of preadoption and postadoption services can enhance adoption as a viable alternative for drug- and alcohol-exposed children and provide the necessary service structure for supporting their adoptive families.

References

Abel, E. & Kintcheff, B. (1984). Factors affecting the outcome of maternal alcohol exposure: I. Parity. *Neurobehavioral Toxicology and Teratology*, 6, 373–377.

Adoption and Safe Families Act of 1997, 42 U.S.C. §§ 620 et seq. (1997).

Adoptive Families of America (1998). International adoption: 1986–1997. *Adoptive Families*, March/April, 7.

Albert, V. & Barth, R. P. (1996). Predicting growth in child abuse and neglect reports in urban, suburban and rural counties, *Social Service Review*, 70(1), 59–82.

American Humane Association. (1994). *Substance abuse and child maltreatment*. Englewood, CO: American Humane Association.

Avery, R. J. (1998). Adoption assistance under PL 96-272: A policy analysis. *Children and Youth Services Review*, 20(1/2), 29–56.

Barth, R. P. (1997). Effects of age and race on the odds of adoption versus remaining in long-term out-of-home care. *Child Welfare*, 74(2), 285–309.

Barth, R. P., Berry, M., Carson, M. L., Goodfield, R., & Feinberg, B. (1996). Contributers to disruption and dissolution of older-child adoptions. *Child Welfare*, 65(4), 359–371.

Barth, R. P. (1991). Trends and issues: Educational implications of prenatally drug-exposed children. *Social Work in Education*, 13, 130–136.

Barth, R. P. & Needell, B. (1996). Outcomes for drug-exposed children four years post-adoption. *Children and Youth Services Review*, 18(1/2), 37–56.

Battiselli, E. S. (1996). *Making managed health care work for kids in foster care*. Washington, DC: Child Welfare League of America.

Beckwith, L. (1990). Adaptive and maladaptive parenting: Implications for intervention. In S. Meisels & J. Shonkoff (Eds.), *Handbook of early childhood intervention* (pp. 53–77). New York: Cambridge University Press.

Besharov, D. (1996). The children of crack: A status report. *Public Welfare*, 54(1): 32–39.

Blakeslee, S. (1990, May 19). Parents fear future of infants born on drugs. *New York Times*: A1, 8–9.

Bowlby, J. (1969). *Attachment and loss: Attachment*. New York: Basic Books.

Brady, J. P., Posner, M., Lang, C., & Rosati, M. J. (1994). *Risk and reality: The implications of prenatal exposure to alcohol and other drugs*. Rockville, MD: The Education Development Center, Inc., U.S. Department of Health and Human Services, & U.S. Department of Education.

Brodzinsky, D. M., Smith, D. M., & Brodzinsky, A. B. (1998). *Children's adjustment to adoption: Developmental and clinical issues*. Thousand Oaks, CA: Sage Publications.

Brown, R. T., Coles C. D., Smith, I. E., Platzman, K. A., Silverstein, J., Erickson, S., and Falek, A. (1991). Effects of prenatal alcohol exposure at school age: II. Attention and behavior. *Neurotoxicology & Teratology*, 13, 369–376.

Carter, L. S. & Larson, C. S. (1997). Drug-exposed infants. *The Future of Children: Children and Poverty*, 7(2), 157–160.

Cermak, S. & Groza, V. (1998). Sensory processing problems in post-institutionalized children: Implications for social work. *Child and Adolescent Social Work Journal, 15*(1), 5–37.

Chasnoff, I. J. (1989). Drug use in women: Establishing a standard of care. *Annals of the New York Academy of Science, 562,* 208–210.

Chavkin, W., Paone, D., Friedmann, P., & Wilets, I. (1993). Psychiatric histories of drug using mothers: Treatment implications. *Journal of Substance Abuse Treatment, 10,* 445–448.

Children's Aid Society. (1996). *Ensuring protection of children of drug addicted or alcoholic parents.* New York: Children's Aid Society.

Daghestani, A. (1988). Psychosocial characteristics of pregnant women addicts in treatment. In I. J. Chasnoff (Ed.), *Drugs, alcohol pregnancy and parenting* (pp. 38–54). Boston: Kluwer.

DeWoody, M. (1994). *Making sense of federal dollars: A funding guide for social service providers.* Washington, DC: Child Welfare League of America.

Edelstein, S. (1995). *Children with prenatal alcohol and/or other drug exposure: Weighing the risks of adoption.* Washington, DC: Child Welfare League of America.

Escalona, S. (1982). Babies at double hazard: Early development of infants at biologic and social risk. *Pediatrics, 70,* 670–675.

Fahlberg, V. (1996). *A developmental approach to attachment.* Evergreen, CO: Forest Heights.

Feig, L. (1998). Understanding the problem: The gap between substance abuse programs and child welfare services. In R. L. Hampton, V. Senatore, & T. P. Gullota (Eds.), *Substance Abuse, Family Violence, and Child Welfare* (pp. 62–95). Thousand Oaks, CA: Sage Publications.

Feig, L. (1990). *Drug exposed infants and children: Service needs and policy questions.* Washington, DC: U.S. Department of Health and Human Services, Division of Children and Youth Policy.

Figdor, E. & Kaeser, L. (1998). Concerns mount over punitive approaches to substance abuse among pregnant women. *The Guttmacher Report on Public Policy, 1*(5), 3–5.

Free, T., Russell, F., Mills, B., & Hathaway, D. (1990). A descriptive study of infants and toddlers exposed prenatally to substance abuse. *Maternal and Child Nursing, 15,* 245–249.

General Accounting Office. (1998). *Foster care: Agencies face challenges securing stable homes for children of substance abusers*. Washington, DC: General Accounting Office.

General Accounting Office. (1994). *Foster care: Parental drug abuse has alarming impact on young children*. Washington, DC: General Accounting Office.

Goldwater, J. (1997, October 24). Adoption: Preparation, education, and assessment of prospective adoptive parents. Presentation, Evan B. Donaldson Adoption Institute conference, *Adoption and Prenatal Alcohol and Drug Exposure: The Research, Practice and Policy Challenges*, Alexandria, VA.

Gomby, D. & Shiono, P. (1991). Estimating the number of substance-exposed infants. *The Future of Children, 1*(1), 17.

Hardin, M. & Lancour, R. (1996). *Early termination of parental rights: Developing appropriate statutory grounds*. Washington, DC: American Bar Association Center on Children and the Law.

Heath, D. T. (1998). Qualitative analysis of private mediation: Benefits for families in public child welfare agencies. *Children and Youth Services Review, 20*(7), 605–627.

Howard, J. & Kropenske, V. (1991). A prevention/intervention model for chemically dependent parents and their offspring. In S. Goldston, C. Heinicke, R. Pynos & J. Yager (Eds.) *Preventing mental health disturbances in childhood* (pp. 119–167). Washington, DC: American Psychiatric Press.

Hughes, D. (1997). *Facilitating developmental attachment: The road to emotional recovery and behavior change in foster and adopted children*. Northvale, NJ: Aronson.

Hughes, D. C. & Luft, H. S. (1998). Managed care and children: An overview. In *The Future of Children, 8*(2), 25–28.

Jaudes, P. K. & Ekwo, E. E. (1997). Outcomes for infants exposed in utero to illicit drugs. *Child Welfare, 76*(4), 521–534.

Johnson, D. & Fein, E. (1991). The concept of attachment: Applications to adoption. *Children and Youth Services Review, 13*, 397–412.

Kaplan-Sanoff, M. & Rice, K.F. (1992). Working with addicted women in recovery and their children. *Zero to Three, 13*(10), 17–22.

Katz, L. (1999). Concurrent planning: Benefits and pitfalls. *Child Welfare, 78*(1), 71–87.

Keck, G. & Kupecky, R. (1995). *Adopting the hurt child*. Colorado Springs, CO: Pinion Press.

Kelley, S. J. (1992). Parenting stress and child maltreatment in drug-exposed children. *Child Abuse and Neglect 16*, 317–328.

Kilborn, P. T. (1997, March 24). Disabled children feel pain of cuts: long-term care is reduced under managed care programs. *New York Times*,p. A10.

Klein, M. (1998, November 30). Personal communication. Supervisor, Special Needs Adoption Services, Spence-Chapin Services to Families and Children, New York, NY.

Kumpfer, K. (1991). Treatment programs for drug-abusing women. *The Future of Children, Drug Exposed Infants, 1*(1), 50–60.

Lester, V. & Tronick, E. (1994). The effects of prenatal cocaine exposure and child outcomes. *Infant Mental Health Journal, 15*(2), 107–120.

McCullough, C. (1991). The child welfare response. *The Future of Children, Drug Exposed Infants, 1*(1), 61–71.

McFadden, R. (1990, June 19). Tragic ending to the adoption of a crack baby. *New York Times*, p. B1.

Murphy, J., Jellinek, M., Quinn, D., Smith, G., Poitrast, F. & Goshko, M. (1991). Substance abuse and serious child maltreatment: Prevalence, risk, and outcome in a court sample. *Child Abuse & Neglect, 15*, 197–211.

Myers, B. J., Olson, H. C., & Kaltenback, K. (1992). Cocaine-exposed infants: Myths and misunderstandings. *Zero to Three, 13* (1) 1–5.

National Center on Addiction and Substance Abuse. (1999). *No safe haven: Children of substance-abusing families*. New York: National Center on Addiction and Substance Abuse.

National Health Law Program, National Center for Youth Law, and National Senior Citizens Law Center. (1996). *An Analysis of the New Welfare Law and Its Effects on Medicaid Recipients*. Special Edition Newsletter, August.

Nelson, L. J. & Marshall, M. F. (1998). *Ethical and legal analyses of three coercive policies aimed at substance abuse by pregnant women*. Charleston, SC: Medical University of South Carolina.

New York Public Welfare Association. (1998). *Recommendations for state legislation to guide the implementation of the federal Adoption and*

Safe Families Act in NYS. Albany, NY: New York Public Welfare Association.

Ornoy, A., Michailevskaya, V., & Lukashov, I. (1996). The developmental outcome of children born to heroin dependent mothers, raised at home or adopted. *Child Abuse & Neglect, 20*(5), 385–396.

Pear, R. (1997, March 10). Congress weighs more regulation on managed care. *New York Times,* p. A1.

Personal Responsibility and Work Opportunity Reconciliation Act of 1996, Pub. L. No. 104-193.

Powell, D. (1991). Family-based intervention with prekindergarten children prenatally exposed to drugs. *The Prevention Report,* Spring, 1–3.

Rodning, C., Beckwith, L., & Howard, J. (1991). Quality of attachment and home environments in children prenatally exposed to PCP and cocaine. *Development and Psychopathology, 3,* 351– 366.

Sameroff, A. (1986). Environmental context of child development. *Journal of Pediatrics, 109,* 192–200.

Schipper, W. (1991, July 30). Testimony before the U.S. House of Representatives Select Committee on Narcotics Abuse and Control.

Simms, M., Freundlich, M., Kaufman, N. D., & Battiselli, E. (1999). Family foster care in the next century: Delivering health and mental health services to children in foster care after welfare and health care reform. *Child Welfare, 78*(1), 166–183.

Singleton, R. (1998, January 12). Disabled kids win back their SSI benefits. *The National Law Journal,* pp. B7–B8.

Social Legislation Information Service. (1997). New rules for children's SSI program. *Social Legislation Information Service, 35*(5), 19–20.

Social Security Administration. (1997). Welfare reform and SSI childhood disability: A Factsheet from Social Security. Washington, DC: Social Security Administration.

Storkamp, B., McClusky-Fawcett, K., & Meck, N. (1993). *The effects of prenatal drug exposure on toddlers' temperament, development, and play behavior.* Paper presented at the meeting of the Society for Research on Child Development, New Orleans.

Streissguth, A. & Giunta, C. (1988). Mental health and health needs of infants and preschool children with fetal alcohol syndrome. *International Journal of Family Psychiatry, 9*(1), 29–47.

Sullivan, A. (1997). *A Conceptual Framework for a Comprehensive Program of Postadoption Services*. Unpublished manuscript. On file with author.

Tarter, R., Blackson, T., Martin, C., Loeber, R., & Moss, H. (1993). Characteristics and correlates of child discipline practices in substance abuse and normal families. *American Journal on Addictions, 2,* 18–25.

Tronick, E. Z. & Beeghly, M. (1992). Effects of prenatal exposure to cocaine on newborn behavior and development: A critical review. In S. L. Quinton, S. A. Johnson, E. M. Johnson, R. W. Denniston, & K. L. Augustson (Eds.), *Identifying the needs of drug-affected children: Public policy issues* (OSAP prevention monograph 11, DHHS publication number (ADM) 92-1814) (pp. 25–48). Rockville, MD: Office for Substance Abuse Prevention; U.S. Department of Health and Human Services.

U.S. Department of Health and Human Services. (1998). Program Instruction, ACYF-PI-CB-98-02. Washington, DC: Administration for Children and Families.

U.S. Department of Health and Human Services. (1996). *Preliminary estimates from the 1995 National Household Survey on Drug Abuse.* Washington, DC: HHS Substance Abuse and Mental Health Services Administration.

U.S. Department of Health and Human Services. (1990). Fetal alcohol syndrome and other effects of alcohol on pregnancy. In *Seventh Special Report to the US Congress on Alcohol and Health from the Secretary of Health and Human Services* (pp. 139–161). Rockville, MD: U.S. Department of Health and Human Services.

Van IJzendoom, M. H. (1995). Adult attachment representations, parental responsiveness, and infant attachment: A meta-analysis n the predictive validity of the Adult Attachment interview. *Psychological Bulletin, 117*(3), 387–403.

Vobejda, B. (1998, November 28). Billy's story: Adopting a child and his demons. *Washington Post*: p. A1.

Voice for Adoption. (1997, February 5). Untitled article. *Washington Update.*

Walker, C. D. (1994). African American children in foster care. In D.J. Besharov (Ed.) *When drug addicts have children: Reorienting child welfare's response* (pp. 145–152). Washington, DC: Child Welfare League of America.

Weston, D., Ivins, B., Zuckerman, B., Jones, C., & Lopez, R. (1989). Drug exposed babies: Research and clinical issues. *Zero to Three*, 9(5), 1–7.

Woolis, D. (1998). FamilyWorks: Substance abuse treatment and welfare. *Public Welfare* (Winter): 24–31.

Yarrow, L. J. & Goodwin, M. S. (1973). The immediate impact of separation: Reactions of infants to a change in mother figure. In L. J. Stone, H.T. Smith & L.B. Murphy (Eds.), *The competent infant: Research and commentary* (pp. 1032–1040). New York: Basic Books.

Zuckerman, B. (1993). The development of drug- and HIV-affected infants. In R. P. Barth, J. Pietrzak & M. Ramler (Eds.), *Families Living with Drugs and HIV* (pp. 37–60). New York: The Guilford Press.

Zuckerman, B. (1991). Drug-exposed infants: Understanding the medical risk. In *The Future of Children, 1*(1), 26–35.

About the Contributors

Kathleen Albus, M.A., is a doctoral student in clinical psychology at the University of Delaware. Her research interests include the study of the precursors of aggressive and other externalizing behaviors and the intervention and prevention efforts aimed at these behaviors. Another area of interest is the conditions under which maternal sensitivity is important in promoting adaptive child behaviors.

Richard S. Barth, M.S.W., Ph.D., is the Frank A. Daniels Distinguished Professor of Human Services Policy Information in the school of social work at the University of North Carolina at Chapel Hill. He was previously Hutto Patterson Professor, school of social welfare, University of California at Berkeley. His books include *Adoption Disruption: Rates, Risks, and Resources, From Child Abuse to Permanency Planning: Pathways Through Child Welfare Services* (Aldine, 1994), *Child Welfare Research Review I and II* (Columbia, 1994; 1997); and *The Tender Years: Toward Developmentally Sensitive Child Welfare Services* (Oxford, 1998). He is on the editorial boards of several research, policy, and practice journals and was the 1998 recipient of the Presidential Award for Excellence in Research from the National Association of Social Workers.

Devon Brooks, M.S.W., Ph.D., is assistant professor in the school of social work at the University of Southern California. He formerly served as a senior research associate for the Center for Social Services Research, school of social welfare at the University of California at Berkeley. His areas of interest include minority child welfare and development, public child welfare policy and innovations, and program evaluation. He has coauthored and written numerous articles on child welfare policy and services and the development of children in the child welfare services system.

Dorli Burge, Ph.D., is a clinical psychologist on the T.I.E.S. for Adoption Project and was instrumental in helping develop the treatment model. She is assistant clinical professor in the psychology department at UCLA. She comes to adoption work with a long interest and experience in parent-child interaction, attachment, and developmental psychopathology, and has published numerous articles on these topics. In her private practice, she treats adults as well as children and their families.

Kristin Riggins-Caspers, Ph.D., is currently a postdoctoral fellow in psychiatric genetics at the University of Iowa. She completed her doctorate in human development and family studies at Iowa State University. Her research interests include gene-environment interaction and gene-environment correlation as conceptual models for predicting childhood aggressivity; conduct disorders; and later substance abuse.

Remi J. Cadoret, M.D., is a Professor Emeritus of psychiatry at the University of Iowa. For over 25 years, he has studied adoptees as a way to learn how genetic factors interact with the environment to result in such complex behaviors as depression, antisocial and other personality traits, and substance abuse and dependency. He is currently director of Iowa Consortium for Substance Abuse and Evaluation.

Mary Dozier, Ph.D., is an associate professor at the University of Delaware. She received her doctorate in clinical psychology at Duke University in 1983. Her research explores the evolution of attachment in adoptive mother-infant dyads and infants. She is particularly interested in how factors such as child age at placement affect attachment quality. She has developed an intervention that helps sensitize adoptive parents to the strategies their children may have developed to cope with the loss of previous caregivers.

Susan Edelstein, M.S.W., is a licensed clinical social worker in the UCLA Center for Healthier Children, Families, and Communities and the director of T.I.E.S. for Adoption. She began her career in child protective services in Los Angeles and then specialized in special needs adoptions for six years. In 1979 she began her work at UCLA Medical Center, directing major service, training, and research projects involving interdisciplinary collaboration, child abuse and neglect, parental chemical dependency, and comprehensive early intervention approaches. She has published extensively in these areas, and is the primary author of Children With Prenatal Alcohol and/or other Drug Exposure: Weighing the Risks of Adoption (CWLA Press 1995).

Madelyn Freundlich, M.S.W., J.D., LL.M., is the executive director of the Evan B. Donaldson Adoption Institute. Her work has focused on child welfare policy and practice for the past decade. She formerly served as general counsel for the Child Welfare League of America. She is the author of a number of books and articles on adoption, child welfare law and policy, and the financing of child welfare services.

Robert B. Hill, Ph.D., is currently senior researcher at Westat, Inc., in Rockville, Maryland. Previously, he was director of the Institute for Urban Research at Morgan University. He has published numerous works focusing on black family issues. His latest is entitled *The Strengths of African American Families: Twenty-five Years Later.*

Stephen Kandall, M.D., trained in pediatrics at Albert Einstein College of Medicine, Yeshiva University, New York City, and in newborn medicine in San Francisco. His 25-year-long interest in perinatal addiction has resulted in 90 contributions to medical literature, many radio and TV appearances, national and international lectureships, elected presidencies of regional pediatric societies, and service on many national advisory bodies dealing with the impact of maternal addiction on infants and children. His 1996 book, *Substance and Shadow,* is the definitive historical study of women and addiction in the United States. He recently retired after 22 years as Chief of Neonatology at Beth Israel Medical Center and Professor of Pediatrics at Albert Einstein.

Judith Larsen, J.D., advocates for children and families through litigation, writing, research and teaching, paying particular attention to the impact of substance abuse on families. In partnership with universities, federal agencies, and organizations such as the American Bar Association and the National Council of Juvenile and

Family Court Judges, she seeks ways to improve the response of legal systems to drug-involved families. Ms. Larsen's law degree is from Georgetown University Law Center.

Carolyn McCarty, M.A., is an advanced doctoral student in clinical psychology at UCLA. She has been active in all aspects of T.I.E.S. for Adoption for three years and has developed a career interest in providing services and conducting research in the area of adoption.

Joseph Pruzak, M.S.W., is the program manager for adoptive parent recruitment for Los Angeles County Department of Children and Family Services and has served as the adoption division liaison to T.I.E.S. for Adoption since its inception.

Harvey Schwitzer, J.D., a 1976 graduate of UCLA Law School, has been involved in adoption and permanency planning since he helped to create the Counsel for Child Abuse and Neglect Office at the Washington D.C. Superior Court in 1980. Mr. Schwitzer is in private practice, specializing in adoption and representation of children and child-serving agencies, and has served as counsel in several wrongful adoption cases. He is legal counsel to the Consortium for Child Welfare and consultant to the Healthy Families/ Thriving Communities Collaboratives in Washington D.C. Mr. Schwitzer teaches juvenile law at Columbus School of Law, Catholic University, and lectures regularly on adoption issues to lawyers and social workers.

Jill Waterman, Ph.D., is adjunct professor of psychology at UCLA and Coordinator of the UCLA Psychology Clinic. She is the mental health coordinator of T.I.E.S. for Adoption and was critical in the development and implementation of the clinical component of the model. Having begun her professional career as an adoption social worker, she has maintained a deep interest in adoption. Dr. Waterman has published two books and many articles on child sexual abuse and other areas of child trauma. She is also a practicing clinician, specializing in treatment of young children and their families.